# PERFORMING KING LEAR

**Jonathan Croall** is a distinguished biographer and theatre historian. He is the author of over twenty books, notably the acclaimed biographies *John Gielgud: Matinee Idol to Movie Star* (Bloomsbury Methuen Drama) and *Sybil Thorndike: A Star of Life*. His other titles include *The Coming of Godot: A Short History of a Masterpiece* (short-listed for the 2005 Theatre Book Prize); *The Wit and Wisdom (and Gaffes) of John Gielgud* and *In Search of Gielgud: A Biographer's Tale*; two collections of his theatre journalism, *Buzz Buzz! Playwrights, Actors and Directors at the National Theatre* and *Closely Observed Theatre: From the National to the Old Vic*; and three books in the series The National Theatre at Work – *Hamlet Observed*, *Peter Hall's 'Bacchai'*, and *Inside the Molly House*.

## RELATED TITLES

*Emotional Excess on the Shakespearean Stage*, Bridget Escolme
*English Renaissance Tragedy*, Peter Holbrook
*A Year of Shakespeare: Re-living the World Shakespeare Festival*,
edited by Paul Edmondson, Paul Prescott and Erin Sullivan
*Shakespeare on the Global Stage: Performance and Festivity in the
Olympic Year*, edited by Paul Prescott and Erin Sullivan

# Performing King Lear

## Gielgud to Russell Beale

*Jonathan Croall*

Bloomsbury Arden Shakespeare
An imprint of Bloomsbury Publishing Plc

BLOOMSBURY
LONDON · OXFORD · NEW YORK · NEW DELHI · SYDNEY

**Bloomsbury Arden Shakespeare**

An imprint of Bloomsbury Publishing Plc

Imprint previously known as Arden Shakespeare

| | |
|---|---|
| 50 Bedford Square | 1385 Broadway |
| London | New York |
| WC1B 3DP | NY 10018 |
| UK | USA |

**www.bloomsbury.com**

**BLOOMSBURY, THE ARDEN SHAKESPEARE and the Diana logo are trademarks of Bloomsbury Publishing Plc**

First published 2015

**British Library Cataloguing-in-Publication Data**

A catalogue record for this book is available from the British Library.

ISBN: HB: 978-1-4742-2386-7
PB: 978-1-4742-2385-0
ePDF: 978-1-4742-2388-1
ePub: 978-1-4742-2387-4

**Library of Congress Cataloging-in-Publication Data**

A catalog record for this book is available from the Library of Congress.

Typeset by Fakenham Prepress Solutions, Fakenham, Norfolk NR21 8NN
Printed and bound in Great Britain

# CONTENTS

# LIST OF ILLUSTRATIONS

# ACKNOWLEDGEMENTS

I am immensely grateful to those many actors and directors who found time to talk to me at length about their experience of working on productions of *King Lear*. This book would not have been possible without their invaluable support and kindness, and in many cases their hospitality. They are listed in the appropriate section of the Sources (page 237).

I am also indebted to the following for permission to reproduce copyright material: The Society of Authors and the Trustees of the Estate of Harley Granville Barker for the letter from Harley Granville Barker to John Gielgud; to Piers Haggard for the extract from his father Stephen Haggard's memoir *I'll Go to Bed at Noon*, and one from the actor's letter to *his* father; to George Byam Shaw for extracts from his father Glen Byam Shaw's notes on his 1959 Stratford production of *King Lear*; to Timothy West for extracts from *I'm Here I Think, Where Are You? Letters from a Touring Actor*; to Richard Eyre for extracts from his lecture to the Royal Society of Literature in 1998; and to Kika Markham and Annie Castledine for extracts from the letters of Corin Redgrave to Annie Castledine.

I'm also grateful to Diana Devlin for alerting me to her father's article on playing King Lear; to Abigail Rokison of the Shakespeare Institute for her valuable talk on 'King Lear in Context'; and to staff at the V & A Museum Theatre and Performance Collections and at the National Theatre Archive for their very helpful assistance.

**John Gielgud** '*Lear* shrieks out to be acted, and I am not terrified by the part. Whenever I play these great tragic characters I know that Shakespeare must have been an actor.'

**Donald Sinden** '*King Lear* is a piece of cake compared with playing a farce like *Not Now Darling*.'

**Timothy West** 'As far as acts four and five go, you can't plan anything, you just have to let those scenes happen to you, they're so wonderfully simple.'

**Tim Pigott-Smith** 'In accepting the part I insisted on two conditions: no rain and no nudity. You don't need rain, and you don't want people talking about the size of your dick.'

**Michael Pennington** 'I think I got all eleven scenes right at some point, but not on the same night. It's like serving at tennis: some of the balls are aces, and some go into the net.'

**Derek Jacobi** 'Normally the storm scene becomes a contest between the sound design and the actor's vocal limits. This time the audience heard every one of those fabulous words.'

**Christopher Plummer** 'Lear is not a noble man at all, he's an absolute bastard, and really a peasant king. I don't know how this idea of his nobility and majesty ever happened.'

**Simon Russell Beale** 'Those blind outbursts of self-indulgent rage in the first scenes are difficult to manage. I have to look very hard to find that rage and power in myself.'

# Introduction

The role of King Lear is seen today as the ultimate challenge for the classical actor, the one that provides the supreme test of his abilities in the theatre. It's a powerful testimony to the immense popularity of *King Lear* that, when I started my research, I discovered that in the UK there were around forty living actors who had played the title-role. During the year I worked on the book I was able to see four of them in action in London alone, playing in a variety of theatres – in the round, in the open air, in a promenade production, and at the National Theatre.

Twenty actors, including many at the top of the profession, talked to me in depth about their experience of playing perhaps the most complex part in all of Shakespeare. They covered a wealth of topics: their reasons for accepting the part, how they prepared for it, the problems they came up against, the nature of the rehearsals, the key question of their working relationship with their director and, not least, their view of their own performance. It's often said that by the time you are old enough to play Lear, you are too old to play him. Yet not all of those featured here were in the later years of their careers: one was twenty-two at the time, while several were in their thirties or forties; all spoke revealingly of how they strived to create a convincing picture of a man supposedly 'fourscore and upward'.

The critic Kenneth Tynan described *King Lear* as 'a labyrinthine citadel, all but impregnable'. The actors and directors I interviewed all testified to the many diverse problems involved in bringing the play to the stage, and the difficulty of deciding how to deal with its many flaws, inconsistencies and absurdities. For the actor the experience is as much a test of stamina as of acting skill. As the Stratford director John Barton has said: 'Lear, like Timon and Leontes, confronts an audience with a kind of verbal overkill which is very hard for an actor to sustain.' It is also a supreme physical challenge, as was made graphically clear when Brian Blessed, aged seventy-eight, recently collapsed on stage in Guildford while playing Lear, and was compelled to withdraw from the production.

As the director Michael Blakemore put it: 'All these Shakespeare plays come with gauze after gauze after gauze of received opinion, and there are so many fingerprints on them.' As practical men of the theatre, the actors I interviewed had an ambivalent attitude to the massive volume of material available to them about *King Lear*, most notably the views of critics and academic experts. Some decided to avoid it entirely, preferring to rely on their own ideas, and on those that emerged during rehearsals. Others found value in reading a certain amount of it, though sometimes only after the play had opened. Peter Ustinov suggested the diminishing value of 'the footnotes of distinguished professors' once the practicalities of rehearsal begin: 'After two weeks you begin to doubt one or two of them, and then the doubt becomes fairly general. When you're actually playing the part, you feel you're rowing out to sea alone in a boat with Shakespeare, and the professors are like bungalows on the seashore; they are getting lost in the mist, and eventually they disappear altogether.'

A small number of actors – and one elusive director – were unable or unwilling to be interviewed, mainly through pressure of work, or a desire to write their own account of their performance. Happily twenty-five directors agreed to share their experience. In doing so they provided another perspective from that of the actors, shedding light on many different aspects of staging the great tragedy. They shared their ideas about the nature and meaning of the play, their reasons for casting the lead actor, how he responded to their ideas in rehearsal, their reasons for deciding on the production's set, costumes and period, and whether their chosen Lear, and the production, lived up to their expectations.

While this book is principally an oral history of *King Lear* over the last half century or so, as remembered by many leading players and directors, it seemed important to look briefly at the play's stage history, and at some of the key performances in the first six decades of the twentieth century. The interpretations of such diverse actors as John Gielgud, Donald Wolfit, Laurence Olivier, Michael Redgrave and Charles Laughton help to bring in to focus the multifarious problems later faced by those whose memories of playing Lear fill these pages.

The watershed moment in the play's more recent stage history came in 1962, with Peter Brook's iconoclastic Stratford production, and Paul Scofield's widely acclaimed Lear. Its influence on the younger generation was widespread and profound. Many of the actors who talked to me described it as the most exciting and revelatory Shakespeare production they had seen. I too saw it in my youth, and one of the great pleasures of compiling this book has been to discover in detail how that memorable production was created by Brook and his company.

With the limited amount of time and space available to me, I was unable to cover several potentially interesting performances and productions. I did see David Ryall's Lear at the Cockpit theatre in London, but illness compelled him, with great courage, to play with a script in his hand, and his condition meant I was unable to interview him. I also caught Edward Petherbridge's *My Perfect Mind* at the Young Vic, directed by Kathryn Hunter, a remarkable show which centred on the actor's traumatic experience of suffering a stroke two days after he started rehearsing as Lear in New Zealand. But I was unable to get to Jonathan Miller's eighth production of the play in 2015, this one for Northern Broadsides with Barrie Rutter playing Lear, since its UK tour coincided with the book going to press.

In 2016, the 400th anniversary of Shakespeare's death, other productions will certainly be staged, among them Anthony Sher's interpretation of the king for the Royal Shakespeare Company at Stratford. One of the most intriguing adaptations promises to be *The Shadow King*, a re-imagining of Shakespeare's tragedy from the Malthouse Theatre in Melbourne, which is coming to the Barbican: set in the Australian outback, with Tom E. Lewis playing the central role, it is told through modern English, Kriol languages, and a score that includes Aboriginal 'dreamtime' songs.

Actors and directors will continue to find new ways of performing and staging *King Lear*. The play's extraordinarily wide appeal shows absolutely no sign of diminishing.

# 1

# A Stage History

*King Lear* has been performed more often in the last fifty years than in the whole of its 400-year stage history. While *Hamlet* was considered Shakespeare's supreme achievement during the first half of the twentieth century, *King Lear* is now seen as his pre-eminent work, and is played more often than the earlier tragedy. In our increasingly violent and fragmenting world, and our increasing exposure to its many horrors, it is widely recognised as Shakespeare's most profound and moving exploration of the nature of man and human suffering, and in its imaginative scope a masterpiece of world literature. As the director Michael Bogdanov observed: 'The more we recognise inhumanity and injustice, the more we witness the disintegration of the family unit, the more urgent and accessible the themes of *Lear* become.'

The play was almost certainly written in 1605–6, and given its first public performance by the King's Men company, probably at the Globe theatre. There was certainly a private performance before James I on 26 December 1606 at the Court at Whitehall. The play was first published in 1608, a year after James succeeded in having the Act of Union passed. This was the Quarto version, which was succeeded after Shakespeare's death by the First Folio edition in 1623. This differed from the Quarto in many important respects: approximately 300 lines were cut, 100 lines were added, Lear's retinue of knights appear for the first time, and scores of minor changes were made. The result was a swifter, more theatrical but also more uncompromising text. It's thought that this edition incorporated the revisions Shakespeare and the King's Men made around 1610, after the play had been staged. Nowadays most directors favour a conflated text, drawing on both versions.

Shakespeare's main source was the anonymous play *The True Chronicle History of the Life and Death of King Leir*. It was performed at the Rose theatre in 1594, and published in 1605. It told of the triumph of good over evil, with Cordelia rescued, Lear restored to his throne, and Cordelia's succession secured. Shakespeare dramatically transformed the story: he introduced the Fool, reduced much of the comic relief, added Lear's madness and the storm, and created the tragic ending. Another key source was Philip Sidney's prose romance *The Countess of Pembroke's Arcadia*, an episode from which he took to use for the Gloucester sub-plot. He also drew on other historical sources, including Holinshed's *Chronicles*, and Montaigne's *Essays*, notably one entitled 'Of the Affection of Fathers to Their Children'.

In 1681 the dramatist Nahum Tate, describing the play as 'a heap of jewels unstrung and unpolished', radically altered the text in an attempt to 'rectify what was wanting in the regularity and probability of the tale'. To meet the taste of the time he shortened it by some 800 lines, simplified the plot and the language, imposed a Christian super-structure, and substantially changed the story to give it a happy ending. He removed the Fool and the King of France, made Edgar and Cordelia lovers who were finally united and ruled the kingdom, and ensured that Lear, Kent and Gloucester retired to a 'cool cell' and a life of 'calm reflections on our Fortunes past'. Although it was modified now and then, and sections of Shakespeare's original restored, except for a handful of performances this popular version held sway on the English stage for more than 150 years.

This was the version performed by star actors such as Thomas Betterton and David Garrick, the latter playing Lear at twenty-five. Samuel Johnson was another who admired it, arguing that an audience would prefer a play which offered 'poetical justice', with virtue triumphing over wickedness. In 1765 he wrote: 'I was many years ago so shocked by Cordelia's death that I know not whether I endured to read again the last scenes of the play till I undertook to revise them as an editor.' Even Tate's sanitised version was banned from the London stage from 1810 for more than a decade: as George III's mental health deteriorated, it was felt the play offered too obvious a parallel.

The poets of the period also greatly admired it. Shelley called it 'The most perfect specimen of the dramatic art existing in the world', while Swinburne declared: 'In this, the most terrible work of human genius, it is with the very springs and sources of nature that Shakespeare has set himself to deal.' But Tate's version came increasingly under fire from actors. Edmund Kean restored the tragic ending in 1823, though his production was not a success, but it was William Charles Macready who took the most significant step. For his 1838 production at Covent Garden he went back to Shakespeare's original version. He rearranged the text, omitted the blinding of Gloucester, but restored the Fool, who was played by the young actress Priscilla Horton.

Other 'improved' versions were used in the decades that followed. Despite spectacular, high-tech stagings, and perhaps because of the continuing uncertainty surrounding these many versions, *King Lear* proved the least popular of Shakespeare's major tragedies on the Victorian stage. In 1883 Henry James thought it 'impossible to imagine a drama that accommodates itself less to the stage'. In 1892 the actor-manager Henry Irving put on an elaborate production at the Lyceum, with elaborate sets and Druidical and

Viking costumes. He cut nearly half the lines, rearranged several episodes, increased the prominence of his role, and reduced the violence and sexuality in response to contemporary values. His production was not a success, prompting newspaper critics to observe that 'Shakespeare is, as a poet and playwright, at his worst in *King Lear*', and that the play 'would not be tolerated if produced without the name of Shakespeare'.

In 1811 the critic Charles Lamb, who had not seen the play acted, complained that 'an old man tottering about the stage with a walking-stick, turned out of doors by his daughters in a rainy night, has nothing in it but what is painful and disgusting'. He concluded: 'The *Lear* of Shakespeare cannot be acted – *Lear* is essentially impossible to be represented on stage'. This idea was reinforced by the influential critic A.C. Bradley, who announced in a lecture published in 1904 that '*King Lear* is too huge for the stage', that it was 'Shakespeare's greatest achievement, but *not* his greatest play'. This view was reflected in the fact that between 1870 and 1920 there were only five West End revivals; at one point the play was not staged for eighteen years.

During the twentieth century this argument was gradually demolished. The counter-argument was forcefully made by the director and playwright Harley Granville Barker, who in his influential 1927 *Preface to King Lear* put the case for the play's actability. The theatrical evidence to support his opinion increased, with the Lears of John Gielgud, Randle Ayrton and William Devlin making a considerable impact during the 1930s. It became a matter of defiance and morale-boosting to continue to stage the play during wartime. In 1917 Russell Thorndike had played Lear, with his sister Sybil Thorndike as the Fool, while bombs exploded all around the Old Vic. In the storm scene he demanded 'All *Germans* spill at once', the topical reference prompting a roar of applause from the audience. During the second world war, as invasion threatened in 1940, the Old Vic re-opened after theatres had been closed with Gielgud's second *Lear*, in which Barker himself was involved as co-director. During these years Donald Wolfit in London and Abraham Sofaer at Stratford offered fast-paced, heavily cut versions, designed to enable audiences to catch their last trains home in the blackout.

After the war *King Lear* grew in popularity, and by the 1960s was accepted as a great stage play. Gielgud, Laurence Olivier and Michael Redgrave all starred in it with varying degrees of success, but the landmark production was Peter Brook's at Stratford in 1962, with Paul Scofield playing Lear. Brook staged an austere, nihilistic version, which carried echoes of the bleakness of Samuel's Beckett's plays in its absurd and grotesque elements and, in contrast to previous productions, offered no hint of redemption. It was a controversial production that was to shift radically people's perceptions of the play, and heavily influence the work of later directors, actors and writers. Jonathan Miller recalled: 'I felt, like many others of my generation, that the speeches had been possessed by a rightful claimant, and that the lines seemed to make rich sense for the first time.'

For Christopher Hampton, aged sixteen, it was 'the cause of my wanting to work in theatre', as it was for Richard Eyre, then at university, and for schoolboy David Hare, who says: 'It was certainly the most influential production that I saw in my life. The excitement was tangible.'

The writer Anthony Burgess wrote in 1986: 'The play presents the modern age more thoroughly than any modern dramatist has yet been able to do.' Shakespearean productions have consistently mirrored the beliefs and values of the day. From the 1980s onwards those of *King Lear* have placed an increasing emphasis on its political and social aspects: on the abuse of power which destroys humanity, on Lear's belated sympathy for the 'poor naked wretches' of whom he had been previously unaware, on the blinded Gloucester's hope for a time when 'distribution should undo excess / And each man have enough.' Many directors have opted to highlight, both on stage and in the accompanying programme, such implicit critiques of society.

The fact that we know little about Lear's past, and that he tells us little about himself, has allowed the part to be given a huge variety of interpretations. James Agate, the leading critic between the wars, declared: 'Lear should look as if he had stepped out of a canvas by Michelangelo or a drawing by Blake.' This 'Ancient of Days' look had been in fashion during the Victorian era, often performed within a Stonehenge-type setting of Druidic stone circles, and it lasted into the middle of the twentieth century.

Recent decades have seen a much greater variety of interpretations, by actors of widely differing ages. Less often now a king, he has been played as a dictator or autocrat, an insensitive or abusive father and, increasingly, a man more sinning than sinned against, shown to be the primary cause of his older daughters' evil actions. Sometimes he has been portrayed at the beginning of the play as a man already showing clear signs of senility or madness.

Unlike other Shakespeare tragedies, *King Lear* is not only about a star actor filling the title-role: more than the others it requires an extensive and high-quality ensemble to play the other ten major parts. This has not always been possible where money has been limited, or the standard of acting not high. In considering how to balance the familial, political and cosmic elements of the play, directors have also been limited by the size and shape of the theatre. Such factors have seen an increasing number of productions focus primarily on the play as an essentially domestic drama, a story of the breakdown of family relationships at the expense of any cosmic vision. Recent London productions in the Donmar, Almeida and Cottesloe, and in smaller theatres and studio spaces around the country, are evidence of this trend.

In recent years the play has been subject to a multitude of adaptations and re-imaginings in various media. In the theatre they have included Edward Bond's *Lear*, and prequels such as *Lear's Daughters* by Elaine Feinstein and the Women's Theatre Group, and *Seven Lears* by Howard

Barker. Radical alternative companies have also staged very different versions of the play. Footsbarn have toured a fundamentally reconstructed *Lear*, using only 25 per cent of Shakespeare's text; Welfare State have put on a site-specific 'critical carnival' called *The Tragedy of King Real* during a residency in Barrow-in-Furness; the Suffolk-based Red Rose Chain have performed an open-air version, apparently 'for all the family', as part of their Theatre in the Forest project.

# 2

# The First of the Moderns

## John Gielgud
### *Harcourt Williams*

*In 1931 John Gielgud played the first of his four King Lears. The Old Vic production was directed by the theatre's artistic director and actor Harcourt Williams.*

The line of modern Lears essentially began in 1931, when two very different actors, John Gielgud and Randle Ayrton, took on the role in London and Stratford respectively.

Aged only twenty-seven, one of the youngest major actors to play Lear, Gielgud was defying the critic James Agate's advice not to play the part. In Agate's view: 'Lear is not, and never can be, a young man's part.' At the time Lamb's opinion that the play was unactable was still supported by many people. Harcourt Williams' production, influenced by Barker's *Preface*, was widely agreed to have discredited it. Gielgud himself dismissed the idea, arguing that the play could only be really appreciated on the stage. 'Certain scenes appear to be very complicated, but they become much clearer when you begin to act them. Lear shrieks out to be acted, and I am not terrified by the part. Whenever I play these great tragic characters I know that Shakespeare must have been an actor.'

He already knew the play well, having walked on in 1922 at the age of eighteen while a student in Robert Atkins' Old Vic production. He was cast as one of Cornwall's attendants, and had to hold Gloucester's chair during the blinding scene. Williams' production cast Leslie French as the Fool and Ralph Richardson as Kent. During rehearsals Gielgud explained: 'Vocally I do not find Lear as trying a part as Macbeth, in which the last act is a terrific strain.' Compared with Hamlet, where 'so much of oneself and one's own emotions get mixed up with the character', with Lear 'one seems to be able to lose oneself, and while on stage to *be* the part. Lear is like a god, whereas there is something of all of us in Hamlet.'

Rather than play him as 'a doddering old man with a long beard', as Lamb put it, he emphasised his physical strength, which remains even after he loses his mind. Robert Speaight, playing Edmund, remembered 'a vigorous old man with a sweeping brow and short wizened beard'. This was a majestic royal Lear, his first entrance down a steep slope between a forest of red spears being of such splendour that it often provoked applause in itself. As Gielgud recalled: 'Trumpets blared in the orchestra, and my way was cleared by spearmen, while lords and attendants kept their distance behind my magnificent white robe.'

Later he criticised his performance: 'I was wholly inadequate in the storm scenes, having neither the voice nor the physique for them. Lear has to *be* the storm, but I could do no more than shout against the thunder-sheet.' But Leslie French, much admired as the Fool, found much to praise: 'It was astonishing, because he was far too young, and yet he gave a tremendous performance.' The poet and playwright Gordon Bottomley was also impressed, writing to Gielgud: 'I cannot believe that you or anyone else can ever be (or can ever have been) more convincingly Lear than you were last night. It was a piece of the greatest kind of art that will go on living in everyone who heard it.'

Among the critics, C. B. Purdom was unhappy with the staging. 'The use of painted curtains to mark changes of scene, the placing of rostrums, the dropping of the proscenium curtains so that action may take place before them, which can be endured in other plays, makes havoc of this one. In short, *King Lear* requires the conditions of the Shakespearean stage.' Another critic J. G. B. underlined flaws in the later scenes: 'The tortuosities of Edmund's schemes become nearly absurd, and Shakespeare's painstaking assassination of half-a-dozen lesser characters takes far too long, comes far too slowly, and signifies far too little.'

Although the critics admired Gielgud for tackling the part so young, they felt this was a Lear who would bend but never break. Several thought he lacked weight and power, most notably in the storm scene; it was, one said, 'like a birch imitating an oak'. It was suggested that his cadences were too youthful, and that his excellent diction tended to get in the way of his attempts to suggest madness. *The Times* critic summed up the adverse views: 'It is a mountain of a part, and at the end of the evening the peak remains unconquered.'

For Peter Fleming 'the imminence of collapse never terrified: the performance has the deliberate threat of distant gunfire, rather than the unpredictable menace of a volcano'. But he added: 'I have never seen a better bit of acting than Mr Gielgud's "Oh fool, I shall go mad." He says the words in a voice suddenly become flat and toneless, quickened only with a chilling objective interest in their no longer contestable truth. It is a brilliant interpretation.' Others felt that, while Gielgud lacked physical power, he overcame this by means of his art. Agate suggested he would conquer the part later: 'In the manifest intelligence displayed throughout, and in the speaking of the verse, it is fine; time only can do the rest.'

*Gielgud played Lear for the second time in 1940 (see page 22).*

# Randle Ayrton
## *William Bridges-Adams/Theodore* Komisarjevsky

*In 1931 Randle Ayrton played King Lear in the Stratford Picture House, in a production directed by William Bridges-Adams, the Memorial Theatre's artistic director. Five years later he repeated the role in the newly built Stratford Memorial Theatre, under the direction of Theodore Komisarjevsky.*

Randle Ayrton was sixty-two when he played his first Lear. The Picture House in Stratford was being used as a temporary stage while the new theatre was being built. It was a simple, direct production by William Bridges-Adams, staged on the cinema's shallow stage with a Stonehenge-style set. J. C. Trewin felt that Ayrton 'never had never enough voice for the part – his tones were dry and gritty – but he developed quite astonishing pathos'.

Five years later Ayrton played Lear in the new theatre, in a startlingly radical, expressionistic production by Theodore Komisarjevsky. The pioneering Russian director had already staged a production in 1927 with Oxford undergraduates, which had helped to shift opinion about the play's suitability for the stage. That production informed the look of his Stratford one, for which he expressed a desire to break with tradition. 'I am producing it for the sake of the acting, not for the *mise-en-scène*,' he announced. 'I have no sets except the simplest, and no *décors*. I am not giving it a barbaric atmosphere or surroundings or costumes, because to my mind there is nothing barbaric about the play. It is inspired by the ideas of the Renaissance period.' He cut the text quite heavily, made textual transpositions, and turned the knights into a chorus, commenting on the action, and repeating the Fool's songs and sayings in unison.

Remarkably, the actors had only six rehearsals. The permanent set was a lengthy, steep staircase of narrow, angled steps, down which Lear and the players, dressed in voluminous woollen cloaks, symbolically descended step by step as the tragedy deepened. The sole piece of furniture was a majestic throne, replete with columns. Komisarjevsky relied a great deal on a dramatic use of lighting, which changed with the different moods. For the storm scene he had no scenery at all, simply scudding clouds projected onto the cyclorama, against which the actors moved in silhouette. His stark but colourful and imaginative staging was praised for reinforcing the cosmic elements in the play.

Ayrton was a short, ugly man, but an actor of considerable range and power. Though he had lost some of his vocal strength, his Lear was widely acclaimed. He played him at the outset as a patriarch already on the edge of senile decay, a snarling, unreasonable, impulsive figure. 'His progress to disillusionment is pitifully rapid and direct, his struggle against complete madness pitifully futile,' wrote the *Birmingham Mail* critic. 'It is a performance in which majesty and helplessness, dominion and pathetic submission to stronger wills, are perfectly blended.' Trewin picked out his qualities: 'He had the gift of simplicity. His Lear was plain and lucid, never a gesture too much.'

The production had its critics, including one of the actors in the company, who thought that 'what Komisarjevsky intended was not necessarily either the intention of the author or the real shape of the play'. He described the Russian as 'a Bernard Shaw amongst producers, ever ready with the shock, and careless of the damage he did, provided he achieved that. In short, his way with the text was monstrous; he cut and hacked it to pieces in a way that not even the great actor-managers of the past dared to do. Whole scenes were transposed, meanings altered, and characters obliterated.'

The actor in question was Donald Wolfit, who played Kent that year and the next, when the production was repeated. Later, when he played Lear himself, he admitted: 'Anything I've ever done as Lear I learned in the first place from Randle Ayrton.'

# Donald Wolfit
## *Nugent Monck*

*With Nugent Monck co-directing Donald Wolfit toured* King Lear *round the UK in 1942 before bringing it to the St James' in 1943, and the Scala in 1944. He revived the play at the King's, Hammersmith in 1953.*

Donald Wolfit was a barnstorming performer, one to whom the word 'ham' was frequently attached. He was often described as the last of the actor-managers, a figure harking back to the nineteenth century in his extravagant style of acting, full of sound and fury but signifying very little. His companies were generally third-rate players, chosen, his critics argued, to give his own acting the greater attention. Yet according to the playwright Ronald Harwood, his dresser and business manager, and later his biographer: 'Nothing came near him for barbaric, Elizabethan power. He was a great actor, as powerful and poetic as any in the twentieth century.'

His wartime Lear was received coolly at first, but then won him sensationally good notices. Wolfit co-directed the production with Nugent

Monck from the Maddermarket Theatre in Norwich. His set was an almost bare, Stonehenge-style affair, his costumes simple, barbaric tunics painted by hand, the swords and shields borrowed from another company's *Macbeth*. Told that the great director Max Reinhardt had used a hundred knights in his production, he explained that he could manage only six.

*King Lear* had not been seen in the provinces for thirty years. The year 1942 was, he felt, an opportune moment in the war to stage the play: 'If ever the sorrows of Lear, the cruelty and the blinding, staggering sickness of this great tragedy could be understood by the mind and heart of the people, surely the time must be now,' he said. 'Half our cities lay in partial ruins; we were indeed on the open heath as a nation, defying the elements.' He began to learn the part in between the air-raids and his Home Guard duties.

He considered his initial performance in Cardiff to be a failure: 'The magnitude of the task and the unnerving cosmic quality of the tragedy became apparent to me as the performance went on. I seemed to myself to resemble a small boy who, wading into a rough sea, sees a big wave coming, jumps in the air to avoid being overwhelmed, and is flung on to the shore. Physically I was exhausted.' To keep himself from hydrating he would drink up to eight bottles of Guinness per performance, while a member of the company stood in the wings with a tray of peeled grapes and a chamois leather to wipe away the accumulated sweat.

Of these early efforts he wrote to an actor who aspired to play the part: 'You have to tear your heart out and it won't come at first – mine resisted for at least twelve performances, and after that it became unbearable until I had to stop.' On tour he played Lear just twice a week, and forty-two performances in all. One day he attempted to give two performances, but found it 'an impossible task'. Later he decided on four performances a week, but found that also too much of a strain.

Arriving in London early in 1943, he staged the play for two weeks at the St James'. The production was received no more than politely. The critic Laurence Kitchin noted: 'He hectors, frowns, licks his lips, sometimes rants.' Others complained of his voice, which was sometimes unpleasantly nasal. The most influential critic, James Agate of the *Sunday Times*, wrote that 'his playing, while it never failed or flopped, never lit on the floor of magic'.

Yet the revival at the Scala the following year provoked a remarkably different response. Some of the reviews were certainly critical: J. C. Trewin decided that 'in spite of its nobility, his Lear suffered from a creeping monotony of intonation', while Herbert Farjeon wrote: 'Too often Mr Wolfit becomes involved in his own tune, which governs and obscures the thoughts instead of emerging directly from them … He was big enough for Lear, but not deep enough.' But these views were more than outweighed by those of other critics.

Beverley Baxter decided: 'There was genius in him that night.' The impresario C. B. Cochran wrote that 'in Donald Wolfit a new giant has arisen'. The anonymous critic of *The Times* saw 'a Lear of outstanding majesty, grandeur and pathos ... His was an emotional tour-de-force lit by a perpetually active intelligence, which flatly contradicted Lamb's contention that Lear should never be acted.' But it was the review by Agate that produced the biggest impact. Unexpectedly reversing his previous judgement, he called Wolfit's performance 'the greatest piece of Shakespearean acting I have seen since I have been privileged to write for the *Sunday Times*'. Later he went even further, describing Wolfit as the greatest actor he had seen since Henry Irving.

Arguing that Lear was the most difficult part in all of Shakespeare, Agate set down what he felt an audience should expect from any Lear: majesty; moral grandeur; a mind; a man, indeed a king, in ruins; and someone with enough voice to dominate the thunder. He added: 'The actor must make us feel in the heath and hovel scenes that we are in the presence of a flaming torch.' Wolfit, he suggested, had all these qualities, and 'created the impression Lear calls for'. His voice always dominated the storm, created by a combination of thunder-sheet, drums, rain and wind machines, and an extra recorded sound of thunder. Harwood, who was a member of the crew who created the storm, says it was never loud enough for Wolfit. 'I want a storm, not a breeze!' he would insist.

Ten years later, on another Stonehenge-style set, he tackled the part again at the King's, Hammersmith. The production, in which Harold Pinter played a Knight, impressed the new *enfant terrible* of criticism, Kenneth Tynan: 'He is magnificent in the early scenes, sulking like a beaten dog when Cordelia refuses to play ball with him.' More ambivalently, Tynan went on to describe him graphically as: 'A great flawed piece of masonry, making up in weight what it lacks in delicacy: a tribal chieftain rather than a hereditary monarch ... His Lear is a brilliant compound of earth, fire, and flood. Only the airy element is missing.' John Osborne remembered that his performance made you 'feel the very roof of the old theatre would split open and the heavens hurtle down upon you'.

Wolfit became celebrated in theatrical tradition for two pieces of advice about playing Lear. When Michael Redgrave was about to take on the part, Wolfit told him: 'Watch your Fool', or as another version has it, 'Be careful of your Fool.' At the King's he put this into practice, making sure that Richard Goolden kept well out of the limelight. He also appears to have been responsible for the dictum: 'Get a small Cordelia', which celebrated advice other Lears including Gielgud, Michael Hordern and Michael Gambon also passed on to their successors.

In 1961 Peter Hall invited Wolfit to play Falstaff at Stratford the following year, but when he heard that Scofield was to play Lear in the same season, he withdrew, announcing: 'Lear is still the brightest jewel in my crown.'

# Laurence Olivier
## *Laurence Olivier*

*Laurence Olivier directed himself as King Lear in his 1946 production at the New Theatre in London.*

It was seeing Randle Ayrton's Lear that had stirred Olivier's ambition, making him decide 'to be the greatest actor of all time'. It was inevitable then that he should eventually take on King Lear. With characteristic bravado he described it as 'an easy part, one of the easiest parts in Shakespeare, apart from Coriolanus. We can all play it. It is simply bang straightforward … He's like all of us really, he's just a stupid old fart.' But at thirty-nine he was young, and his performance was felt by many to lack stature.

In his book *On Acting* he explained how he prepared for such a part.

> First I exercise my chords by shouting full out in the open air, probably to an audience of cows. I try to extend my vocal range and make sure I can manage eight or more lines without pausing for breath. Then I practise the role in detail to myself. It is a great mistake to take up rehearsal time with technical matters. By the first rehearsal of *Lear* I knew exactly where to take a breath, how to light and shade my voice, and how to tonalise it at certain moments in order to get the utmost variety. At the rehearsal I like to work full out, to try my complete range, so that I can eventually produce my final performance by a process of selection.

In addition to playing Lear, he directed the play, a fiendishly difficult undertaking. Here again his preparations were meticulous, and clearly limited the actors' freedom to invent. Margaret Leighton, playing Regan, recalled: 'He astonished me by having everything worked out in great detail. He explained his plan for the play, and in particular for my part. He had planned every single move for Regan, and each move was in accordance with the text, and helped to explain it.' He went so far as to visit an eye specialist, to get the medical details right for the blinding of Gloucester. For that scene he also suggested that Regan should appear to have an orgasm when Cornwall trampled on Gloucester's eyes.

Combining acting with directing was far from ideal. During the early rehearsals Olivier partly got round the obvious difficulty by asking his stage manager to walk through the part and read for him. But the set-up inevitably became more problematic at the technical and dress rehearsals, when he needed to concentrate on his performance while simultaneously assessing the overall effect of his production. Unexpectedly, on the first night he experienced none of his usual fears, feeling that the odds against him were so great that they ceased to be terrifying. How realistically could he hope to succeed in every aspect of such a complex part?

With the wartime Lears of Gielgud and Wolfit still relatively fresh in the critics' minds, his performance provoked wildly divergent reviews. Some critics called it the best Lear yet, faultless and great, full of vigour and pathos, with Olivier exercising a new control, and solving all the problems the part threw up. They wrote of his quicksilver rapidity, daring changes of tempo, and shifting of mood. Harold Hobson felt that 'the cries and the lamentations that are torn out of his breast are like the crash of thunder and the stab of lightning ... They are the groaning and the weeping of the universe.'

Others felt his performance to be a failure: remote, eccentric, technically brilliant but lacking in depth and tragic weight. Tyrone Guthrie called it 'sentimental rather than monumental'. Laurence Kitchin saw a technical performance: 'He was impersonating an elderly psychopath, but he was impersonating him out of the play.' Tynan was also disapproving, suggesting he merely introduced us to some unpredictable moments in the private life of Justice Shallow in *Henry IV Part II*, a role he had played the year before. Describing Olivier as 'a player of unparalleled animal powers miraculously crossed with a player of extreme technical cuteness', he criticised him for his 'over-worked tricks', such as the stabbing finger and the nervously nodding head, deciding that 'instead of the pathos of crumbling strength, he offered the misfortune of bright wits blurred. He could not give us more than a fraction of all the massive deluded grandeur.'

Olivier injected grim humour into the part, especially in the opening scene, which he played as a whimsical father rather than an impetuous king. As he entered through a line of guards he paused to poke some of them in the ribs, with a chuckle. As a director Peter Brook was not amused: 'Of course he got his unexpected laughs, but the price was high. There was nowhere to go for the rest of the long play; there was no tragedy, and it was only the superb Fool of Alec Guinness that saved the day.' This comic element led Agate to comment: 'I have the conviction that Olivier is a comedian by instinct and a tragedian by art. He keeps his sense of fun under control in his tragic parts, but I can see him controlling it.' Tynan made a similar point, writing: 'He cannot play old men without letting his jaw sag and his eye wander archly in magpie fashion – in short, without becoming funny.'

Guinness' strange, sad, white-faced, expressionless Fool attracted the best reviews. Trewin compared him to a 'half-frightened bird', writing: 'The Fool is neither prancing jester nor piping grotesque, and Guinness, wry, quiet, true, with a dog's devotion, restored it to its proper place. When at last he slipped from the play we felt for a moment that the candle was out.' Guinness himself observed: 'The Fool has sixty lines and Olivier wisely cut them down to thirty, so that you couldn't get bored with the doggerel that goes on. Every time he came on stage the lights went up in his vicinity. All I had to do was just stay very close to him.'

Harry Andrews, who played Cornwall, remembered the impact of the blinding of Gloucester. 'It was pretty horrendous. After the first night, with the audience fainting and being taken out, Larry agreed we had gone over the top and toned it down a bit.' The storm was powerfully done, staged in complete blackness with just flashes of lightning to illuminate Olivier. But there were problems. Owing to technical difficulties involved with the cyclorama, half of the visual effect of the two main interior settings had to be abandoned at the dress-rehearsal, leaving an unintentionally stark set. In addition, the incidental music by Herbert Menges failed to cover the noise of two low platforms on wheels being moved around the stage.

Later Olivier wrote: 'I was determined to be heard in Trafalgar Square and I'm sure the effect was electric, for I stood in jet blackness shot through with lightning ... I was able to get tremendous power vocally, so in the storm scene the thunder and lightning were in the king himself as well as in the elements.' For the Dover scene he entered with naked bleeding feet, dressed like a tattered scarecrow, vines clinging to him, and a wreath of flowers set at an angle over one ear. For many this was an intensely moving scene, as Lear hugged and shared his grief with the blind Gloucester.

Olivier later compared his performance with Wolfit's, stating: 'Wolfit stressed the senility of the character, whereas with mine the octogenarian's body still pulsed with life and passion.' Wolfit himself, after watching the performance, concluded with evident satisfaction: 'Not Larry's part, I fear. Lear's a bass part, and Larry's a tenor.' Gielgud, another tenor, took a more balanced view: he thought Olivier 'brilliantly clever and absolutely complete in his characterisation', but 'without majesty or awesomeness'. In hindsight Olivier thought he was wrong to direct the production.

In the immediate aftermath of the war, with the horrific pictures of the Nazi death camps engraved on people's minds, the novelist Rosamund Lehmann pointed up the play's topicality: 'This is the time, the age, to take in *Lear*, isn't it?' she told Olivier. 'It seemed prophetic for our day – the gigantic moral anarchy – every word true.'

# 3

# At the Old Vic

## William Devlin
### *Henry Cass*

*William Devlin played King Lear in 1936 at the Old Vic, directed by Henry Cass.*

Although he was only twenty-four, this was already William Devlin's second Lear. Two years previously, having been on the professional stage for just seven months playing minor parts, he had made his debut as Lear at the Westminster, and achieved a remarkable success. His performance, directed by Hugh Hunt, prompted James Agate to suggest that 'it may be that here is the new great actor for whom the English state has impatiently waited since the death of Irving'. Praising Devlin's 'magnificent voice full of oak-cleaving thunderbolts', he concluded: 'Setting it against the performances of mature actors in the part, I find that, with the exception of Benson's Lear, it is incomparably the best I have known.'

The young actor was enthralled by the play, describing it as he prepared for the 1936 production as 'surely the greatest masterpiece ever conceived by the mind of man'. He suggested that 'the farther one probes into it, the greater is the appreciation of its beauties … Shakespeare's native genius soars far above the historical or legendary plots on which he bases his plays. He welds their garbled incongruities into a tremendous whole by the strength of his human insight.'

His director was Henry Cass, who set the play in an arid landscape of Ancient Britain. This connected well with Devlin's rugged features. 'This Lear had a head like the Job of Blake, and his features seemed hewn out of the Druid pillars of Stonehenge,' noted the critic Audrey Williamson. 'In voice and physique it seemed more than life size, and if this a little limited its humanity and range, it gave a livid power and anguish to the scenes of the storm.' However, she thought him 'insufficiently crazed in the mad scenes; something in that noble and intellectual head defied the impression of mental distraction.' She added: 'The main portrait was one of dignity and passion, not of pathos ... The heart that cracked was a king's heart, the man a giant to the last.'

A decade later Devlin appeared again as Lear in Hugh Hunt's 1947 revival at the Embassy, co-produced by the Old Vic and the Bristol Old Vic, and the following year repeated the part in a BBC television version, directed by Royston Morley. In the Old Vic's 1952–3 season he took over the part from Stephen Murray, also under the direction of Hugh Hunt. He also played Lear in America, as a guest in 1950 for the Brattle Theatre Company in Cambridge, Massachusetts. One critic wrote of his performance there: 'Devlin's portrayal is one of tremendous emotional intensity and compelling human qualities. His delivery is clear, sonorous and wonderful to hear.'

# John Gielgud
## *Lewis Casson/Harley Granville Barker*

*In 1940 John Gielgud played his second Lear, again at the Old Vic. The production was co-directed by Lewis Casson and Harley Granville Barker.*

In March 1940 John Gielgud reported to George Rylands: 'Granville Barker comes to work on *Lear* with us (in the deepest secrecy).' The arrangement was for Lewis Casson, playing Kent, to co-produce, but appear as sole producer in the programme. Barker, who had not directed for many years, came over from Paris and worked for a fortnight on the play. Gielgud read his part to him, weeping during the more emotional scenes. Barker told him he had read only two lines correctly, adding: 'Of course you are an ash and this part demands an oak, but we'll see how this will serve you.'

With Barker temporarily back in France, Gielgud, Casson and Guthrie laid the foundations of the production, using Barker's *Preface* as a guide. Barker then reappeared, and scrapped nearly everything. 'He was like a god coming back,' Gielgud remembered. 'Guthrie and Casson were absolutely thrown out of the window by the force of his personality. You felt if you could satisfy him, the puzzle was solved for ever.' For ten days the company worked intensively, sometimes from 10.30 in the morning to midnight. 'Barker's knowledge of the stage, of the tricks, of the ways and vanities of the actors, is enormous,' Gielgud explained. 'If you think you are going to see the old-time ranting Lear next week, you are mistaken. I shall rant hardly at all.'

Gielgud later observed: 'I don't think about what may or may not have happened to the characters before the play begins. I remember Barker saying that Shakespeare wasn't worried whether Lear was married twice or not.' Barker told the actors to think of the play as something from the Old Testament, or as one of the great fairy stories: 'Once upon a time there was an old king with three daughters ...'. Gielgud found this illuminating. He also admired Barker's meticulous methods, so different from his own mercurial style of directing.

> He inspired and dominated everyone like a master-craftsman. He began to work with the actors, not using any notes, but sitting on the stage with his back to the footlights, a copy of the play in his hand ... quiet-voiced, seldom moving, coldly humorous, shrewdly observant, infinitely patient and persevering ... He neither coaxed nor flattered, but at the same time, though he was intensely autocratic and severe, he was never personal or rude. The actors had immediate respect for his authority. They did not become paralysed or apathetic, as can so often happen when a strong director is not excessively sensitive ... Tempo, atmosphere, diction, balance, character – no detail could escape his fastidious ear, his unerring dramatic instinct, and his superb sense of classic shapeliness of line.

But Barker could also instil fear. Alan MacNaughtan, just out of drama school and playing the King of France, recalls: 'He was an absolute martinet, and for Gielgud and the others their God. They were just like children, they were all petrified of him.' Stephen Haggard, cast as the Fool, wrote to his father of 'nine ecstatic days' of rehearsals: 'Oh my! how exhilarating he is to work for. He has taken the whole dead thing and made it sit up and look at you ... He's an object of reverent admiration for the whole cast (and that's a feat in itself).'

Haggard reflected later on playing the Fool, which Barker said was the most difficult part in all Shakespeare.

> And except perhaps in the first scene it is a thankless one too. To have one's best scene first, to have no scenes at all except when Lear – that terrific figure – is also on the stage, to be summarily and unexplainedly dismissed halfway through the play: these are grave disadvantages to any part, but especially to so slight and wistful a creature as the Fool, surrounded as he is by almost titanic characters.

Meanwhile Gielgud was absorbing everything from 'the finest audience and the severest critic I ever had to please'. His confidence in Barker was absolute: 'When Barker told me anything was good, I never wanted to change it,' he admitted. 'He was the master, the Toscanini, the absolute genius. He had an enormous knowledge of the scaffolding of the work, not only as a student, a professor, but also as a stage manager and stage director. There was a feeling that he was ready to improvise, and that he summed up your possibilities almost the first day.'

Barker was also open to ideas, such as Gielgud's suggestion that in the final scene he should find the rope that hanged Cordelia in the soldier's hand. He tried to get Gielgud to be less declamatory, not to twist the

melodic line, to hold his emotional power in reserve, and to find the witty
and sly side of Lear. Once he told him: 'You did some fine things today in
that scene: I hope you know what they were!' – then produced a page of
what Gielgud described as 'shattering, critical notes'. Yet he relished being
pushed hard: 'Barker was like a masseur who forces you to discover and
use muscles you never knew you possessed.'

The final dress-rehearsal finished at 3 a.m. To the actors' dismay Barker
left for France straight afterwards: there was growing anxiety in Paris about
the German advance. But before the opening he wrote to Gielgud: 'Lear is
in your grasp. Forget all the things I have bothered you about. Let your own
now well-disciplined instincts carry you along, and up, simply allowing the
checks and changes to prevent your being carried *away*. And I prophesy –
happily – great things for you.'

Just before the opening Gielgud wrote to his father about the value of
playing Lear at such a momentous time: 'I am in the usual chaotic despair
before a first night. Barker has tried us hard – and still demands further
ideals – but his work is fine – I have learnt much this week – and everyone
has struggled bravely and uncomplainingly ... Nothing but such a master
as Barker and a mighty work like *Lear* could have kept one so concentrated
these ten days with such a holocaust going on around us.'

*King Lear* opened as the phoney war ended. Hitler had invaded Norway
only days before, and the atmosphere in the Old Vic was tense and
expectant. One critic wrote: 'People crowded every seat, stood all down
the aisles, hardly dared breathe, certainly dared not cough.' Afterwards
Guthrie wrote to Gielgud's parents: 'I think John's performance is *very* fine
– a really memorable achievement and a contribution to the sort of theatre
that is worth fighting and tussling to preserve.' Herbert Farjeon praised the
'gallant actors' for working for next to nothing, declaring that they had
'put Shakespeare and the Old Vic on their feet again', and 'restored the
self-respect of the theatre'.

Gielgud later wrote: 'You have to decide from the outset whether Lear
is a great man who loses his position, or that he acquires greatness and
wisdom through suffering.' His performance provoked a mixed critical
reception. *The Times* critic observed that 'he acts with a nervous force, but
is inclined at times to fall something short on physical toughness', while
Farjeon wrote: 'We feel for the words Lear speaks rather than for Lear
himself.' Agate, who had clearly heard of Barker's comment, thought there
was too much ash and not enough oak. Yet he found Gielgud's performance
one of 'great beauty, imagination, sensitiveness, understanding, executive
virtuosity, and control', though concluding 'this is Lear every inch but one'.

There was praise for the way he conveyed Lear's progress from worldly to
spiritual authority, and for the pathos of his final scenes with Cordelia. Alan
Dent was impressed, writing: 'This acting gives us much of the terror of the
play, and still more the pity of it. It is only in the easiest and least important
scenes, occurring early, that we faintly detect the young actor in his thirties

behind that old and most authoritative beard.' But he took Gielgud to task for one scene: 'As done at present, you look a little too like an old gent at the Athenaeum having his final heart attack.' Audrey Williamson thought his performance 'the most powerful, moving and imaginative of Gielgud's Shakespeare portraits, in which beauty of elocution, nobility of presence and emotional range combined in an unforgettable degree.'

The poet Stephen Spender told Gielgud. 'You have made such a profound study of the part that your acting transcends itself, and one forgets altogether the sense of a performance, and has instead an impression of the poetry itself come to life.' Gielgud suggested to his friend Gabrielle Enthoven that he had improved on his last Lear: 'I do now feel I have some of the range and gradual ebb and flow of the character.' He gave full credit to Barker, telling the novelist Hugh Walpole: 'I have never before had so much care taken with a performance by someone on whose critical judgement I could absolutely rely.'

His playing gave people the courage to face the imminent threat of bombing and invasion: 'It is wonderful that people are so ready to come, and seem to be so still and moved – even with all the troubles in the world,' he told Enthoven. 'I think the superb poetry is a sort of comfort and release.' He asked people how they could bear the blinding, the cruelty, the death of the king. They would say: 'There's a kind of catharsis, and when we come out of the theatre we are uplifted, like after hearing Beethoven. It shows that with all the appalling things going on, there is some glory, and something that is worth everything.'

# 4

# A Stratford Decade

## John Gielgud
### Anthony Quayle

*In 1950 John Gielgud played his third Lear, this time at Stratford, where Anthony Quayle acted as his co-director.*

This was John Gielgud's Stratford debut. The schedule was to be a gruelling one, with eight performances a week, including two matinees. Gielgud immediately made clear his approach. 'I have very careful notes of the Granville Barker production, which Mr Quayle and I intend to follow,' he explained. Andrew Cruickshank recalled a moment during a rehearsal that underlined his reliance on Barker's ideas. As they worked on the Dover cliff scene, Gielgud checked his notes, and then shouted from the stalls: 'Barker told me I should play this scene as though there was a pain shooting through my head.'

But one actor rebelled against this Barker-worship. Alan Badel, aged twenty-six, wanted to play the Fool as a merry, dancing and singing boy, prematurely aged, who worked in Lear's kitchen and was unable to tell a lie. Gielgud reluctantly gave him his head, and the result, which impressed the critics, was a terrified, emaciated, suffering Fool, 'the very embodiment of pathos, loyal as a mongrel, frightened as a lost child', as one put it.

Gielgud wrote later: 'Many Lears have tried to rationalise the coming madness by making him also senile, showing an unhinged mind from the very start, but I think the first scene should be simple and majestic. For all the rash things he does, Lear has complete control at first.' At Stratford he adopted this approach, starting as a firm, proud monarch with no hint yet of madness, or of a capricious tyrant. But on the first night he was nervous and exhausted, and his playing seemed to several critics subdued and detached, though still intensely moving in the reconciliation scene with Cordelia.

J. C. Trewin wrote: '*King Lear* is an Ancient Monument, but in the early stages Gielgud behaves like a guide who is showing us around … Until the end the actor, intellectually commanding, illuminated the part from without rather than from within.' Philip Hope-Wallace observed: 'The poetry had a crystal clarity, and I cannot imagine a more intelligent or a more fastidious Lear,' but felt that 'his rages are sarcastic rather than thunderous, and he bears his wounds with dignity and a thin-lipped nervous grief'. For Harold Hobson, Gielgud displayed 'the pathos of a Don Quixote grievously deceived, rather than a god magnificently overthrown.' He was not helped by the loud recorded music, which drowned out his words at the start of the storm scene.

Ivor Brown admired his fidelity to Shakespeare's intentions. 'He gives no embroidery of character acting in Olivier's way. He is the text incarnate.' T. C. Worsley compared his qualities to those of two earlier Lears: 'Both Mr Wolfit and Sir Laurence Olivier strike harder, clearer, louder at the note of the majestic or the terrible,' he suggested, whereas

> if Mr Gielgud is the great tragic actor *par excellence* of our generation, is it not by virtue of his ability to exhibit the particular kind of simplicity that lies at the heart of passion in highly conscious, complicated personalities? ... It is the weight that he gives to the ironies, the irresolutions, the subtleties, that gives the still moments when they come their extra turn.

There were then no previews at Stratford, which made the first night additionally stressful for the actors. Fortunately Worsley returned the following night, and found a Lear transformed. On the first night, he wrote, 'you admired Gielgud's performance intellectually; on the second it drew you in emotionally, so that he no longer seemed to be acting.' He also described the production as one that 'might convert those, if there still are any, who prefer reading *Lear* to seeing it'.

*Gielgud played his fourth Lear five years later (see page 31).*

# Michael Redgrave
## *George Devine*

*Michael Redgrave appeared as King Lear in 1953 at the Stratford Memorial Theatre, directed by George Devine.*

While a student at Cambridge, Michael Redgrave had appeared in a Marlowe Society production of *King Lear*, directed by George Rylands. Cast as Edgar, he had been praised for his sensitive verse-speaking. Five years later, while a teacher at Cranleigh, a public school in Surrey, he had moved up to the title-role, preparing for it in the Lake District by 'spouting Lear on a fell above Borrowdale'. He directed the production himself, seeing the play as essentially a pagan one. His acting drew praise from two eminent Shakespearean scholars, G. Wilson Knight and J. Dover Wilson, and from Rylands, who told him it was 'a performance of exceptional beauty and understanding'.

In the mid-1930s he wrote an article in the theatre magazine *Rep*, stressing the importance of a quality cast:

> In order to interpret the triumph of Lear's spirit it needs a small group of fine actors who, even if they do not realise the end in view, can combine together with an intensity that is called for by no other play in the world. Team-work is a poor word for such fusion. The third act of Lear in performance is the greatest experience of group acting that there is. There is no part for a star in Lear. Lear himself is a constellation.

Ironically, when he came to play the part again in Stratford in 1953, his performance was treated by the critics as a star solo effort, despite the high quality of the cast. George Devine placed the story firmly in pagan antiquity, echoing Redgrave's Cranleigh production. He wanted the sculptor Henry Moore as designer, but when he declined he commissioned Robert Colquhoun. The Scottish artist's set had a primitive, monolithic Stonehenge-style structure, which was used for both Lear's throne and the hovel. Two gigantic doors, placed on either side of the stage and leading into the castles of Albany and Gloucester, suggested a later period, hinting at the Christian element in the play. The costumes were the colour of stone, earth and heather, decorated with scrolls like Celtic runes.

Tall, intellectual and still relatively young at forty-five, Redgrave presented an ancient, lonely and heart-weary Lear, a man, according to Robert Speaight, 'stooping and frail and immense in stature, wearing all the weight of his four score years'. Unfashionably infirm and ineffective, already 'a fond and foolish' old man in the opening scene, he offered a morbidly clinical picture of senility, reflected in his struggle to draw his sword while castigating Kent for opposing him.

He achieved this state, wrote T. C. Worsley,

> not by conventional 'old age business', but by the voice and bearing, by giving off somehow in the way he sits and stands and listens the very feel and, as it were, the smell of old age ... This is the old age of a despot still unreconciled to the loss of power and vitality, whose resigning of his office is only another whim of his never crossed authority.

Yet not all critics were convinced: Alan Dent had the impression of 'an accomplished young actor impersonating an old Gentleman suffering from asthma'.

The production was commended for its lucidity and restraint, and Redgrave praised for a performance of great humanity and breadth.

Speaight concluded: 'Time and again we are caught up by the sweep and the surprise of great acting.' Several critics measured his performance against those of Wolfit and Gielgud. Philip Hope-Wallace wrote:

> Others have found more striking power, or more simple poetry, but none an interpretation at once so full (in the sense of histrionic volume) and so consistently bringing all the aspects together, without any shirking or pruning away of what is inconvenient ... Taken as a whole, his Lear must be counted the most satisfying interpretation of the allegedly unplayable part since the war ... If sheer acting ability and intelligence can make Lear live for us in the theatre, then his interpretation is one of the most interesting and vivid lessons in the way to play it.

Speaight suggested he had never been so moving: 'His voice rumbled, spurted, and subsided with the ebb and swell of passion, whimpered or thundered with alternating rage and grief.' In the past Redgrave had been criticised for lacking passion, for over-intellectualising a part, for being deficient in pathos and 'keeping one foot outside the character'; Tynan suggested that 'the technical apparatus with which he besieges his parts has sometimes looked a little over-elaborate'. But this flaw, he decided, was not in evidence here: 'Lear is a labyrinthine citadel, all but impregnable,' he wrote, 'and it needed a Redgrave to assault it. On Tuesday night the balloon went up.' However, Trewin felt there were still signs of detachment in his performance: 'He has the intellectual measure of the part, but he is cold', was his verdict.

Some critics suggested vocal mannerisms marred the clarity of his verse-speaking; Cecil Wilson drew attention to 'careful cracks of the voice' and 'great hissing intakes of breath'. Vocally he lacked the lyric quality of Gielgud, but also the kind of bass voice that could help him outface the storm. As with many Lears, he was felt to be at his weakest here, though he had to contend with more elements than some: as well as the effects of the thunder-sheet and the rain box, he had to battle against a musical accompaniment. Richard Findlater observed: 'English directors pay far too much attention to the weather and too little to the verse.'

Most critics felt Redgrave came into his own in the later stages. Tynan wrote of the Dover cliff scene: 'Is it a backhanded compliment to say that this actor is best when maddest? Lear's drifting whims, his sudden, shocking changes of subject, his veering from transcendent silliness to aching desolation, were all explored, explained, and definitively expressed ... Give Redgrave a scene like this one, which is the higher mathematics of acting, and he solves it in a flash.' The final scene with the dead Cordelia was heart-breaking for many critics, notably when he used a wisp of his hair to test whether she was still breathing ('Look there!'). Speaight reckoned that 'of all the modern Lears – and there have been many fine ones – Mr Redgrave is, I think, the finest.' Worsley asked: 'Is there anywhere in dramatic literature so perfect a dying close as the phrases of these last pages of *Lear*? And is there anything more moving than to hear them perfectly delivered as they were on this night? Certainly I don't remember an audience so deeply stirred.'

Looking back on his performance, Redgrave noted. 'If it is in your power to be great in a part, you can nearly be great quite a number of times. But there is that other time – maybe once a week – when you know, and the audience knows, that it is magic.' In *King Lear* he felt this occurred too rarely. Suggesting a degree of disappointment with his performance, he added: 'I think it will be better when I play it again.' He never did so.

# John Gielgud
## *George Devine*

*In 1955 John Gielgud took on his fourth Lear, playing it again at Stratford, this time with George Devine as his co-director. The production also played at the Palace in London, and toured the UK and Europe.*

This controversial production caused a furore. It was quickly labelled the 'Noguchi Lear', in reference to the futuristic sets and costumes designed by the internationally celebrated American/Japanese sculptor and furniture designer, Isamu Noguchi. While in New York Gielgud had seen Noguchi's sophisticated but simple designs for Martha Graham's ballets: 'The whole set-up gave me a very new feeling about the possibilities of combining tragedy with stylised movement, which I should greatly like to experiment with in *Lear*.'

He decided to change his conception of the play. In his recent Stratford production of *Macbeth* he had been moving towards a more abstract design, less anchored in a specific time or place. Here was a chance to develop the idea further with an innovative designer. He persuaded Devine, who also admired Noguchi's theatre decor, to commission sets and costumes from him. Noguchi produced a set of startling abstract and geometric designs, including egg-forms, triangular caverns, bright-coloured moving screens, airborne prisms and a large floating wall, the shapes and colours of which reflected different aspects of the story.

Both directors were impressed. The costumes, however, were another matter. Devine's idea in the brief to Noguchi was that the costumes would define the essence of each character, but change to mirror their development. 'The gloves are gradually removed,' he explained, 'so that by the end of part one no one is any more pretending to be anything but what he is.' However, Noguchi had never designed costumes before, neither could he draw. He therefore submitted paper maquettes, painted and cut to scale, and dressed in miniature versions of the costumes. These were hurriedly made up, but when the actors put them on for a dress parade they were aghast at the bizarre designs, and their impracticality. Gielgud tried unsuccessfully to persuade Devine to abandon them, and create instead 'nondescript cloaks' to give a Blake-like effect to go with the settings.

According to the two directors' hopeful programme note:

> Our object has been to find a setting and costumes which would be free of historical and decorative associations, so that the timeless, universal and mythical quality of the story may be clear. We have tried to present the places and the characters in a very simple and basic manner, for the play to come to life through the words and the acting.

Not surprisingly, the effect was precisely the opposite: the bizarre costumes and intrusively weird sets all but obliterated the performances.

Gielgud, his face surrounded by dense white horsehair, wore a crown resembling an upturned milking stool, carried what looked like a hearth-brush, and was trapped in a cloak full of holes, which symbolically grew larger as Lear's mind disintegrated. Several critics pointed to Lear's remark 'I do not like the fashion of your garments ... let them be changed'; others sneered at what they saw as a science-fiction, outer-space landscape inhabited by aliens. Gielgud himself was variously compared to the Wizard of Oz, a gruyere cheese, and a Henry Moore sculpture, while Emlyn Williams dubbed him 'Gypsy Rose Lear'.

The actors found themselves caged in lattice-work armour, or wearing overcoats with lifebuoy-like waistbands. The critics were almost unani-mously scornful. One observed that the designs were so distracting that 'John Gielgud's Lear is for some time neglected in favour of Kent, who is wearing india-rubber water-bottles; the Knight, with a gumboot on one leg and a hockey-pad on the other; and other men, draped with sausages. There are also "things" that descend from heaven, including a large black banana, and at least one hat straight out of *The Mikado*.'

Peggy Ashcroft, playing Cordelia, felt that without the Noguchi costumes *King Lear* 'would have come off magnificently', but that with them 'I didn't see how anybody could act'. Helen Cherry (Goneril) remembered the problems created by the Minoan dresses she and Moira Lister (Regan) were compelled to wear, which prompted comparisons with Alice in Wonderland versions of caterpillars. 'They were like tents, and you had to put your hands on them to stop them swaying as you walked. The critics said it was a new stylised way of acting, but we were just trying to keep these awful costumes under control.'

Devine was in revolt against the style of the Stratford Memorial Theatre, which he described as a 'death trap' and 'a great lump of masonry, standing on the riverbank, imposing itself on everyone who has to work there'. He was looking for a more detached, less rhetorical style of acting to match the oriental-style decor. But according to David Conville, who played one of Cromwell's servants: 'He was so thrilled by the set design and costumes that he didn't really direct the play. At the first rehearsal he said that we had to find a new style of acting to fit the set and costumes, but he gave no indication of how we should do that.'

Gielgud re-thought his interpretation of Lear. He now saw him as much more of a stubborn and obstinate old man, the victim of his own tyranny. Yet his heavy, cramped costume all but destroyed his performance, which hovered between two styles. According to the designer Jocelyn Herbert, who later lived with Devine: 'George tried to get Gielgud to control his voice, and in rehearsals he was fine, but he got cold feet, and soon went back to his old style.'

T. C. Worsley was one of the few critics to defend the production: 'Experiment is the lifeblood of any art, and the English theatre is not so noticeably lively at the moment that we can afford to scoff when it tries to be adventurous,' he wrote. Others accused Gielgud of breaking up the poetry into fragments of prose, or losing it altogether by adopting a thin, dry and frequently rasping voice. There was, as one put it, 'not a damp eye in the house'. Gielgud wrote to Olivier: 'It was obvious that the different style of the production had to be matched if possible by a performance that goes with the make-up and general pictorial effect. But the clothes and furniture are both very hard and exhausting to manage, and with the emotion and vocal strain as well, I find it a very wearing business.' This last point was underlined in a slip inserted in the programme, stating: 'Sir John Gielgud has requested that for this performance of *King Lear* patrons do not smoke, as it is injurious to the voice.'

Gielgud wrote to the designer Cecil Beaton: 'The production is very original and powerful. It will cause a lot of controversy, but I'm sure it breaks new ground, which is what we hoped.' During the tour he publicly defended the production: 'At least we can say we have done something experimental and fresh – and there hasn't been much of this in our theatre for a long time. Experiments such as this can have a lasting influence. They can encourage others to do better and go farther, and people can learn from our mistakes. I think it is nonsense to say that men such as Granville Barker would turn in their graves if they could see this *Lear*. On the contrary, they would be the first to be interested and understanding.'

His words proved prophetic: when seven years later Peter Brook directed *King Lear* at Stratford, he told Gielgud it was this production that had given him the basic idea for his own one with Paul Scofield.

# Charles Laughton
## *Glen Byam Shaw*

*In 1959 Charles Laughton played King Lear at the Stratford Memorial Theatre, directed by its artistic director Glen Byam Shaw.*

During his years as a Hollywood star Charles Laughton became obsessed with Shakespeare. He never stopped thinking about the plays, and dreaming about them. As his biographer Simon Callow put it: 'In a sense, Laughton had been preparing for *King Lear* all his life. From the moment he started giving interviews, he had been alluding to the play, sometimes representing it as the ultimate summit, sometimes as a byword for the irrelevance of Shakespeare to the modern world, depending on how defensive he felt.'

It was Gielgud who, turning down the offer from Stratford to play his fifth Lear, suggested to the theatre's artistic director Glen Byam Shaw that he approach Laughton. He had been away from England since the 1933–4 season at the Old Vic, when his unconventional interpretations of Macbeth and Angelo had infuriated the critics, and he had withdrawn from the London stage. Now, arriving in Stratford in the summer of 1959, he hoped to restore his reputation as a leading actor in the English classical theatre, and fulfil his long-standing ambition to play King Lear.

Once he had agreed to the role, his preparations were remarkable. At his home in California he studied the play alone, even reading it in bed. He then spoke it aloud many times with his wife, the actress Elsa Lanchester: he read Lear, while she read all the other parts. They flew to Hawaii for several weeks, to work solidly on the play away from all distraction. He even bought some peyote, telling her, 'I want to get as far into the character of Lear as I can.' Once in England, and before rehearsals began, he and his wife took a trip to Portmeirion in Wales. Laughton knew the part well by then, but they still spent many hours developing it. 'Lear was always with him,' she remembered.

Glen Byam Shaw, who was directing the play, had decided to set it in pre-historic times. So Laughton and his wife visited the pre-historic circle of stones at Rollright outside Stratford, which according to local legend represented a king and his knights, turned into stone by a witch. He was to visit the place later with young members of the cast: Julian Glover, playing Albany, recalled driving him there: 'He went and lay down in the middle of the stones. He was wearing an oatmeal coloured smock against those white stones, and he was very portly, and there was this boulder in the middle of it all, and that was Charlie Laughton.' Ian Holm, cast as the Fool, was also there one night, and reported that Laughton 'was awe-inspiring when he declaimed his speeches under the stars'.

Laughton persuaded Byam Shaw to go with him to Stonehenge, where in similar vein he imbibed the atmosphere of the famous standing stones. Continuing on this spiritual search, and with the play's Dover cliff scene in mind, the two men went together to Beachy Head on the south coast. 'It was a beastly day, a very high wind, and raining,' Byam Shaw recalled. 'We struggled to the top of the cliff. I hate heights, and stopped well short of the edge. But Charles staggered on until he was within a few feet of it. Standing there alone being battered by the wind and rain, he looked remarkably like King Lear.'

In Oxford they booked rooms in a hotel, and Laughton insisted on reading the play to his director. 'It was two in the morning when we finished,' Byam Shaw remembered.

> At the end of each scene we discussed various points. Laughton said: 'I feel that for this scene I must be seated, up high and very near to the audience – like this.' He clambered on to the upright piano that stood against the wall, and sat on top of it with his feet on the keyboard. 'It will be rather difficult to achieve that,' I said, looking up at him and realising how right he was about the position. 'You'll think of something,' he said.

Laughton had shown Peter Hall, who was to direct him as Bottom in *A Midsummer Night's Dream*, how he saw the storm scene. 'It was not created by a collection of noisy drums and thunder-sheets,' Hall recalled. 'He spoke the words quietly and distantly, muted by an enormous sense of strain, drowned by an unheard wind. The eyes bulged, the voice was hoarse, and I seemed to hear the winds cracking their cheeks. I *imagined* the storm because I could hear every word.'

Even before rehearsals began he would come into Byam Shaw's office during or even after a performance of one of the plays he was not involved in, and act Lear's speeches. 'It was then that I realised how superb he could be,' Byam Shaw noted. 'The mad scenes were overwhelmingly tragic and moving.' But he wondered if Laughton would have the physical and vocal strength to sustain the whole part and fill the theatre with his performance.

Rehearsals proved to be a strain, and a test for their relationship. Byam Shaw had reluctantly agreed to Laughton's request that Elsa Lanchester attend, after Laughton claimed she knew the text better than he did, and understood it better. She was there every morning, and Laughton would often consult her. Byam Shaw found to his surprise that her potentially awkward presence was actually useful: 'She never interfered, and only gave advice or criticism when asked to do so either by Charles or myself,' he recalled. 'He trusted her judgement completely, and so, after a very short time, did I.' But Robert Hardy, playing Edmund, had a rather different memory: 'Clasping a first folio, and using his wife as a meddlesome go-between, Laughton drove the hapless director to distraction.'

Laughton did indeed prove difficult: 'He was not easy at rehearsals,' Byam Shaw observed. 'He was never satisfied with his own work, and was continually experimenting and exploring.' At times he became moody, and began telling the company that Byam Shaw had lost heart in the production, and that he himself was doing all the work. When Byam Shaw got wind of this he denied it forcefully, and a blazing row ensued. 'I think it was partly his way of goading me on, and getting all that he could out of me,' he suggested. Julian Glover was given a glimpse of the actor/director relationship. 'During rehearsals Charlie said to me: "The thing about Albany is that he's just like our director." By this he meant he was somebody who seems to be rather weak, but actually has a backbone of steel when you challenge him.' According to others, Byam Shaw was much too deferential to his star actor.

Despite these problems Laughton showed occasional flashes of brilliance. Michael Blakemore, then a young actor before becoming a director, was playing Lear's Knight, and remembered one rehearsal:

> There was one scene I doubt I shall ever see better played, when Lear with the blinded Gloucester expatiates on his newly acquired insight into the world's darkness. Charles played it with an understanding and simplicity that almost transcended acting. I sat watching him in the rehearsal room, spellbound. It was mesmeric, absolute magic. If I was asked to nominate one thing in the entire season that approached the condition of art, it would be this scene that morning.

Determined to conquer the iambic pentameter, Laughton had spent years reading Shakespeare out loud, to the ticking of a metronome. But in Stratford, as Blakemore recalled:

> It was apparent as soon as he opened his mouth on the first day of rehearsal that he didn't have a stage-ready voice. He didn't have what Olivier had so superbly, the grasp of making the iambic pentameter work for him, the ability to let a line go right to the back of the house. He wasn't into that at all, he was into the motives, the impulses, and the emotional drive of the thing.

There was a particular problem with his method of verse-speaking. Laughton had become convinced that, in the Quarto and Folio editions, the use of initial capital letters for certain words meant that the actor should stress them. But the modern consensus was that this erratic choice of capitals was the printer's rather than Shakespeare's. A worried Byam Shaw asked Peter Hall to try to persuade Laughton to abandon this nonsensical idea, but the actor wouldn't budge. 'He stuck to it doggedly,' Hall recalled, 'producing many strange stresses which made nonsense of the rhythm, and certainly didn't help the sense.'

Before leaving America, Laughton had told a friend he was to play Lear at Stratford. 'But I shall fail, of course,' he said. Still insecure as the first night loomed, he wrote to his agent:

> *Lear* approaches ominously. The further you get into that play, the more you feel that never, never will you, or any other damned actor, be able to act it fully. From all that I have read of the past, no actor has succeeded, and I am not vain enough to think that I will. One wishes the play wasn't there at all as a challenge, but there it is mocking me and I have just had

to try it, because it would be sitting on my chest when I took my last breath, saying I am a coward.

Byam Shaw felt he gave a superb performance at the dress-rehearsal, but had a shaky first night. 'He started badly, but played the mad scenes better than he had ever played them, and had the great success he deserved.' But as the run continued there were other opinions within the company. Glover remembered: 'He was tremendously nervous to start with, and was always tentative.' For Blakemore: 'He could never really manage the big rhetorical moments, such as the storm scene or when he curses his ungrateful daughters. He simply didn't have the voice.'

Zoe Caldwell, as his Cordelia, watched his entire performance every night from the wings, hoping to learn from his great experience. 'He would play Lear definitively in one scene, but you never knew which scene it would be. He was sometimes extraordinary in the storm scene, and sometimes not. His best scenes were the final ones with Cordelia. But if you're playing Lear you need an extraordinary amount of energy, and he was grossly overweight.' Ian Holm, playing the Fool in the image of a Picasso harlequin, found him 'an embarrassingly inept Lear'. From the stage he noted his lack of energy and power, observing that 'he did little to suggest the struggles Lear was enduring. There was no madness, no struggle against the elements, nothing.' He put forward the original suggestion that 'he gradually became more like himself than Lear, his performance becoming an expression of self, and a self moreover that was in dread of being found out, exposed, as if the performance was something so personal it might perish.'

There was a consensus among the critics that his performance lacked grandeur or majesty, that he was unable to compete against the storm despite Byam Shaw toning down the sound effects, but was very moving in the final scenes. Some felt he was too gentle a Lear, too tubby and loveable, a near relation to Old King Cole. Eric Keown suggested: 'His snow-white hair and beard form an almost complete circle round a podgy face of the utmost benignity, giving him the air of an innocent Father Christmas.' Harold Hobson observed: 'That the universe should single out so small a figure for its wrath gives a lurid splendour to the performance; it is as if an ordinary man was called to crucifixion.'

His voice was sibilant, his delivery rapid, and it became a prose Lear, at odds with the verse. Alan Brien wrote in the *Spectator*: 'At his best he sounds like the wind in the willows rather than the brass section of the music of the spheres. At his worst, he mumbles and groans with the threadbare moan of an old violin.' For some it was a performance of extreme care that lacked a final emotional drive. Robert Speaight spoke for many:

> The production suffered from a displacement of gravity due to Laughton's domestication of the opening scene, and a deprivation of poetry due to

his inability to speak. Words and meaning were huskily hammered out, but melody was missing. He was at his best in the scene with Gloucester, and in the arms of Cordelia, all passion spent, secure upon the summit of a second innocence. His mistake was to arrive there too soon.

During the run Laughton was troubled by nightmares associated with the play, which a psychiatrist thought were connected to the opening speech and Laughton's own fear of death. Blakemore recalled: 'He used to dread coming into the theatre to play Lear. I would stand beside him in the wings while we waited to go on, while he sighed, huffed and puffed and groaned, to dramatise the enormity of this great spiritual journey he had to go on.'

Nor was he helped by the cruel scheduling of the play, as Byam Shaw admitted: 'On matinee days it made my heart bleed to see him battling his way through two performances of that exhausting part.' At one matinee he 'dried' just six lines into his opening speech. The actor standing next to him gave him the line very quietly, and then right in his ear, but to no avail. Laughton turned to the prompt corner, asking for the line, but when the prompter obliged, he said: 'No, further back.' It was every actor's nightmare, but he dealt with it with composure.

Peter Hall believed that

at another time, and if he acted the part in an intimate space, he might have been one of the great Lears. The pathos and the ribaldry of his unhinged mind were certainly extraordinary. But in the storm he became, on the huge stage of the Stratford theatre, an aging actor whose voice had weakened, and who no longer had the equipment that was needed. He had been away too long. Playing Shakespeare is like athletics; you have to keep in training.

Michael Blakemore concluded: 'I don't think I've ever seen a Lear where I've thought, "That's it." All the Lears I've seen have come to grief somewhere along the line.' Elsa Lanchester later summed up Laughton's feelings about the experience: 'Charles knew he had only touched the surface. Once you've reached a certain point, it's hopeless, and you realise you have twice as far to go as before. He wanted to work on it all over again. He died thinking he'd play Lear again.'

# Paul Scofield
## *Peter Brook*

*In 1962 Peter Brook directed Paul Scofield as Lear for the Royal Shakespeare Company at Stratford. The production moved to the Aldwych theatre in London, then toured to France, West Germany, Eastern Europe and Russia before visiting America, playing finally in the New York State Theatre in the Lincoln Centre.*

For Peter Brook, *King Lear* was at the pinnacle of all European writings, because it contained almost all of social, familial, political, personal and inner life. It was, he argued, a play about sight and blindness – 'what sight amounts to, what blindness means – how the two eyes of Lear ignore what the instinct of the Fool apprehends, how the two eyes of Gloucester miss what his blindness knows'. He also described it, controversially, as 'the prime example of the Theatre of the Absurd, from which everything good in modern drama has been drawn'.

Looking back at the production as he reached ninety, Brook remembered: 'I had no idea how to do it; I only knew what I didn't want to do.' He had already directed a heavily truncated version for American television in 1953, in which Orson Welles had played Lear. In 1962 he directed the play at Stratford for the Royal Shakespeare Company, with Paul Scofield playing the king. Brook believed the play to be Shakespeare's greatest, and also the most difficult to stage. He saw it as essentially an ensemble piece, requiring a high standard of acting from the other major characters. As rehearsals began he underlined the great task that lay ahead. *King Lear*, he explained, was a mountain whose summit had never been reached; on the way up you found the shattered bodies of others who had failed to get there. 'Olivier here, Laughton there; it's frightening.'

Still only thirty-seven, he had long wanted to stage *King Lear*, but had waited until he found his ideal actor. He had already worked many times with Scofield, beginning with Shaw's *Man and Superman* in 1945. 'The real decision to do a big Shakespeare play is that you have to believe in the actor,' he said later. 'And there was Scofield at forty, at the full height of his powers, absolutely right and ready to play this much older man needing all the vitality and skills of a mature actor.' Scofield saw *King Lear* as 'undoubtedly the greatest play ever written by Shakespeare – or anybody else for that matter. *Hamlet* is certainly great, but it doesn't contain as many elements of humanity as we see in *Lear*.'

Deciding to design the play himself, Brook had been preparing the production for a year, wondering what period to set it in.

The whole problem was to make a world the audience would believe in. The characters breathe a real air and yet it's a world we don't know, it's a world that's close to us, and yet it's far, far away. If you try to put it in a historical period you come unstuck. If you set it in Ancient Britain, you go right back to pre-historic England and you paint the characters in woad and give them sandals and naked tops, and so that's Ancient, and it becomes completely absurd. It doesn't breathe that sort of world.

He rejected the traditional Stonehenge, Druidic option, feeling this would lose the essential cruelty of the story, the cruelty of turning a man out of doors who was already used to sleeping there. 'The play is about indoors and outdoors, the warmth of the interiors, and the desperate barren cold of being out of doors.' He also noted that the language of the play was that of the Renaissance, and that the characters speak 'present-day Elizabethan'. So his first set design reflected an elaborate, beautiful but harsh Renaissance world.

The Stratford workshops started to construct it. But late in the day he changed his mind, deciding that the play was pre-Christian in nature, that the imagery and the gods that are continually invoked were essentially pagan. Abandoning his initial design, he created a model for a very different kind of set. It was simple and austere, with three large white walls which opened out on to a black cyclorama, sparse furniture made of rough wood, and a minimum of props. He also sought simplicity in the costumes, believing that any kind of 'romantic decoration' distracted the audience from the plot. So Lear would have a rich robe at the start, and then shift into a simple leather jacket and trousers like the other men, before donning a simpler robe for the final scenes. Brook's aim with both set and costumes was to 'follow what Shakespeare does on the page, which is to put completely different styles and conventions side by side without any feeling of uncomfortable anachronism'.

Reinforcing this austere design, he preferred not to use any music, arguing that there was no place for it in *King Lear*. He declined to stage the storm scene realistically, which he felt never worked, and all too often caused the actor's words to be drowned out. But he was opposed to the idea of the storm taking place in the audience's imagination, believing the essence is Lear's conflict with it. Eventually he decided to have three rust-coloured thunder-sheets hanging in full view, each fitted with a small motor which enabled them to vibrate. This, he felt, would be disturbing both visually and aurally, and provide Lear with a clear source of conflict. He orchestrated the storm so that the thunder complemented Lear's lines rather than competed with them.

In making these key decisions, Brook was influenced by the 1962 essay 'King Lear, or Endgame' by Jan Kott, which later appeared in his book *Shakespeare Our Contemporary*. The Polish critic believed the play was about 'the disintegration of the world', and likened it to the bleak vision of Samuel Beckett, with its grotesque elements – a madman, a fool, a blind man and a feigned demon. He argued that Beckett and Shakespeare have more in common with each other than either has with the romantic, naturalistic theatre that historically separates them. For *King Lear*, he argued, the stage must be empty and sterile.

Brook was impressed by Kott's writings, and read the essay in French when it appeared that year. According to Charles Marowitz, Brook's assistant director, who kept a log during rehearsals, 'our frame of reference was always Beckettian. The world of this *Lear*, like Beckett's world, is in a constant state of decomposition.' But Brook later attempted to downplay this influence, claiming that he used the Beckett analogy merely as a shorthand device in rehearsal in order to make his ideas clear. Scofield later said that the actors themselves were not much influenced by it.

Brecht's plays were also in fashion in the British theatre, and his notion of 'alienation' informed Brook's production, both in its almost bare staging, and in the director's desire to remove the audience's sympathetic responses. 'A play must leave you in a more receptive mood than you were before,' he insisted. 'It isn't there to "move" people. That's a ghastly idea. You cry, you have a bath of sentiment. You come out saying you've had a lovely time. I prefer the notion of disturbance.'

He was determined to break away from the tradition whereby

everyone concerned had made up their minds as to who were the good and the bad characters. How often have Goneril and Regan been reduced to comic-strip caricatures, as two slinking, evil sisters? An actress playing Goneril knew, and the director knew, that this was the monster of all time. In fact if one wants to make new discoveries in Shakespeare, there are simple methods there. Try to read the plays without preconceptions, without placing the characters in a certain bracket. The moment you do that, the characters leap out of you.

He gave as an example Goneril's first speech which, if not pre-judged by the actress or director, could be seen as the words 'of a lady of style and breeding accustomed to expressing herself in public, someone with ease and social aplomb', rather than those of 'a macabre villainess'.

He was also concerned to highlight the difference between the steely, dominant Goneril and the softer, weaker Regan. 'Sometimes on stage you see them played almost identically. But they are not twins, they are totally different people. Goneril wears the boots and Regan wears the skirt.' He also took a fresh view of Cordelia's character: instead of stressing the saintly, truth-telling young woman, he wanted to suggest her similarity to Lear, to emphasise in her stubborn defiance of his wishes the 'uncompromising strength of her father in her blood'.

He believed it was a mistake in the opening scene for Lear to be played as a feeble old man in his dotage. His decision to divide his kingdom was, he believed, the practical reflection of a hard-bitten man of the world. That 'future strife may be prevented now' was the action of a shrewd ruler, and having three rather than two parties to share the kingdom made for a much better balance of forces. He felt Lear needed to be a strong, obstinate, powerful king with no apparent chinks in his armour, though of course they were there, and would soon be revealed.

According to his working philosophy, the crucial insights into the play needed to come from the actors in rehearsal. Scofield appreciated this collaborative method, recalling: 'Peter nourishes growth in his actors, he has a prodigious acceptance of their contribution, he literally encourages not by praise, but by a tacit endorsement. With *King Lear* he was wonderfully patient, he waited to see what was on offer, and then incorporated that offering into his own unique conception of the play.' His relationship with Brook was now firmly established. 'The communication between us was now so deep that it required few words,' Brook explained.

At the first read-through Marowitz was impressed by Scofield's attempt to grapple with the text. 'One was immediately aware of the actor's resolve and caution. Scofield circled Lear like a wary challenger measuring out an unbeaten opponent, and it was apparent from the start that this challenger was a strategist rather than a slugger.' For the first week they just read the play. As the rehearsals progressed Scofield gradually worked his way into the role in his distinctive manner, discarding conventional readings, and constantly testing the scansion, inflections and accents to make sure the sound corresponded to his emotional intention. His concentration was intense; he even asked for a prompt in character. He was confident enough in his own method and instincts to resist some of his director's intellectual ideas.

One day Brook outlined his view of the pattern of the play, citing Lear's gradual loss of his kingdom, his authority, his trust in his daughters, his reason, and so on. But Scofield felt this wouldn't help him as an actor: 'I can't play negative actions, I can't show *not* having. I have to find a different way to mobilise my energies, so as to be fully active, moment after moment, even in loss, even in defeat.' Similarly, when Brook continually chided him in rehearsal for not playing Lear older, he refused to do so, and remained hugely energetic. Brook was eventually satisfied, reflecting: 'He remained himself, but by the force of inner conviction he projected the exact image that he had in mind.'

Brook's style in rehearsal was to experiment, to try all kinds of possibilities before settling on one interpretation of a speech or a scene. 'You just can't go about things as if you knew all the answers,' he said. 'New answers are constantly presenting themselves, prompting new questions, reversing old solutions, and substituting new ones.' He would offer the actors hints about their characters, prompting them to reappraise them, but not providing them with alternatives himself. When their moves were inconsistent with their lines, he preferred the actors to discover this for themselves, rather than for him to point it out to them immediately.

He sought ideas from the actors, as Clive Swift, playing Oswald recalls: 'He said to me: "If you were allowed one prop, what would it be?" My answer was, a badge of office. I wanted to have something distinctive, as Oswald thinks rather a lot of himself. So I was allowed to have a medallion. That was the kind of principle on which he worked.' In rehearsing the hunting scene, Brook encouraged the knights to choose a name for themselves, and to sketch in some relationships between them. When Lear, admonished by

Goneril for their behaviour, overturns the dinner table and storms out, the knights followed suit, tipping up chairs, throwing plates, and generally creating pandemonium. But when Brook told them their behaviour was not barbaric enough, they replayed the scene with such violence it caused considerable damage to the set, and made a chandelier above the rehearsal stage come crashing to the ground and splinter into pieces.

Improvisation was a key part of Brook's directorial armoury, and he asked Marowitz to devise some specific exercises for the leading actors. However, most of the cast disliked improvising, or simply thought it a waste of time. Scofield refused to take part, an attitude which Brook respected, acknowledging that he had enough on his plate. 'Paul is already struggling with what is essential in Lear. For him, improvisation would only be a diversion of energy.' Alec McCowen secretly admired Scofield's stance, and was reluctant to take part. Brook wanted the Fool to be 'an inspired zany' displaying an ethereal quality, but McCowen preferred to create a more homely, domestic relationship with Lear: 'I thought of myself as a small boy trying to entertain my father, as if he's just come home from work, so I'd perform for him to stop him being bad-tempered.' Marowitz thought he was giving a thoroughly professional reading of the part, but one that lacked the required demonic touch; improvisation would, he believed, encourage this element.

Diana Rigg and McCowen were asked to improvise Cordelia's relationship with the Fool, to help to build up an affectionate relationship between them. She too was evidently reluctant, but felt unable to defy Brook: 'He did a Svengali on me,' she remembered. 'I fell in with everything he told me to do. I felt trapped.' In another exercise she was asked to work on her relationship with France, played by Hugh Sullivan. Brook asked them to imagine they were driving away in a carriage after their wedding. They felt awkward playing the scene, sitting in their seats and waving at the crowd – until Sullivan had the bright idea of pulling down the blind, so bringing the exercise to an abrupt halt.

James Booth and Brian Murray were also required to improvise. The aim here was to help Booth, as the villainous and cunning Edmund, to improve his ability to play different roles in different situations. In Murray's case, the aim was to encourage him to play Edgar less stiffly in his first scenes, in order to make his physical change to Poor Tom more convincing. Marowitz noted: 'The results were partial, but a sense of relationship sprang up between the brothers that had not existed before.'

After the first tentative run-through on the stage, Brook commented: 'All the bones are there.' But he warned the cast to beware of what he called the law of falling inflections. 'Each time you make a downward inflection, the rhythm of a speech comes to a halt,' he explained. 'You are ending your last speeches with a downward inflection, so the play seems to be coming to a halt after every scene. You must keep in mind that when your particular scene is finished, the play still goes on.'

At this stage Marowitz, a rigorous observer, thought Scofield's Lear deficient in characterisation. 'It is over-ridingly reasonable, but lacks the epic quality the play demands. It is still without the weight and age of the crumbling monarch.' But by the first dress-rehearsal he felt his Lear was beginning to emerge. He remained dissatisfied, however, suggesting Scofield was still playing certain scenes in a studied, over-reasonable manner, producing a dry, monotonous effect. Brook agreed, but remained unfazed, confident that he would eventually shift into a higher gear. 'Anything he is not sure of he will simply mark out drily, as he is doing now. He refuses to throw himself into something he does not feel and cannot answer for.'

A significant moment came on the afternoon of the first night, when the actors were asked to give a scaled-down, quieter run-through in order to save their voices. According to Marowitz, this served to improve the level and clarity of the verse-speaking, and clarify some of the relationships, as well as highlight certain flaws. Clive Swift remembered the occasion: 'We were called for a whisper-through before the first night. We were doing it in what is now the Swan, and afterwards Peter Brook said: "In a few years' time Shakespeare will be done in a lot of very intimate venues like this."'

The production provoked considerable controversy. It was widely praised by many critics for its freshness, depth and lucidity, its absolute modernity in catching the spirit of the time – at a moment when the Cuban missile crisis was prompting a widespread fear of nuclear destruction. W.A. Darlington called it 'the best all-round performance of this tremendous play in modern times'. Scofield's arrogant, despotic Lear, a brooding, cantankerous, bullet-headed warrior, with short cropped hair and beard, was highly rated, as he moved from brusque domination to frail pathos. Harold Hobson saw a real man rather than a Druidic myth, 'a man capable of tramping twenty miles a day over sodden fields, and arriving home at nightfall properly tired and in a filthy temper, insulting the servants and cursing his relations'. The *Daily Telegraph* reviewer praised his 'unsentimental, awesome, rasping delivery', while *The Times* critic commented on his 'grating low tones, the powerful air of authority'. Margaret Drabble, who understudied Diana Rigg as Cordelia, remembered 'Scofield's deep gravel voice of angry suffering ... catching and breaking as he neared the unbearable ending'. Philip Hope-Wallace wrote of the later scenes: 'Scofield possesses as few other Lears I have seen the ability to make the pathos of old age utterly convincing, terrible and touching, without a hint of sentimentality.'

But it was Tynan's ecstatic notice in the *Observer* that underlined the radical nature of the production. 'Lay him to rest, the royal Lear with whom generations of star actors have made us reverently familiar;' he began, 'the majestic ancient, wronged and maddened by his vicious daughters; the felled giant, beside whose bulk the other characters crouch like pygmies. Lay also to rest the archaic notion that Lear is automatically entitled to our sympathy because he is a king who suffers.' He praised Brook for provoking questions, not providing answers.

> A great director has scanned the text with fresh eyes and discovered a new protagonist – not the booming, righteously indignant Titan of old, but an edgy, capricious old man, intensely difficult to live with. In short, he has dared to direct *King Lear* from a standpoint of moral neutrality. The results are revolutionary. Instead of assuming that Lear is right, and therefore pitiable, we are forced to make judgements, to decide between his claims and those of his kin. And the balance, in this uniquely magnanimous production, is almost even.

But Brook's nihilistic version annoyed or angered others, who felt Shakespeare's play had been distorted to fit in with the director's bleak vision. Laurence Kitchin complained that 'the royal tragic hero gets elbowed out of this rendering far too often'. T. C. Worsley disliked the production's 'fatal mixture of stylisation and realism'. Bernard Levin described as 'impossibly cavalier' Brook's decision to increase the cruelty and bleakness of the play by making certain cuts, such as the servants' sympathetic words after the blinding of Gloucester. Rather than help Gloucester ('I'll fetch some flax and whites of eggs / To apply to his bleeding face'), they showed indifference to his suffering, and simply pushed him off the stage. The same point was made about the cutting of Edmund's last-minute repentance of his order to have Lear and Cordelia killed ('Some good I mean to do'). Brook emphasised the bleakness by the startling decision to have the blinded Gloucester groping towards the wings as the house lights went up for the interval.

Marowitz was not fully convinced by Scofield's performance: 'Lear the ruler is there, as is Lear the madman; but Lear the father and Lear in those supreme final moments, where the play transcends itself, is only sketched out ... Scofield forces the verse to adjust to his patterns of delivery, and as a result great chunks of it are distributed wholesale instead of being individually packaged.' This view was echoed by Clive Swift, who recalled: 'On the first night there was a feeling that he hadn't really caught fire.' But by the end of the London run Marowitz decided that 'Scofield had become one with the role'.

In the new year the production transferred to the Aldwych in London where, according to one recollection, Scofield was said to be profoundly moving because 'he broke free of the production'. The company then moved to the Sarah Bernhardt theatre in Paris before touring elsewhere in Europe, where British productions had rarely been seen since 1945. The play provoked enormous enthusiasm; Brook later recalled: 'The production was steadily improving and the best performances lay between Budapest and Moscow.' He praised the quality of the audiences' attention, which expressed itself in silence and concentration, a feeling in the house that affected the actors as though a brilliant light were turned on their work. As a result the most obscure passages were illuminated; they were played with a complexity of meaning and a fine use of the English language that few of the audience could literally follow, but which all could sense.

After the tour Scofield shed light on the differing audience reactions in Europe, where Shakespeare was revered:

After half an hour of a performance an audience begins to unify – whatever it's getting from a play, it's sharing, and the minute it begins to share it becomes like talking to one person. You begin to get a very strong sense of an audience's personality. Bucharest, for instance, provided a strong emotional feeling. It was a very highly strung, warm, temperamental audience. In Poland they were very reserved, very intelligent, very listening. In Hungary there was a kind of melancholy attentiveness ... The emphasis shifts according to the response you're getting.

During the tour Brook described the reaction in Budapest when Lear brought on the dead Cordelia: 'I felt the audience was moved by something much more considerable than the sentimental image of a poor old father howling. Lear was suddenly the figure of old Europe, tired, and feeling, as almost every country in Europe does, that after the events of the last fifty years people have had enough, that some kind of respite might be due.'

In America the production played in Washington, Boston and Philadelphia before moving to New York. But audiences in these cities, many of whom treated theatre as more of a social than an artistic event, were less responsive to the austere, unconventional quality of the production, with the result that, according to Brook, 'the actors played louder and cruder, and whipped past those intricate passages that the non-English audience had so enjoyed'. There was further trouble when the company moved to the Lincoln Centre in New York. The play opened the vast New York State Theatre, which had a wide and shallow stage, with the audience seated in long rows far to the right and left of the acting area. The acoustics had apparently never been tested and were terrible, and the audience felt their contact with the stage was poor. Brook was furious, but felt the actors had no choice but to play less subtly: 'They faced the front, spoke loudly, and quite rightly threw away all that had become precious in their work.'

Gielgud saw the production in Philadelphia and wrote to Irene Worth, who played Goneril: 'One cannot hope in such a mighty work to achieve more than two-thirds perfection – and that I think this production does.' He thought both she and Scofield magnificent, but was critical of certain specifics, such as the decision for Lear not to look at Cordelia during the awakening scene, which he felt destroyed any chance of pathos. Olivier, by contrast, admitted to not being an admirer of Brook's work, or this production: 'He rid Lear of his glamour, kingliness; he made him down to earth,' he complained. 'People nicknamed the play "Mr Lear". Whether you liked that or not, the fact is that the image of *King Lear* has had its expression slightly changed.' Among living actors, Oliver Ford Davies had reservations: 'He was the best Lear I've seen. But I thought he was a little bit too iron, I think he boxed himself in a bit, because he was such an impressive figure, with that strange voice and wonderful face. But he was a little bit implacable.'

Scofield, looking back many years later, reflected: 'It's a grim play and our work on it was grimly enjoyable. Actors always find much to laugh about in this kind of play.' Sometimes he felt the need to release the tension during a performance. At one moment he and McCowen would whisper to each other the names of actors in the BBC Radio Repertory Company: '*Lear* – Marjorie Westbury; *Fool* – Rolf Lefebre; *Lear* – Belle Chrystall; *Fool* – Carleton Hobbs.' Diana Rigg recalls the reconciliation scene at one performance when, in response to her line, 'Had you not been their father, these white flakes did challenge pity of them,' Scofield replied under his breath: 'Are you suggesting I've got dandruff?' In similar vein he and McCowen, as they stood in the wings before the storm scene, would sing Arthur Askey's comic song 'I'm a busy, busy bee'.

Scofield summed up:

> Attempting to encompass this play and his character must be a rite of passage, a journey into the tragedy and absurdity of human life, a rigorous examination of the actor's perceptions and his capacity to project them … Again and again during performance there is a sense of exultation, that we are close to something uplifting and immense, whether or not we are close to conveying this to the audience. I have had no larger experience in the theatre.

In 1990 Peter Hall tried to persuade him to play Lear again at the age of sixty-eight, but he declined. In 2004 the *Daily Telegraph* published a survey in which members of the Royal Shakespeare Company voted for the greatest Shakespeare performance in history. On being told that his Lear had come out on top, Scofield commented: 'Playing Lear was a tremendous challenge and I was extremely apprehensive about taking on the role. However, Peter Brook is an immensely inspiring character, and I had utter faith and trust in him as my director.'

*For his performance as King Lear Paul Scofield won the Evening Standard award for Best Actor. In 1971 Peter Brook directed a film version, with Scofield again playing Lear, and some of the original cast also involved. It differed greatly from the Stratford production: filmed in a snowy landscape in Denmark, it was considerably shortened, with some scenes rearranged and many lines reallocated.*

# 5

# For the Royal Shakespeare Company

## Eric Porter
### *Trevor Nunn*

*In 1968 Trevor Nunn, newly appointed the RSC's artistic director, staged the first of his three Stratford productions of* King Lear, *with Eric Porter cast as the king.*

> The story of Lear is so horrific and tragic that it can hardly be faced. It is the hardest, cruellest, most uncompromising message that any dramatist has ever presented to an audience.

Such were Trevor Nunn's thoughts about Shakespeare's tragedy, as his first production of *King Lear* opened in Stratford. Aged just twenty-eight, he had recently taken over from Peter Hall as the RSC's artistic director. 'The stripping of Lear is to my mind one of the unique feats of structure in all drama,' he suggested. 'As he stands naked, without possession of any kind, we see how a king may make progress through the guts of a beggar. We have watched All become Nothing, or Nothing become All. For Lear, further discovery can only occur in madness.'

He and Eric Porter made a young team: Porter was only forty, younger even than Scofield. He was returning to the stage where at seventeen he had begun his career as a spear-carrier. He had already played Lear once at the age of twenty-eight at the Bristol Old Vic, where he was directed by John Moody. A versatile actor, his grave demeanour and features had enabled him to play characters much older than his real age without having to resort to heavy make-up. Much respected for his classical roles at the RSC, he had recently gained wider recognition for his brutal portrait of Soames Forsyte in the BBC's acclaimed version of Galsworthy's *The Forsyte Saga*.

In considering whether to use the Quarto or Folio text, Nunn consulted his fellow-director at Stratford John Barton, and decided on a conflated version. Like others of his generation he was greatly influenced by Peter Brook's production, including his innovatory take on Goneril and Regan. 'It was a production that tried explicitly to exonerate the sisters. I remember that the impact of revealing Lear's behaviour as frequently unacceptable hit home very strongly.' He set the action of the play against a black wall, mirroring Brook's bleak interpretation with a stage devoid of all but the most essential props. Of the play's opening he observed: 'Critics have bewailed that the first scene is inexplicable and ludicrous. Unfortunately that is the whole point. Lear's action is irrational, it is virtually a denial of reason.'

His conceptual production, set in no particular time, lasted nearly four hours. Diane Fletcher, cast as Cordelia, recalled one rehearsal: 'We improvised the opening scene, and came up with a lot of innovative ideas. Trevor asked us to find something in the rehearsal room and then worship it. I worshipped a chair.' In the performance of the scene Porter was carried in on a litter, sitting cross-legged, with Michael Williams' Fool cowering at his side like a pet dog, and the courtiers abasing themselves all around him. A dour, hunched, white-bearded but vigorous monarch wearing golden garments, and seated on a golden throne, he met Cordelia's refusal to speak her love with a thundering rage. Later in the storm scene he created something of a sensation when he stripped down to just a G-string, a Lear more naked than any previously seen on the English stage. Early in his career he had toured with Wolfit's company, and was able to observe his mighty Lear at first hand. His own playing was along similarly majestic lines, although unlike Wolfit he opted to wear a false nose.

The critical response was mixed. Milton Shulman wrote: 'Eric Porter's magnificent Lear, raging at fate with demonic fear and futility, has about it at times the agonising, authentic cry of eternal pain one associates with a painting by Goya or Francis Bacon.' Gareth Lloyd Evans was less impressed, seeing 'a traditional interpretation of Lear, a clear, logical portrait, which lacks emotional engagement with the poetry'. Irving Wardle called it merely 'workmanlike', while J. C. Trewin concluded: 'Eric Porter is sensitive, intelligent, sympathetic, yet there always comes a moment in the great parts when he can't face the undressing of his soul in public. The heath scene is just an actor ranting.' But his final scenes were praised for their dignified suffering; Stephen Wall noted his 'heartbreaking whimper' as he carried in his dead daughter. Tim Pigott-Smith, a later Lear, recalled: 'It was a slow, rather long production, because it was interrupted by the visual aspects. Porter was an egghead Lear, vicious and vituperative and crotchety, not unlike the man himself. He was brilliantly clear with the text, and very moving, hollowed out with misery, broken and weak in his mighty fall.'

Michael Williams, who was to play the Fool again in Nunn's next production, drew his inspiration for his first Fool from a visit to the monkey-house at the zoo. There he met Alec McCowen, Scofield's Fool, who pointed to one monkey and said: 'That was mine.' Williams explained:

'I thought of the Fool as a young man, clinging rather like a monkey to Lear. He's not remotely whimsical, which can happen to the Fool – he remains an earthy man who comes from peasant stock.' John Shrapnel, playing the Gentleman, remembered 'a tiny, Puck-like person, a strange boy-man, a slight small figure, with a great music-hall comic sense, which worked very well with Porter's gravitas'. While some critics thought him too jerky and restless, Shulman felt he provided 'an eerie counterpoint to Lear's tottering grandeur'.

His performance made a great impact on the young Anthony Sher, making his first visit to Stratford and experiencing an epiphany about Shakespeare and theatre: 'The character was beautifully played by Michael Williams with a grin permanently frozen on his face, as if the clown had wiped off his cartoon make-up only to find that the crude outlines had stuck.' That interpretation remained with him when he came to play the part himself fourteen years later.

Porter later told Sher that he had been unhappy in the production, telling him it had not been well-received critically, and failed to transfer to London. According to Pigott-Smith: 'He didn't enjoy the experience, feeling there was too much intrusion by the play's upstart young director.'

*Eric Porter played Lear again in Jonathan Miller's 1989 production at the Old Vic (see page 86).*

# Donald Sinden
## *Trevor Nunn/John Barton/Barry Kyle*

*Donald Sinden played Lear at Stratford in 1976, under a trio of directors, John Barton, Barry Kyle and Trevor Nunn, the RSC's artistic director. The production moved to the Aldwych in London in 1977.*

> Donald was desperate to play the part. *King Lear* is actually the Palace of Bishops: actors know that if they get the chance they must pass into it. That was one of the things that inspired Donald.

In Barry Kyle's view Donald Sinden's Lear was going against the tide of RSC practice, which by 1976 had been given a whole new direction by the Scofield/Brook *King Lear*, and more recently by Buzz Goodbody's revolutionary work at The Other Place. 'He was of that generation of actors who remembered what Olivier had done, and believed this was the birthright of a classical actor of dimension. He was a very gifted comedian, who wanted to redefine himself as a classical actor. But he was very much at the end of a tradition; his Lear was really a kind of nineteenth-century turn.'

Looking back at the production at the age of 90, Sinden implicitly accepted this view, citing the influence of Wolfit.

> I'll never get over his performance at the Scala. It inspired me: it was so large, so awe-inspiring; there was something magical about it. I learned that you cannot be too big. This is what I must do, I thought. His storm scene was monumental. He had all the sound effects – thunder, lightning, rain – that you could imagine. He had the most wonderful voice, which went right over the top of them. When he cursed Goneril, I was petrified: I thought there would be a flash of smoke and she would disappear. It didn't matter about the later quieter scenes; you had seen something enormous.

A popular film star and comic actor of the 1950s, he had already appeared in several RSC productions since 1963, in roles such as Malvolio, Henry VIII, and as a widely acclaimed Benedick. John Barton had been the director on the productions of *Twelfth Night* and *Much Ado about Nothing*, while Trevor Nunn had directed him in other plays, including Vanbrugh's *The Relapse*, in which he scored as Lord Foppington. But it was only after playing Dr Stockmann in *An Enemy of the People* at Chichester that he felt ready for Lear. 'I knew then I could do it, but I didn't suggest it to anybody. So Trevor's offer came as a total surprise.'

Kyle outlined the essential challenge of the role: 'You have to pull off this transformation from somebody who is initially a bully or a monster, into somebody who goes through so much and yet remains standing, so that he arouses compassion. So when we begin to see the signs of spiritual re-birth and love we are cheering him on, and don't want this monstrous hanging to happen and to have to watch him deal with it.'

There was a precedent at Stratford for having a directing triumvirate: when Nunn had staged the four 'roman' plays he had brought in Buzz Goodbody and Euan Smith to share the load. For *King Lear* Nunn was in overall charge, Barton looked after textual matters, and Kyle handled the Gloucester sub-plot. Sinden remembers: 'I never read any authorities, so John was wonderful for individual lines of the verse. Trevor's speciality was theatricality, on which he was very helpful. When you work with a director you admire, you don't have to talk about it much. So we didn't analyse the text, or at least only very little.'

The text used was, at Barton's suggestion, a conflation of the Quarto and Folio, which Nunn had used in his 1968 production. In deciding on the period setting he steered well clear of the Stonehenge idea, observing: 'It seems very odd that Lear should make such a fuss about being out on a heath in a storm when his normal domestic condition appears to be open to the elements.' He set the play in 1914, the last era, he thought, in which a monarch could conceivably give away his kingdom. It was an environment which had, he suggested, resonances of Tsarist Russia and the Austrian autocracy of the Emperor Franz-Joseph. Sinden recalled: 'I was happy to go along with Trevor's idea. My uniform was like the emperor's, all covered in medals; I even had his sideburns. For the opening scene I came stomping on in jackboots smoking a cigar, a tyrant who brooked no interference.'

His powerful, rich and resonant voice undoubtedly helped him with the storm, for which he took on board Kyle's suggestion that Lear's words were a commentary on what was happening.

> I went back to the script, and it was an eye-opener. 'Blow winds …'. It dawned upon me that wind doesn't make any sound, unless it hits something. So for the first line he's not fighting a storm, he's just imagining it, and so it's silent. 'Cataracts' – that's the rain, which makes a sound. 'Thunderbolts' – sound again. These three steps influenced me enormously, and it worked a dream.

John Barton recalled a discussion during rehearsals about one key question: 'I remember asking Trevor: "At what point can we say with assurance that Lear actually goes mad?" He's frightened of going mad, therefore he's trying not to go mad, that's obvious enough, but I'm not sure that he goes utterly mad. He says too many wise things in the course of undergoing a massive mental crisis and breakdown.' Sinden shared this opinion: 'I was convinced Lear had dementia, and that extreme anger was there, but not that he was mad.'

Michael Pennington, who played Edgar, recalled:

> People were surprised at how very good Donald was given his earlier reputation in comedy and films; they were taken aback by his tragic range. But he was the most serious and committed Shakespearean actor you could imagine. He was so diligent and concerned and interested in all the performers. He used to listen very carefully on the tannoy to everything that was going on.

Sinden worked extremely well with Michael Williams' ancient, bald-pated, scrofulous Fool, whom John Barton twenty-five years later called 'the greatest Fool I've seen. He had all the skills of the music-hall clown, but he also had a great humanity and a sort of cosmic wisdom.' Sinden remembered him as 'very ancient and very funny. He played it like the north-country comedian Robb Wilton, whom he greatly admired – he used to do him as a party piece.' Williams himself recalled:

> I developed the idea of the Fool as a busker, and made him North Country for no better reason than my knowledge of some of the Northern comics. Besides, since he is Lear's conscience, it makes much more sense to play him as the same age as the king. Lear and the Fool have grown old together. He has always been allowed to speak his mind, even if his opinions have had to be cloaked in comedy and humour. He

is the character who is closest to Lear, and his plain speaking is born out of his great love for him. One critic complained that it was illogical to have them as contemporaries, since they constantly address each other as 'nuncle' and 'boy'. But these are terms of endearment rather than a reflection of any age gap, and it shows the depth of their mutual affection. When the Fool disappears, it is to die of a broken heart.

One casualty of the production was Judi Dench, who played Regan. Sinden remembers her problem: 'Regan is one of the most evil characters in the whole of Shakespeare, and Judi didn't like to be evil.' Pennington recalled: 'She didn't like the cruelty of Regan, but she played her brilliantly.' But the actress, who was also to play Goneril in the 1994 Gielgud radio version, confessed to finding both roles difficult:

> The problem is that the moment they come on stage they are plotting away. You don't get a chance to explain to an audience how their past history might influence their behaviour – an audience instantly grasps what kind of women they are. It's so hard to make a case for them, to point out that Lear is a very difficult old man and that they are being asked to put up with him and his hundred, badly behaved knights, when in the first scene they are putting their heads together in a conspiratorial huddle.

She felt she simply couldn't get Regan right. 'I had this theory that Regan couldn't be all bad. I thought maybe it was all to do with her relationship with Lear, so whenever she was with him I gave her a stammer.' In Kyle's recollection: 'Judi stammered through five weeks of rehearsal. I thought it was just great, but she got very anxious about it. In the last week she cut it, because she thought people would think she couldn't remember her lines.'

She left the company on the production's transfer to the Aldwych. She had found the physical cruelty hard to stomach, especially the blinding of Gloucester, which in rehearsal had been particularly violent. At one session John Woodvine as Cornwall took a false eye out of a hidden bag on the line 'Out vile jelly!' and flung it at the wall, where it stuck. 'It was too awful,' Sinden recalled. 'John Barton intervened, and they had to scale it down. It's such a terrible scene.'

In London there was a problem with the length, as Paul Shelley, who took over as Edmund, remembered: 'The first preview ended at about 12.15 in the morning. Donald and Michael played their scenes as old and slow, which made the production endless. People used to come out saying, "God I'm exhausted!"' Watching the final Aldwych performance, Peter Hall was critical of the company's pace: 'Again there was this slow, over-emphatic, line-breaking delivery of the text. The actors are so busy telling us the ambiguities and the resonances that there is little or no sense of form. You cannot play Shakespeare without a sense of line. RSC Shakespeare is getting slower and slower.' Barry Kyle admitted the production was far from perfect:

'It had some wonderful actors in it, but it lacked a singularity of purpose, which may well have come from the experiment with three directors. The dilution that happened amongst us meant we did a respectable show, but not an urgent one. There wasn't really a reason for doing that Lear except to let Donald play it.' Bill Alexander, a young assistant director for the London transfer, recalled Sinden's view of the set: 'The floor was duckboard pathways on top of mud made of dyed polystyrene. Donald said to Trevor: "About the floor – could we keep the old one? I find it impossible to bounce my voice off this one."'

For the critics, Benedict Nightingale noted approvingly: 'Sinden half-pranced, half-stumbled on stage in Ruritanian epaulettes, looking like a caparisoned, gouty circus horse, but proceeded to find the pain behind the pretension.' Bernard Levin, who had described his performance at Stratford as being half an inch from greatness, qualified his remark, saying he was now a quarter of an inch from greatness. Trewin concluded that 'none, after this, will deny his right to be among our first classical actors'.

Michael Billington was more equivocal: 'He conveys madness's strange blend of muddle and clarity, chilling the heart with his sudden recognition of Gloucester in the Dover scene. The externals of old age and insanity are faultlessly captured. What I miss is the authentic cry of a cornered human soul: Sinden acts torment without, for me, instinctively embodying it.' Greg Hicks was then a young actor: 'Just to see a man like Sinden strutting around, bellowing his stuff out there was really rather inspiring. Something of that must have seeped into my bloodstream; there were things about him that I think enriched my sense of kingship when I came to play the part.'

At the time Sinden announced: '*King Lear* is a piece of cake compared with playing a farce like *Not Now Darling*.' Reflecting on the experience nearly forty years on, he concluded: 'I think I gave a truthful performance.' Pennington agreed: 'Donald was an extremely powerful and autocratic Lear, and on occasion very moving. He played the Dover cliff scene with a wind-up gramophone in long combinations, rather than with flowers. It was pitiful to see, and quite wonderful.'

*Donald Sinden won the Evening Standard award for Best Actor for his performance as King Lear.*

# Michael Gambon
## *Adrian Noble*

*In 1982 Michael Gambon played King Lear for the RSC, in Adrian Noble's production at Stratford. The following year it transferred to the Barbican in London.*

Thirty years or so after his production, Adrian Noble reflects on the nature of the challenge for any actor playing Lear. 'The intellectual and emotional journey that's required is extreme, and the technical challenges facing the actor are unrivalled. The play attracts not just great actors to play Lear, but great casts. Other very fine actors will cluster round many productions of the play.'

They certainly did so on this occasion. 'They were all serious heavy-weight actors,' Noble points out. 'Michael Gambon was relatively young at forty-two, but they gave him security.' This was clearly welcome to Gambon, who said of *Lear*: 'The play is so majestic it makes you feel insignificant in measuring yourself against it. When you wake up in the morning and you've got King Lear that night, your whole day is destroyed. I've always been frightened of these big parts, but you've got to do them. If you shied away from them, why be an actor?' He also confessed to being uneasy with directors, of even being 'rather frightened' of them; but Noble says he found him easy to direct.

Large and solidly built, with a strong and confident bearing and voice, Gambon was an imposing presence on stage. Like Olivier, he liked to develop a character by first concentrating on externals. 'I have to find out what the man looks like, and what he's wearing, and then everything else seems to fit into place.' In the case of Lear, he had firm views about his age. 'I don't like to see him played unless he's the proper age. That man is eighty years old. So we put a lot of make-up on, and wigs.'

As all actors do, he found some scenes extremely demanding. 'It varies with different actors as to which they are,' Noble says.

> It can be quite unrewarding as a part. I thought Michael absolutely astonishing from the Dover cliff scene until the end, and very moving. The first half was trickier for him. It's absolutely unremitting, and almost unplayable: the pain is so great, the vocal demands so huge. It gets actors down a lot, because it magnifies your failures. I'm not saying Michael didn't do it well, but the journey to madness is very hard to play. The dreadful break with Cordelia, the cursing of Goneril – these are difficult areas for an actor, because they have to do and say really toxic and horrible things.

In his introductory talk to the company he stated that *King Lear* was the cruellest play he had ever read. He wanted to stress two elements of the story, the savage cruelty and the sense of the absurd. For the latter he cited two examples: the Fool's strange speech in the storm ('This prophecy Merlin shall make') – lines often cut, but not in this production – and Gloucester's attempted suicide at Dover. 'I was very influenced then by Brecht and Beckett – and Michael is a great Beckett actor; he seems to be able to inhabit quite comfortably that bleak landscape, that frontier land between sanity and insanity.'

The production was staged in repertoire with Edward Bond's *Lear*, with considerable overlap in the casting of the two plays, including that of the three principal actresses doubling as Lear's daughters. This gave the company the rare luxury of three months' rehearsal time. Noble saw this as a chance for the basic production concept to emerge during rehearsal, rather than be imposed by him beforehand; for the moment, he explained to the actors, he had only vague ideas about the set, and none yet about the costumes.

His intention as director was to create a vengeful, godless universe, a world which would literally disintegrate in parallel with Lear's mind. The eventual result was an opening scene marked out by power, order and authority. The floor was covered with a paper map on which the lines of the division of the kingdom were painted; as the action wrenched apart family and country, so the map was shredded and torn. The final scenes, which featured searchlights, sandbags and combat boots, offered visual reminders of a bombed-out East European city, suggesting the aftermath of war or revolution. The costumes eventually chosen were eclectic and deliberately anachronistic, moving gradually from the medieval to the nineteenth century, and finally to the modern.

Noble saw the need to balance the familial and the cosmic elements of the play as an exciting challenge.

> The intricacies of the plot up to the interval – which I placed after the blinding – revolve around family matters. So one has to get that right, and in rehearsal one spends a lot of time chiselling out those relationships quite precisely. I'm always very chary of the cosmic aspects, but the two are intertwined. Shakespeare just lobs to a director the idea that there is a tangible connection between Lear's madness and the elements, the chaos, the natural disorder. So we made that manifest.

A key decision for any director is to decide when Lear crosses the border into madness. Noble identified this as the moment when the king meets Edgar disguised as Poor Tom, who now becomes the key protagonist and replaces the Fool. Noble had him exploding out from below the stage like a fiend from hell, and wrecking the set, which then became the basis of the hovel. 'Edgar appears to occupy this domain of insanity and irrationality. At that point everything went completely silent, all the sound effects stopped. Then Lear says, "Didst thou give all to thy two daughters?" He's gone into the other world, and it's peaceful and quiet.'

Another unusual touch was Noble's decision to include the Fool in the opening scene.

> It struck me as interesting to ask, Would all this have happened if the Fool had been there? I had him hiding behind Lear's chair. But in the pre-show that I set up I thought it was important that we get a sense of

who's who, and of the relationships between the characters, which is not easy for a modern audience to grasp. I had this idea that Cordelia and the Fool would be great friends, so you saw them playing with a rope round both of their necks, making an interesting pre-echo of Lear's later line 'And my poor Fool is hanged'.

During rehearsals he set the actors various tasks. One evening he, Gambon and Anthony Sher, playing the Fool on his RSC debut, went out to Dover's Hill, a local beauty spot, to work on the storm scenes. Gambon attempted to project Lear's 'Blow winds' speech against the deafening noise of jets passing overhead – this was the time of the Falklands War. Another day there was a further rehearsal on location, as Gambon recalled: 'Adrian had us sitting in a church at Stratford saying the fucking lines of the speech at the end when they're arrested, and Lear says he'll pray and sing and laugh at gilded butterflies. I went along with it, but I didn't understand it.'

The extended rehearsal period gave the actors plenty of time to explore various ideas about their characters. One who benefited greatly from this was Sher. Although he had played the Fool ten years earlier at the Liverpool Everyman, he had no desire to repeat that interpretation. As he observed: 'The role is so inextricably linked to Lear himself, as a master-servant relationship, a double-act, that the two performances have to grow together in rehearsals, both the actors and the director making their discoveries simultaneously.'

The Fool was a part that fascinated him. 'I had seen Michael Williams play it beautifully to Eric Porter's Lear. But when I came to do it myself I found it frightening. It's hard at first to know what direction to go in, because there's not much in the text to tell you what he is.' The break-through for him came when, in order to release the wildness of the action in the heath scene, Noble asked each actor to choose an animal to play. 'I chose a chimpanzee,' Sher recalled, 'chattering and clapping hands, hurling myself around in forward rolls, and finding this very liberating.' He then visited London Zoo to observe the animals' behaviour, and became convinced the chimpanzees 'had all the requisite qualities for the Fool – manic comic energy when in action, a disturbing sadness in repose.' While at the zoo he came across Gambon, 'presumably also in search of his character, leaning against the plate-glass of the gorillas' cage, man and beast locked in solemn contemplation of each other'.

Noble explains how Sher created his Fool:

He did some research, and found that sometimes Fools were disabled, so they had to live off their wits. He saw that as an interesting way in to the character, so he made him disabled. Then we were keen that he should be regarded as a professional Fool, who was funny. One morning I brought in a whole load of stuff, including hats, a mask, a mime artist's white face, and a red nose.

Sher immediately took to the red nose, which led him also to adopt the bowler hat, baggy trousers, long shoes and a tailcoat, and an out-of-tune violin. He and Gambon then investigated various music-hall routines, though not any based on the work of a particular clown. Having added his crippled walk, Sher decided 'the mixture was complete – the accoutrements of a clown worn clumsily but defiantly by a little crippled outcast'. Noble approved, but told him: 'If only you could be as dextrous with your voice as you are with your body.'

Happily, Sher and Gambon quickly developed a rapport and a friendship in rehearsal, which fed into their stage relationship. They became a double act, made explicit by their playing one scene as a ventriloquist and his dummy, and by going through a music-hall, front-cloth routine as they waited for their horses to go to Gloucester's home. 'It was a brilliant notion of Adrian's,' Sher observed, 'enhanced by the use of footlights and giant shadows, the two characters and their relationship illuminated in a bold piece of expressionist theatre.'

The most controversial moment came during the mock-trial scene, when Lear distractedly mortally stabbed the Fool, mistaking him for Regan during a pillow fight. The idea emerged one day from an improvisation designed to reflect the lunacy and panic the characters were experiencing, when Sher suddenly jumped into an oil drum. This seemed a way of making sense of the Fool's subsequent line 'And I'll go to bed at noon', after which, mortally wounded, he tries to get out of the oil drum, but falls back dead. 'A lot of productions do that nowadays,' Noble said. 'I gather some kids at school believe that this is what Shakespeare wrote.' Some audience members disliked the incident, arguing that it wasn't in the text.

Gambon was said to have given an off-the-scale performance at the last run-through; some people who were there say he never got anywhere near it again. Certainly the critics were not all convinced by his first-night performance. Barber noted 'a vigorous, strong-voiced and angry Lear', but Robert Cushman thought he had 'more violence than authority', and Billington argued that 'he chills the blood more than rends the heart'. Some thought he failed to suggest Lear's spiritual recovery, though Michael Coveney argued: 'He releases great emotional depth charges in the reunions with Gloucester and Cordelia.' Others raised the question of whether Sher's virtuoso Fool unbalanced the play, making it about him rather than Lear – one review's headline ran 'Lear in the Fool's Shadow'.

In David Hare's opinion 'Gambon could have made a great Lear, but I don't think the production enabled him to be that. His Lear was rather old-fashioned: stagey, trembling, with a lot of make up.' Barry Kyle had a different perspective: 'Gambon wasn't happy in the production, I do know that. He recognised in a way that he was more suited to comedy. If *King Lear* contains a multi-faceted and poetic spiritual connection to the universe, that's not him. He was a born Falstaff, but Lear was another matter.'

A legend grew up that Gambon had resented Sher's very original Fool. Asked later whether he felt he was giving something away by allowing the Fool to be so prominent in their scenes together, he replied: 'It's not a question of giving something away. That's how we played the scenes in the rehearsal room. I didn't think in terms of that. The better the player you're opposite, the better you are. The meaning of a play is the principle of the thing, not who is winning.'

He made certain changes when the production moved to the Barbican in London, mainly to do with playing down the clowning. According to Noble: 'Michael felt it was tricky to navigate the choppy waters of the first half, and that some of the stuff he did with the Fool wasn't helping that navigation.' There was another factor. Halfway through the Stratford run, as he was alone on stage delivering the Fool's Merlin speech, Sher's Achilles tendon snapped. During his subsequent recuperation he spent some months on crutches, an experience which provided 'a personal association of being disabled', and led to his playing his next role, Richard III, on crutches. His part was taken over by his understudy, Ian Talbot, both in Stratford and London. Gambon says he got into a different rhythm with Talbot, and when he and Sher teamed up in London he continued to play it in that way. 'I changed bits, but it was never as fulfilling.' But Pete Postlethwaite, playing Cornwall, thought he hit the heights at the Barbican. According to Rupert Goold, who would later direct him as Lear: 'Pete watched the second half in the rehearsal room, and it was about the total humiliation of being an actor. He said it was like standing on the side acting next to a huge i-max cinema screen.'

Later Gambon admitted he might have been reacting to Sher's brilliant reviews. 'I think that might be true, that I wanted to reassert myself.' He concluded: 'It's a part that makes you want to play it again – you can never grasp all of it.' But he was never to do so.

# 6

# Around the Regions

## Michael Hordern
### *Jonathan Miller*

*Jonathan Miller mounted his first production of* King Lear *at the Nottingham Playhouse in 1969, with Michael Hordern as Lear. It transferred to the Old Vic the following year.*

Like many other actors, Michael Hordern found it impossible to turn down the great tragic role. 'It was not something I was planning to do all my life,' he said. 'But if someone comes up and asks: "Do you want to play Lear?" you don't ask questions. I accepted immediately.' Jonathan Miller offered him the part because he admired his style of acting. 'I'd always been impressed by his performances, by his playing naval officers and such like in films. He seemed so wonderfully natural and unpretentious.'

This was Miller's first Shakespeare production with professional actors (he had previously directed a student production of *Twelfth Night*). 'King Lear is the Shakespeare play I enjoy directing the most,' he says. 'It's one of the best plays Shakespeare wrote, which is one reason why it's being increasingly performed nowadays. But it also seems to reflect more vividly than *Hamlet* does certain aspects of our time, such as the prevailing nihilism.' But he was attracted to the play for a more personal reason. 'I have a sort of atheist pessimism about the world, which is why I think I identify closely with *King Lear*. It has a pessimistic view of the fact that we're the playthings of cosmic forces, and don't really leave much more than a scratch on the surface of the universe'.

In staging the play he reacted against the style of earlier productions, including those of the nineteenth century, which reflected the Victorians' love of violent natural spectacle. '*Lear* is not what it's thought to be about, a great cosmic drama,' he says. 'People get misled by the thunderstorm, which lasts about four minutes, if that. If you make Lear a cosmically suggestive role, it may satisfy people who are looking for operatic bullshit,

but that's not what it's about. It's really about what happens if you lose
everything, about the learning that results from the chastening loss. We
discover throughout the play that, for Lear and for many of the other
characters, the experience of nothing becomes everything.'

Miller believes the play is relevant to our own day, not just in relation to
the issue of homelessness, and Lear's belated realisation of the plight of the
'poor naked wretches' in his land, but also because of the lack of awareness
of those in authority.

> He becomes struck by something that had not previously occurred to
> him, and that has not occurred to David Cameron either, that a large
> majority of the population do not live like the sovereign, and certainly
> not like what I call the Bullshittingdon Club. From his high point in the
> social order Lear has not seen what the unentitled, the underprivileged,
> the unemployed and the beggars endure. It's only by going through
> this chastening experience of deprivation and loss that he discovers the
> essential nature of the human soul.

Other themes, he believes, include the relationship of paternity to sovereignty,
and the nature of the social order.

> The play anticipates what Thomas Hobbes later wrote about the
> absolute necessity of sovereignty. It deals with the authority that a father
> exercises over his children, male or female, and the authority which a
> sovereign exercises over his subjects. Shakespeare is pointing out if a
> sovereign doesn't behave with the authority and control that he has over
> himself, as exemplified by what he does with his children, the state will
> fall to bits.

In deciding in which period to set the play, he avoided 'the boring clichés
of precedent, of which I think the most depressing one was the Druidical
representation of the ancient, pre-Christian Lear – the long white beard
surrounded by a retinue of figures swathed in savage leather.' He argues
that the Christian symbolism in the play makes this choice nonsensical:
King Lear is a play about statecraft and its breakdown when authority is
removed, and there was no concept of a state in ancient times; also, he finds
the play's language 'saturated' with the Book of Revelation and the imagery
of the Gospel of St John.

> If you set it in pre-Christian England you also lose another aspect, which
> is the relationship between Edgar and Edmund, whom I see as glosses
> upon Christ and Lucifer: an intelligent Lucifer set against the sacred
> idiocy of his Christ-like brother. If you look at the history of lunacy at
> the beginning of the seventeenth century, a significant proportion of the
> mad who are out on the heath or not in asylums – of which there were

very few anyway – take on the role of Jesus. That's why I've dressed Edgar in a loincloth with stigmata in his hands, because then he would convince people he was mad, as people would so often see these lunatics out in the country thinking they were Jesus. And at the end when the third trumpet sounds and Edmund comes to defeat him, he's the devil. It's Armageddon. But if you ignore that aspect of contemporary Christianity, you've missed one of the points.

Instead he chose to set the production during the Thirty Years War (1618–48), a time of chaos and upheaval:

Shakespeare was writing about his own time, about seventeenth-century ideas, and foreshadowing the political upheaval that was soon to come with the civil war in England. Here we have a play written only a few years before people begin to question the right of someone to be a sovereign, to the extent that they chop off his head. So I wanted to bring to light themes which seemed to be absolutely contemporary with that period.

Seeking inspiration from the work of painters and writers, for the costumes he used as a source the etchings of the great French artist Jacques Callot, whose masterpiece *Les Grandes Misères de la Guerre* recorded the horrors and savageries of the Thirty Years War.

Apart from the decision about scale, and the appropriate period and costumes, he planned little in advance, preferring to wait until he started work with the actors.

I will have some ideas to offer in rehearsal: I will say 'I don't think it's about this, that or the other.' Otherwise it depends so much on who the actors are. Each one brings their own thoughts, but there's also something about his or her aspect which reminds you of something which you had not previously seen in the character they are pretending to be.

According to Penelope Wilton, who played Cordelia: 'One of the best things was Jonathan's ability to make the play very much a story about a family – he knows how to reduce Shakespeare from the epic to the intimate.' He found a willing collaborator in Hordern, who recalled:

I realised as we began that Jonathan had the most amazing grasp of the play. Although we didn't have any in-depth discussions about it beforehand, he produced the intellectual fuel for me to run on. He displayed such incisive understanding of an old man's state of mind, seeing Lear in a very human and sympathetic light. Being not only a doctor but deeply versed in psychiatry, he was able to explain the whole geriatric aspect, and he wanted me to play him very mad indeed.

He remembered their collaboration being fruitful:

> Moving as much as he does between arts and science makes Jonathan immensely open-minded as a director. He never dictates, and like Tyrone Guthrie he is very innovative and fresh, taking what you can give him and using it if it is any good. We worked terribly well together. My having my feet on the ground was something he could use, while his intellect was something I could use. The best thing was his spontaneity, his using improvisation, but always with a clear end in sight.

For Frank Middlemass, playing the Fool, it was Miller's humour that he enjoyed. 'He was formidably intelligent but as silly as anybody, and daft as a brush.'

Miller believed that as a director

> the more you open yourself up to the unforeseeable, the more spontaneous and interesting the performance becomes. My best ideas on productions are never ones for which I have sat down and consciously asked myself: how shall I do this scene? Often a few seconds into the scene material surfaces from some part of me and I suddenly know what needs to be done. It's like the discovery of some buried treasure.

He also believed that 'actors cannot be treated as marionettes. I positively want to encourage the unpredictable eruptions of inspiration that can come at the most unexpected moments, purely because a different group of people is working together under pressure. I see the rehearsal room as a playroom; it's rather like a nursery where I am the supervisor. I let things emerge within a framework.'

Penelope Wilton approved of this collaborative method:

> He doesn't tell you what to do. He's not worried about his status, and therefore you're all in it together. His approach is very practical and down to earth, with everything focussed on the characters. He brought out all the relationships with great clarity. He always makes the smaller roles come to life by casting very interesting actors and giving them a lot of attention. And he tries to avoid people attitudinising on stage – he wants them to be simple, natural and clear.

This desire for clarity extended to the verse-speaking, as Miller explained to the actors during rehearsals:

> I don't want to hear poetic verses, I just want to hear you talking. Don't feel when you're uttering verse that you have to speak it in a separate, actorish voice. No one ever talks like that. If you speak it more naturally,

we can hear you thinking to yourself. Otherwise it's just versifying, and verse to me is of no interest at all.

He started work on Lear himself with the idea, as Regan says, that 'he hath ever but slenderly known himself'. He wanted Hordern's king to be 'a cantankerous, petulant, weak-willed foolish old man, paranoiac, depressive but vigilant, on the look-out for slights'. His medical background enabled him to draw heavily on his knowledge of geriatric behaviour and madness, which was valuable in relation to Lear, but also for Edgar's scenes as Poor Tom. 'I gave Michael Hordern a model and a description. I only wished I could have taken him to an old people's home, so that he could have incorporated a kind of ranting incontinence into the performance. I wanted to roughen the madness and restore its horribleness. He was very mad indeed.'

Encouraged by Miller, Hordern also found the comical element in Lear's behaviour.

> Jonathan's view was that if you don't approach it as a funny play about people going gaga, you missed a dimension, and all you got at the end of the day was rather a depressing tragedy about madness and old age. You can't keep your intellect at a desperately intellectual level all the time, and we laughed a great deal. He brought out a lot of humour which surrounds Lear, unkind, ironic humour, but there nevertheless, particularly in his scenes with the Fool.

As the Fool, Frank Middlemass was only slightly younger than Hordern. 'Jonathan saw Lear and the Fool as mirror images,' Hordern explained. 'Despite the fact that one of them had been brought up in the palace and the other in the stables, they had obviously developed a very close relationship over the years.' Middlemass played the Fool in white face, as a broken-down, cockney, music-hall performer with a touch of Max Miller.

Miller was reacting against the tradition of the Fool being played by a young man, believing that 'this clichéd rendition removes the force of the Fool's wisdom and pathos'. Instead he saw him as Lear's contemporary.

> Because Lear calls him 'Boy', people have tended to play him younger than he is, forgetting that in many countries adult black servants are always referred to in this way. That sort of ironic wisdom that the Fool has is something you can't credit a young person with. This romantic idea of the defective juvenile who is a prophet is just twaddle. The two men are mirror images of folly, distinguished from one another only by their social station. A foolish old king shadowed by a wise old fool.

Like other recent directors of the play, he was keen to differentiate clearly between Goneril and Regan:

They are not a duo of evil sisters, they're very separate identities. If you treat the two of them as serpentine villainesses, as exponents of some abstract principle of vileness, they inevitably become cartoon figures. It's quite clear that Regan's behaviour is much more cruel and venomous and nasty than Goneril's. So we have to make them different, and there are intimations of how they differ.

The two older daughters, he suggests, are thoroughly taken aback by Lear's testing of their love for him. 'They've no idea that he's going to ask them to speak about that. When he actually says to them, Tell me how much you love me, they just look at each other. They're absolutely disconcerted by his demand.'

He suggests that Lear set up the love test in order to humiliate Cordelia, 'anticipating the rebuttal from the daughter he loves best, and from whom he can never obtain enough expressions of love. She is the daughter he wants the most from, possibly because she was the one whose mother died bearing her, as so many women did at that time.' He was looking to get away from the traditionally virtuous and sweet Cordelia, and emphasise her obstinacy. 'You find yourself wanting to say about her silence: "Hang on, why not say something? Have a go, it won't cost you too much. Why do you so value your moral chastity?"' Penelope Wilton duly played her with a cold, stubborn streak.

Cordelia is taken aback at being asked to express in public the extent to which she loves her father. 'She takes it for granted that of course she loves him, but it's not something she wishes to speak about in public. She's thinking, If you don't know that I love you, then you have failed to understand me, and possibly yourself.' He suggests she is one of Shakespeare's 'tuitional' female characters – like Portia, Viola and Rosalind – who teach stupid or blinkered men a lesson in morality, in her case by means of her silence, the initial trigger for Lear's disintegration. Only when he has learnt wisdom does she return.

He was clear that the physical staging at Nottingham was far less important than the emphasis put upon the characterisations in performance. With this in mind, and influenced by his memories of Brecht's *Mother Courage*, he opted for a set of striking simplicity, a bleak, almost empty stage with the minimum of props. Initially he wanted no set at all, but his designer Patrick Robertson persuaded him to have a moveable black box, consisting of screens of black gauze which moved on tracks above the stage, giving different spaces within a black void. There were no scenic effects, so that, with the help of the atmospheric lighting, everything was concentrated on the actors and the essential moral arguments.

Some of the critics felt Hordern lacked the full passion the part required. Irving Wardle observed: 'There is no *hysterico passio*, no climbing sorrow, and it is a huge gap; he scrambles through the thunderous storm speech, and even delivers the curse on Goneril in the style of an icy legal sentence.'

Others felt his and Miller's take on madness was convincing. 'Hordern slipped into a clinical senility, twitching, bronchially hiccoughing, laughing and even clutching his genitals,' Benedict Nightingale noted. Martin Esslin wrote: 'Michael Hordern's king is a magnificent creation ... Jonathan Miller, using a simple set of shifting plain dark gauze screens, has wonderfully concentrated the play upon its essentials: the morality of man and man's wits and the depth of insight which can spring from madness.'

*Jonathan Miller directed Michael Hordern as Lear twice more, on two BBC television versions of the play, the first in 1975, the second in 1982 as part of the BBC Shakespeare series, of which Miller was the producer.*

# Kathryn Hunter
## *Helena Kaut-Howson*

*In 1997 the director Helena Kaut-Howson cast Kathryn Hunter as King Lear. The production opened at the Leicester Haymarket, then moved to the Young Vic in London before visiting Japan.*

Casting a woman as King Lear was, Helena Kaut-Howson insists, definitely not a feminist statement. The idea was actually prompted by her Jewish Polish mother's final years, and her admiration for Kathryn Hunter's remarkable abilities as an actress.

'It was my mother's recent death at the age of eighty-seven that gave me the desire to direct *King Lear*,' she says.

> She had survived the revolution and the holocaust, and became a communist in Poland. She was a forceful and vital woman in a responsible position, hiring and firing people. But then she went into an old people's home. Her decline was a collapsing of everything: in her last year or so her memory went, and she refused to acknowledge what was going on around her. That transition and her loss of power must have been traumatic for her, as it was for me. As a single parent – my father was killed by the Nazis – she was both father and mother to me, so I never thought of her in terms of gender. When I was selling her house I dreamed of her shaking the walls while a storm raged outside, and I found a note in which she cursed me. I saw her very much as a Lear figure. That was my impulse to stage the play.

Kathryn Hunter had her own reason for taking the part.

> I became obsessed with the play when I was fourteen and studying it at school. I strongly identified with Lear rather than Cordelia: with his rage, rejection and refusal to compromise he's not unlike a teenager. He's

a tyrant and pig-headed, but I felt there was something heroic about his willingness to forgo security. That connection with the play never left me. At drama school I wasn't attracted to those little ingénue parts, but I did have this abiding fantasy of playing King Lear.

So it came as a shock when Kaut-Howson offered her the role. 'Helena knew nothing of my feeling for the play. I was only thirty-nine, and I thought it was madness. But I also thought it was not going to happen again.'

Hunter had recently finished a spell with the Complicite company, during which she had once played Paulina, the boy Mamillius and the Old Shepherd in a production of *The Winter's Tale*. The two women had worked together before at Theatr Clwyd in north Wales, in a production of John Whiting's *The Devils*. Hunter describes the director as 'like quicksilver, mercurial and seemingly eccentric, but actually very deeply rooted and passionate, and with a very strong visual sense.'

Kaut-Howson insists she chose Hunter for her acting skills rather than her gender.

Kathryn is one of those protean actors who can embrace a range of personalities. She's wonderfully imaginative. She has this ability to transform her body completely, to transcend gender. She has tremendous flexibility; she can play anything. But it's pure art rather than impersonation, in the way that classical Japanese theatre made actors capture the quintessence of femininity rather than do an imitation. There are few other actors who can accompany the diversity of notes in *Lear*, with its tragedy and grotesque, Bosch-like comedy. With Kathryn drama is always present in her comedy, and comedy in her drama. I wanted her to play Lear because I knew she was intellectually and emotionally capable of the necessary leaps of imagination towards old age and death.

Just over five feet tall and slight of build, Hunter was determined to play Lear as an eighty-year-old, and to capture his fragility.

As a young person I was very close to old people, and I think that helped. At school we were involved in Task Force, where we used to go and look after elderly people, and I developed an affinity with them. I realised that advancing age isn't necessarily just a decline, that it's quite turbulent becoming aware of a series of losses, and how to confront them.

But she faced an obvious physical challenge in creating a convincing figure of authority and power. She found unexpected encouragement one day during a break in rehearsals, when she followed an old man into a Leicester supermarket. 'He was quite small and frail, but he had a real sense of authority. I thought, "If he were wearing a crown and was surrounded by dignitaries, why couldn't he be King Lear?"'

She also had to make sure she achieved the right mindset.

> I had to keep checking that I wasn't thinking like a woman, and was attending to a male mentality. But although there has to be a certain amount of transformation, it mustn't be to the point where you lose the feminine element. As an actor you try to enter the appropriate frame of mind, and then the physical action looks after itself.

She used her own family background – her parents were Greek – in carving out Lear's relationship with Cordelia. 'In Greek families there's more of a sense than there is in Britain of a father knowing better than a daughter, so that for a daughter to defy his authority is both humiliating and outrageous.'

Kaut-Howson set the play in the world of her mother, 'who spent the war being hunted, continually running from place to place, hiding and working in the fields'. Her set evoked the feeling of war and the harsh landscape of war-torn Eastern Europe, suggesting both the second world war and the recent conflict in Bosnia. Controversially, she added a framing device to the story. An old woman is seen watching television in a nursing home, when she has a heart attack and is rushed into intensive care. This causes her to hallucinate, and at that moment she has a vision of her life, which becomes the play.

The Fool was played by Hunter's husband, the Italian actor and clown Marcello Magni, who had already played Shakespearean parts such as Autolycus, Dromio and Lancelot Gobbo. 'This was a very different comic role, and I struggled to give my own version' he says.

> Helena was giving me lot of images from a world that I didn't understand, such as that of a Jewish mother or a Russian Holy Fool. I played him younger than Kathryn's Lear, as an open-hearted Italian clown, not one with a wise, cunning and acute mind, which I think is more English. But I don't know if I got the Fool at all.

Hunter found acting with her husband valuable.

> It did help that I knew Marcello so well. I know it's often played differently, but I feel there has to be a great love and care between Lear and the Fool, and that came easily to us. I think that sharpens the whole sense of wanting to wake someone up with those riddles and the truth. Physically Marcello played that a lot in the storm: he's much bigger than me, and was very protective.

Her Lear had shoulder-length white hair, a tiny goatee beard, and a three-piece suit several sizes too large. Her low, husky voice enabled her to embrace a masculine pitch, but using it to rise above the storm was a problem; in rehearsal she lost her voice trying to compete with some very loud sound effects. The eventual solution was for her to start 'Blow winds and crack your cheeks!' without any background effects, and for the storm to be gradually introduced on 'Rumble thy bellyful!' As she remembered it: 'There was a sense of my summoning up the storm. Lear is calling for the end of the world as well as the destruction of himself. You don't have to play mad: it's someone talking to the weather.'

She remembers the reaction to Lear being played by a woman.

There was a lot of fuss about it in the press. Some questions put to me were less than sophisticated, such as 'Are you going to go naked in the storm?' Anyone playing Lear is nervous before they go on, but this was fantastically scary, because I had the additional pressure of knowing people were sitting there going, 'Oh really? Well prove it.' So the concentration required was huge. I was interested in exploring what imagination means in theatre. If an audience can accept that an actor is a king from the distant past, why can't they imagine that a woman has made that transformation?

At the time only three other actresses had played King Lear professionally, Maria Casares in Paris, Janet Wright in Toronto, and the German Marianne Hoppe, at the age of seventy-nine. (In 2014 at the Union theatre in London, Ursula Mohan played her as a woman, a very different concept.) Some critics were not happy with the idea, arguing that an actress tackling the part 'goes against the grain'. Paul Taylor decided that Hunter 'looks like an eccentric midget in a freakshow' giving 'a mannered and distancing impersonation of male old age', but he also thought she achieved 'extraordinary vocal and physical precision', and that 'she makes a persuasive case for gender-blind casting'.

Others felt her Lear had been justified. Charles Spencer noted her 'rare authority and presence', stating: 'What might have been a fiasco turns out to be an interesting experiment. At the end of the play you do, just about, feel you've witnessed *King Lear*, rather than a meaningless exercise in modish casting. After a few minutes Hunter's sex ceases to be an issue.' She was praised by the *Leicester Mercury* for creating 'an almost genderless person wrestling with the confusion of being old', while Michael Coveney wrote: 'She brings off the big moments with panache, intelligence and welling emotion.' Looking back, Magni speaks highly of her performance. 'Kathryn loves playing old people. I felt her transformation into Lear was totally believable, and her madness devastating. I could see her father in it, and other old people. There was an extraordinary tenderness in the Dover cliff scene with Gloucester, which was perhaps not the tenderness of a man.' The director Dominic Hill pointed out: 'There's such a mythic element to the story which is non-naturalistic, and I thought she was incredibly moving.'

Hunter felt the question of her gender was eventually not a problem. When the company took the play to Japan the response was very different. For Japanese audiences accustomed to theatrical forms like *kabuki*, in which men play all the roles, female as well as male, a woman playing Lear was never a problem. 'I did a couple of interviews, and they said, "How interesting, we usually do it the other way round, with men playing women." After that I really felt I could play the part with authority.'

She and the company visited a Shinto shrine, to observe the behaviour and absorb the body language of elderly Japanese worshippers, after which she added new details to her performance. She also noticed a significant cultural attitude to old age. 'Old people's homes were then very new and very few. The idea of rudeness to an elder person and a parent was palpably shocking. They wouldn't dream of sending them off to a home.'

The framing device was heavily criticised. Charles Spencer called it 'an irritating gimmick' and an idea of 'monstrous arrogance', while for Michael Billington it went 'right against the Shakespearean grain'. Kaut-Howson remembered:

I thought the device was a good way of making the play accessible. Young audiences responded very well: they completely understood how you can move from dream to reality, from reality to fantasy. But the critics hated it and were very rude and vicious about it. So when we moved to the Young Vic I shrank it and made it more abstract, though the play still took place in the woman's mind.

Hunter sees the play in a more hopeful spirit than some actors do. 'People say it's the most painful of his plays, but because of Lear's spiritual awakening I don't see it as one of total loss. He has a genuine kinship with the poor naked wretches.' After Lear she played another major Shakespearean part, Richard III, in an all-female production at the Globe. 'There's no redemption for Richard as there is for Lear. Richard is so vitriolic and evil under the playfulness, whereas Lear actually feels more familiar to me than some female parts. He's not just a great giant of a man, but an expression of the human spirit. My heart and soul were much more connected to his journey.'

# Warren Mitchell
## *Jude Kelly*

*In 1995 Warren Mitchell played King Lear at the West Yorkshire Playhouse in Leeds, in a production directed by its artistic director, Jude Kelly. The play then transferred to the Hackney Empire in London.*

Goneril and Regan are very difficult roles. It's a very male play and they're trapped in the middle of it. I've been frustrated by the way they have been portrayed in the past, so as a woman director I wanted to attend to their stories more fully than a man might do.

While rehearsing her production, Jude Kelly and her company explored the back story of Lear's two oldest daughters, played by Tricia Kelly (Goneril) and Alexandra Gilbreath (Regan), to try to identify the cause of their dysfunctional behaviour. She was keen that they should only make use of ideas that could be validated by the text. One conclusion was that the sisters had probably been set up in competition with each other throughout their lives, that 'a lifetime of aberration' had destroyed their happiness and well-being.

'It's impossible to think that Goneril and Regan go round being vile just because they feel like it,' Kelly suggests.

I think they were always in fight or flight mode, either for Lear's attention, or to get away from his anger. They were needy of their father, but they also harboured deep resentment of him, because he never allowed them to have their own independent lives. What he's done to his family is terrible. He destroys Cordelia, but he's already destroyed Goneril and Regan. We know that if you are a child who is publicly less loved, that can destroy your life, making it difficult to be a balanced human being. So you can see why underneath they hated him.

It was important, she felt, to show that there was nothing in Lear that understood or cared about anybody's welfare except his own. This is highlighted in his insistence on clinging to his hundred knights. 'When you hear the word knights now, you think of nice men with polished armour, but that's not what you've got here. These are mercenary thugs, hanging about everywhere, dominating Goneril's servants, being absolutely sexist and vile and horrific. Nobody could cope with that, and it puts her in an impossible position.'

Cordelia, she feels, is less damaged than her sisters, since Lear obviously dotes on her.

I came to the conclusion that the doting wasn't suspect or physical, but that she was probably so different and separate from her sisters because she was the result of another marriage, or perhaps just because she was Lear's last little girl. So she was shielded from the pressures and emotional cruelty that he put upon Goneril and Regan. But her refusal to play Lear's game in the first scene is not simply a matter of ethical purity, but defiance. She's immensely stubborn, and doesn't want to give Lear power over her, or to lie about how she feels. And when she comes back as the leader of the French army, you can see she's got a will of iron.

Warren Mitchell had played Lear before, in Australia in 1978 for the Queensland Theatre Company in Brisbane. Of that production, a conventionally pagan, Druidical one, he remembered: 'The director said it was a long play, so we would have to deliver the verse at so many words a minute.' Best known in Britain for playing the bigot Alf Garnett in the hugely popular television series *Til Death Us Do Part*, Mitchell had also worked extensively on the stage both in Australia and the UK, most notably as Willy Loman in *Death of a Salesman* at the National Theatre in London.

Kelly had originally wanted Cyril Cusack to play the part, but then he died. Soon after she had a letter from Mitchell, asking if he might be a suitable replacement.

> I agreed, because I thought he was a great actor, and I could see there were some qualities in his playing of Alf Garnett that would be appropriate for Lear: the elements of the dictator, the plaintive and misunderstood man who liked to make himself the centre of the story. Most actors who have played a major Shakespearean part think they know what it's about, and want to play it again. And of course Warren was now twenty years older. As we know, with each decade you go through your understanding about old age changes phenomenally. I think Warren was at the stage of thinking about frailty and vulnerability.

Now approaching seventy, he had undergone hip replacements, but kept fit by swimming and playing tennis. When offered the role, he made it clear what kind of Lear he could best play. 'I said I couldn't play a regal king. I could play a warrior, a tribal chieftain – but not a gracious royal. I look like what I am, the descendant of a Russian Jew.'

At first Kelly found it difficult to wean him off his previous interpretation, to relinquish those ideas and start again.

> A certain amount of 'unrehearsing' went on. I've had this with directing opera, where singers who have played the role before say, 'I play it like this.' I have to tell them that even if we arrive at the same conclusion, we still have to go through a process of investigation. Warren still knew the lines, which initially made it more difficult for him to start again.

But eventually he did so. 'He believed in collegiate rehearsing because he comes from that tradition, so it was actually great working with him.'

She says that he and Toby Jones, who played the Fool, had a fantastic relationship, which was quite like that between Lear and the Fool. 'Toby, who was very young, was solicitous and teasing and loyal to Warren in rehearsal, taking him through his lines, and generally looking after him.' But she also had to deal with the perennial problem of actors wanting to be loved: 'It was difficult for Warren to accept the idea that Lear needed not to be centre stage, being adorable.'

Her fresh directorial look at both Lear's and Gloucester's children resulted in some startling characterisations. Goneril, seen as starved of both love and sex, expressed her frustration in obsessively arranging flowers. Regan, abusively fondled by Lear in public, was constantly on the edge of a breakdown. Avoiding the usual smooth and calculating Machiavellian villain, Damien Goodwin played Edmund as a sad, shambolic, near psychotic figure. A bumbling, bespectacled student raging in his bedsit to the sound of sleazy jazz, he practises committing suicide by putting a plastic bag over his head, and takes out his frustrations on a rag doll of his legitimate brother. By contrast Robert Bowman's Edgar came over as an unusually cool charmer before morphing into Poor Tom. Initially laid-back and humorous, he first meets Edmund holding a bottle of brandy, and mimes yawning and vomiting in recollection of his conversation with their father the night before.

Like other directors, Kelly cut many of Poor Tom's lines.

The question is, is he feigning madness, or just on the borders of feigning madness? But you can't sustain madness for too long: there's nowhere to go with it except to observe it, and there's a limit to an audience's attention. It's a situation that offers an actor the chance to give a virtuoso performance of madness, which is great for him, but less interesting for the audience.

The surprises in the production were not confined to the two families. Albany, sporting a Hitler hairdo and a fanatic demeanour, displayed a grim, repressive piety, prayer book in hand. Kent became in his disguise as Caius a vicious, green-haired psychopath, a tattooed Nazi thug, who made monkey noises at Oswald, played by a black actor. The King of France was also black, and in another unconventional touch appeared menacingly at the end of the play, seemingly ready to take over the kingdom. After Lear and Cordelia were taken prisoner the Fool was shown to have hanged himself.

To give more weight to her production, Kelly recruited some fifty local people, who played Lear's knights, the beggars whom Poor Tom encounters on the heath, and the army soldiers. For the storm scene she used water to create a huge rainstorm, in which Mitchell became completely soaked. 'We were trying to show how horrific it was to leave this man out in the pouring rain, and for him to take his clothes off and prance around naked; to show the wildness of him being ejected from hearth and home into the wilderness, as a metaphor as well as a reality.'

She set the play in a timeless period, with mixed costumes. In the opening scene Lear wore a red coat in the style of a Chelsea Pensioner, and open-toed sandals. The members of the court wore a mixture of medieval helmets and shopping-mall suits, while the soldiers in battle carried pikeshafts and were dressed in chemical-warfare suits. 'I didn't want to set the play in period, I just wanted to show this could happen any time, any where,' Kelly stresses. Mitchell welcomed this decision, explaining during rehearsals: 'The tone of the production is specifically unspecific, which gives you far greater freedom of expression. It allows me to think: "How would Prince Charles react in a situation such as this? Or Louis XIV? Or Henry VIII?"'

The unorthodox production annoyed some critics. Paul Taylor felt 'it was much too busy to be truly affecting'; Benedict Nightingale thought 'the emotional essence disappears beneath too much distracting detail and frantic business'. Mitchell's Lear provoked more mixed reactions. Charles Spencer felt 'he misses tragic grandeur and emotional depth', while Nightingale found the end 'unmoving'. But Michael Coveney thought it 'a performance of outstanding warmth, character, pathos and sensitivity', while Robin Thornber called it 'a virtuoso display of histrionic knowhow – deeply felt and carefully thought through.'

Kelly was pleased with Mitchell's performance. 'I thought he was tremendously moving. Even though he was small he was physically powerful, and frightening when he lost his temper. He communicated marvellously the loss of power, and being pained and baffled by the resulting loss of his identity, and being infantilised by it.'

She denied that people were seeing it as a feminist production. 'For most people it was just the play, and as far as they were concerned it seemed to stack up.' But she was not entirely satisfied with her work.

> I didn't feel the production and meaning completely held together. The thing that is hard about the play is its length, and trying to make the pace work well. There are also those long arias in the storm, and the speeches of Poor Tom, which are very difficult to create. If I did it again I think I would set it in a specific time and place, because I think in a weird way that gives people a greater sense of the play's universality.

# Pete Postlethwaite
## *Rupert Goold*

*In 2008 Pete Postlethwaite played King Lear at the Liverpool Everyman. Directed by Rupert Goold for his company Headlong, the play subsequently transferred to the Young Vic in London.*

> With Shakespeare I like to bring out the social context, in order to give the actors a foothold.

Rupert Goold's way of demonstrating this approach in his Everyman production, which he set in the broken Britain of the late 1970s and 1980s, proved hugely provocative, both to the critics and to his lead actor. He chose to start the play with a recording of Margaret Thatcher quoting from the prayer of Saint Francis of Assisi. He had Lear sing a snatch of 'My Way' when dividing his kingdom, which he did with the help of a Hornby train set. He made the Fool break into 'Singin' in the Rain' after the storm; put Lear in a floral dress for the Dover cliff scene; used an Elton John song playing on a transistor radio during the reconciliation scene; and turned Lear's knights into violent, face-painted football hooligans.

All these ideas provoked considerable fury from the critics, who denounced the production as wayward, gimmicky, clumsy, obtrusive, and generally flawed by misjudgements and facile theatricality. Susannah Clapp wrote: 'It looks like a string of unrelated incidents. Here people seem to be barging on to the stage from different dramas: you might be channel-hopping.' Charles Spencer, who thought Goold's recent RSC *Macbeth* one of the greatest Shakespeare productions he had seen, concluded: 'On this occasion his bright ideas often seem self-indulgent and reductive, drawing flashy attention to the director's role of theatrical razzle-dazzler without serving the text.'

Pete Postlethwaite's Lear also came in for considerable criticism. While Christopher Hart thought him 'unusually moving', Michael Billington stated that 'he lacks the vocal heft or dominant presence to hold the production together', and that 'he suggests less a testy autocrat than a mildly angry Rotary Club president'. Spencer argued that 'his creaky, mechanical voice isn't up to the demands of the role' and that 'he often misses the pulse of the poetry, rarely illuminates its meaning, and almost totally fails to catch the desperate king's heart-rending terror of madness'.

The actor had been deeply unhappy about the production, and generally agreed with the reviewers' criticisms. 'There was too much gimmickry, and I told Rupert as much,' he recalled.

> Our first responsibility is to tell the story Shakespeare intended. That's our duty as actors, not to impose our theory as to what the story is about. The kitchen sink was being thrown at our performance, with props, songs, overt politics, and more besides. As a company we found ourselves divided over the way we were approaching the production. There were continual disagreements, with changes being made up to the opening night and throughout the first week. We seemed to be lumbered with a production that we didn't really want and didn't really believe in. Being King Lear became really hard. You can't have someone playing him who doesn't endorse every bit of the production.

Seven years on, Rupert Goold reveals some of the reasons for the many differences that arose.

> It was probably the most volatile time I've had in any rehearsal room. Pete was beloved as a northern folk hero, but ironically for this great

working-class, left-wing actor, he felt this was the moment for him to play a 'proper' King Lear. So he was shocked by the huge arguments I had with him about playing Lear in his own accent. In the end I managed to budge him slightly off doing it in received pronunciation, although he got at me as being a middle-class boy trying to impose some working-class ideal. He wanted our show to stand comparison with the RSC productions of the 1980s.

Postlethwaite had reason to be nostalgic, having played Cornwall in Adrian Noble's 1982 production at Stratford. He had also understudied Gambon's Lear. 'I adored the role,' he remembered. 'It seemed the most complete part that Shakespeare created, the most accomplished, four-dimensional role in all of theatre. I longed to test myself against Shakespeare's moving and complex text. There seemed to be no greater examination of an actor's skill than the fragile, tormented, doomed king.'

He also believed the destruction inherent in the play made it pertinent for the present day.

What you have essentially, once the sluice-gate holding back the poison is removed, is civil war and anarchy and carnage, lies upon lies, brothers turning against brothers, father against daughters. All of which is precisely what is happening in Iraq at the moment. Nobody is telling the truth about that situation, but what we've done is release complete anarchy in that part of the world. So we've ended up with a situation where nobody wants to carry the can for what's happening there, rather like with Lear, who wants all the trappings of statesmanship without any of the responsibility. I strongly believe Shakespeare knew that what he was writing would make sense four hundred years later.

Goold had several reasons for casting Postlethwaite.

He was incredibly emotional, a man who totally wore his heart on his sleeve. He had a real danger in him, a genuine explosivity. He also had this great capacity in both his life and work to show humility. No actor I've ever worked with or seen did an emotional epiphany like Pete, that moment of going, 'What have I done?' after realising he had been wrong over a conflict with somebody.

One such conflict he recalls was with Amanda Hale, playing Cordelia.

They were both strong personalities, and they clashed horribly over what constituted good acting. Pete's was all about liveliness, saying, I need to connect with you and something that's happening between us in the moment. Amanda wanted to be allowed to give her performance and not to have it re-shaped and dictated to by a slightly bullying father figure.

It got worse and worse, until each of them came up to me and said they were leaving, they couldn't work with the other one. That made the reconciliation scene much more complicated than it normally is.

He and Postlethwaite did a great deal of work together before rehearsals started, studying and analysing the text, deciding on cuts, modernising the odd word, and structuring it as three acts, labelled Dissolution, Anarchy and Recovery. 'Pete loved being involved with all that. In the rehearsal room he was very exciting, he had incredible energy. He was off the book the day we started, and he lived it more than any other actor.' He also came up with many of the ideas for which Goold was severely criticised: the 'My Way' moment, the floral dress, Lear's masturbation during the Dover cliff scene with Gloucester. 'Critics have so little idea how plays are made,' Goold says. 'They think a director comes in and maps out all the business, and the actors do the performances. It's just not like that, it's much more collaborative.'

It was also Postlethwaite's idea that Goneril should be eight months pregnant in the early scenes, and give birth during the storm. So Lear delivers his curse on her fertility to a very obviously expectant mother; we hear the sound of the birth during the night of the storm; and later Goneril is seen kissing Edmund over the baby's pram. Goold remembers: 'The show finished with just the sound of the boy crying, abandoned because his mother was dead. It was a slight gesture towards the question, What is this future generation going to be?'

In the face of the widespread critical hostility, Goold made substantial changes when the play moved to London. 'I think some of the criticism was unfair, but I didn't get the beginning of the play right, and if you don't do that people feel uncomfortable.' So Margaret Thatcher was dropped, as was the Hornby train set, while much of the politics disappeared. He re-staged the opening scene more conventionally, and put a throne on the set to give Lear more status. 'That was a big change, and I think it was an improvement. But I missed the Thatcher recording, I thought the show was better with that opening. However, when you then hear the first lines of Shakespeare uttered, it is a bit dislocating.'

John Shrapnel, playing Gloucester, remembers that 'in London the production dropped into place and settled down. Its shape became clearer and more defined, with more confidence. Rough edges were ironed out, and a few grace notes tidied up. It was a cleaner production than it had been in Liverpool.' Postlethwaite was greatly relieved that Goold was prepared to re-think: 'It was like a bonfire of the vanities. Anything that we found unhelpful, distracting, not true to the story, was washed away.'

The reviews this time were much more positive. Dominic Cavendish decided: 'For much of the evening it is gripping, inventive, assured – and revelatory ... The journey Postlethwaite takes is beautifully shaded: by turns semi-serious, pensive and pained before arriving, touchingly, at some dazed, carefree state where madness has become his sole means of self-preservation.' Fiona Mountford wrote: 'Mercifully, this 1970s dress production has managed to shed its tricksy excesses. What remains is a lovely, easy fluidity. Goold brilliantly dislodges the play from the daunting realms of the mythic where it too often nests, and gives it instead the compelling, accessible-to-all stamp of a quality soap opera.'

For Postlethwaite the relief was considerable. 'Having come through the experience of an unsuccessful opening in Liverpool, the success in London was actually sweeter. Lear is a very brutal and exhausting role, and by the end of the run I was exhausted, both emotionally and physically. But it had been a redemptive experience; the light had followed the darkness.' Goold remains puzzled by the gap between his views and those of the critics. 'I've done shows that have been not well received, and I've said fair enough. But I think *King Lear* is the best Shakespeare I've directed – and yet I've got miles better reviews for other ones.'

# Tim Pigott-Smith
## *Ian Brown*

*In the autumn of 2011 Tim Pigott-Smith played King Lear in a production at the West Yorkshire Playhouse in Leeds, directed by its artistic director Ian Brown.*

> *King Lear* is a masterpiece, one of the greatest works of literature. Whatever you think of it, whether you like it or whether you don't, it's there, and has to be negotiated. But it's a tough play to get to know well, and I was quite daunted by it.

In planning his Playhouse production, one of Ian Brown's principal aims was to make sure the story was comprehensible to a modern audience. Before rehearsals began he and Tim Pigott-Smith worked on the text, cutting some seven hundred lines, notably a substantial number of Edgar's as Poor Tom, but including the mock-trial scene, which is omitted from the First Folio. Pigott-Smith recalled the process:

> We went through it and took out every sentence we didn't understand immediately. We ended up with a very clear text, and keeping all the essential elements. We had no concept in mind; we just wanted to make the play work. We found that there were quite a lot of places where you could use the old word and the audience would know exactly what it was from the context. But some of Poor Tom's stuff is incomprehensible, and that took the biggest savaging. As a result people could understand the story, rather than have to say, 'Oh my God, this is Shakespeare, and nobody is guiding me.'

As an experienced Shakespearean actor he had had the part in his sights for some time. In fact the idea had first been put to him several decades earlier. 'When I was at university I played the bearded Hermit in *Next Time I'll Sing to You* by James Saunders. Someone said to me afterwards: "You should play King Lear." I suppose that planted the seed in my mind.' Brown's offer was not one he felt able to refuse. 'If somebody says here's a mountain and you're a mountaineer, you've got to scale it.' At sixty-five he felt he was the right age to tackle the role. 'I thought I should do it before I was too old. I don't think I could have played it when I was younger. And if I'd waited until I was much older I wouldn't be strong enough.'

He was conscious of the play's dark nature.

You get this fantastic sense of bleakness coming through at the end, and a savagery and barbarism which you don't find anywhere else in Shakespeare. There is absolutely nothing redeeming about the play. It starts with people talking to the gods, and by the end there are no gods; man is on his own and, as Lear says, a poor bare forked animal. The only thing that distinguishes him from the beasts is the ability and the power to love. Lear finds that very late on, and then it's taken from him. I think that's part of the essence of this great tragedy, that what makes us human is the ability to love.

For Ian Brown the attraction of the play was clear.

It was written at a time of unrest, and that has echoes for today. The use of language is phenomenal, and very complex. You just wonder how Shakespeare had all these frames of reference. The imagery is very strong, and the nihilistic aspect of the play speaks very powerfully to me. Also there's a fairy-tale element to it; it feels like a mythic story. It's dealing with images and symbols and archetypes, but within that there is a reality, a bleakness that can be there in people's lives.

Deciding against staging a modern-dress production, he set the action in the early Jacobean period.

It seems to be a play that emerges from a particular time, written as a warning to King James, a fairly new king, to try to hold everything together. So the production reflects the period in which the play was written, with a version of Jacobean dress, though not a slavish repro-duction, that gives it a lot of weight and power. It gets you over certain problems, such as the sword fight between Edgar and Edmund.

In the wide expanses of the Playhouse stage, designer Ruari Murchison's set for the first half was deliberately tilted and off-kilter, with walls set at lopsided angles, suggesting Lear's fracturing kingdom. The second half had just a bare stage, a vast expanse which, Pigott-Smith says, 'gave you the sense of being on the edge of the world'. A huge moon hung at the back of the set, reflecting a theme on which Brown wished to focus. 'The planetary influence that's referenced right at the beginning with an eclipse was really strong, and I wanted to highlight that. You see these human beings under the planets, these poor naked wretches trying to make their way in the world, in this uncaring and unforgiving universe.'

Director and actor agreed on the basic quality in Lear that needed stressing at the outset. Pigott-Smith explained:

> We both felt he had to begin as a very powerful king. You have to start off with all the trappings of power and wealth, to establish a sense of his total authority. He really does believe he's God's representative on earth, so you have to believe that what he says goes. People prostrate themselves on the floor when he comes on, there's a big sense of power about the man. That's absolutely crucial, because the journey of the play is Lear discovering how hollow and absolutely unimportant that power is in the scale of things.

During rehearsals they discussed the back story of Lear's family. Brown recalled their conclusions:

> I think poor Goneril suffered most for not being born a boy. When Lear was busy being a king, having battles and not spending much time at home, she was neglected. Then Regan came along, and the pressure on her to be a boy was not quite the same. She seems to have a way of playing Lear, making him feel uncomfortable, whereas Goneril by this stage has become a tricky child. And then Cordelia arrives and becomes the apple of Lear's eye. So there was a lot of sibling rivalry going on, it's just not a functioning family. There's definitely something unhealthy in Lear's attitude to women, something very twisted, and the play is an exploration of what happens if women are evil. Even in our culture there is something particularly repellent about women doing evil, because we look to women to save us flawed men; when they behave like men we are very shocked by it.

Pigott-Smith pondered on Lear's attitude to his two older daughters.

> It's a phenomenally powerful and diseased relationship. He's vile to Goneril, but not half so vile to Regan: he's shocked by the way she behaves, but he's nice to her, he says: 'You can't do this to me, you're a nice girl.' But with Goneril he's never like that; it's terrible, violent stuff from the beginning. So why does he reserve his most violent, horrendous language for her? Our solution was that Mrs Lear died giving birth to Cordelia. At that time Lear was very lost, and turned to Goneril, and

that very close relationship developed into an incestuous one. Then by the time Cordelia becomes an adult he loses interest in Goneril, and transfers all his affections to the younger, idolised daughter. So you have a ghastly, rejected sister, who's then motivated throughout as to what she has to do. And you also have that scene where Lear gives that massive curse about the organs of increase. I used to kneel down, hold her and curse her womb, then drag her down to the floor, so we were in a pretty nasty sexual position.

When Brown suggested that Lear should display some very elementary sign of dementia in the first scene, he was happy to go along with the idea.

I'd seen dementia, so I didn't have to research it. My Dad had it – not very badly, but enough for me to know what it was, and to be able to spot the clues. He had that thing of getting halfway through a speech and not knowing where he was going with a sentence, and just stopping. His mind was beginning to fade, but he always knew who you were. So in the opening scene I made it clear that Lear was suffering in this way. I deliberately got very, very lost. I didn't know where I was physically and mentally, and it took me a while to get back on track. I could do it very easily, just pause in the middle of a speech, and then carry on, and everyone knew where you were. Even if they thought I had dried, I wouldn't have worried about it, because Lear could have dried. Afterwards I had lots of letters from people saying: 'It was really interesting, I never realised Shakespeare wrote so clearly about dementia.'

Brown considered doubling Cordelia and the Fool, but decided against the idea. He made Lear and the Fool (Richard O'Callaghan) be contemporaries, who had known each other for a long time.

We talked about Max Wall, that kind of old-style British comic, seeing the world in a sardonic kind of way, not necessarily trying to be funny. It was a very bleak vision of the Fool. He does his best to show Lear that he's done wrong, but he can't cope, he's really had enough, and eventually he leaves Lear, and maybe hangs himself.

Brown explained his thinking on the storm scene:

There's a bit of an Old Testament image for me there, it feels as if there might be one of those figures in the corner of a map, blowing with his cheeks. I think he's having a conversation with the gods, because he's a king, and they are listening to him when they don't listen to ordinary human beings. We wanted to use the theatricality of the scene, so we had the thunder machine in view, and human-made percussion. We did without real rain, which never really works for me.

Pigott-Smith agreed with this decision. 'In accepting the part I insisted on two conditions: no rain and no nudity. You don't need rain, and nudity just distracts. Wearing long coms is fine. You don't want people coming in and talking about the size of your dick, as happened with Ian McKellen and Ian Holm. It's stupid.'

Another directorial decision was to position Gloucester's blinding after the interval, rather than before, as is generally the case. And when Pigott-Smith entered with the dead Cordelia, there was another unusual touch. 'The fight director came up with the idea that I should carry her on my back,' he explained. 'I was pleased with that, because it meant I could just lower her down and put her where I wanted, without anyone interfering. I didn't need anyone to help me, and as an actor I didn't want anyone near me at that moment. It was a matter of: "Stay away, I've worked all evening for this moment."'

The critical reaction to his Lear was positive. Heather Neill observed: 'Piggott-Smith is every inch a king and, more significantly, a suffering human being too.' Jonathan Brown wrote: 'He is avuncular, needy, vengeful, raging, and ultimately lost to confusion, hitting each mark near perfectly during Lear's long descent into madness.' Alfred Hickling stated: 'The reunion of Olivia Morgan's iron-willed Cordelia and her broken father is among the most moving I have seen.' Dominic Cavendish suggested this Lear could stand comparison with those of Ian McKellen and Derek Jacobi, adding: 'There are many moments when you get a terrifying flash of what it's like for age, unreason, dementia even, to steal up on you unawares.'

Brown observed of Pigott-Smith's performance:

> I think Tim brought great humanity to Lear. All the different facets of his journey through the play – the madness, the wrath, the vindictiveness, the pettiness, the lavishness – you have to find all of those things, and great sensitivity too, and the terrible lessons he has to learn in order to become a better human being. That needs an actor of Tim's range.

Pigott-Smith himself was awed by the power of the play. 'There can't be a set of scenes anywhere in dramatic literature of such depth and wonder. In the mad scenes you can turn on a sixpence, you can be very mercurial, you can go anywhere. I had a ball; it was an exhilarating part to play, because you release so much energy.' In general he was satisfied with his performance.

> I've spent my acting life playing authority figures, so that aspect of Lear comes quite easily to me. The greatest challenge was his disintegration in the second half, and that staggering emotional scene when he wakes up and sees Cordelia. It's a very hard part, and you need to be strong. But since then I've not played any part that has intimidated me. You think, If I can do Lear, I can do anything.

An experienced director himself, he was full of praise for Brown's production.

> Every aspect of it was thought through. It was all of a piece – set, sound and design, and that's rare. Ian included me in its creation in a way that I really appreciated, and I felt we did something valuable and honest. If someone asked me if I would play Lear again, I think I would say no, because I doubt if I could be in a better production.

# 7

# At the Old Vic 2

## Anthony Quayle
### *Toby Robertson*

*In the 1978–9 season at the Old Vic, Anthony Quayle played King Lear for the Prospect Theatre Company, in a production directed by Toby Robertson, its artistic director.*

Anthony Quayle was a distinguished Shakespearean, not only because of the major roles he played – among them Othello, Iago and Coriolanus – but because he turned down a Hollywood contract to run the Shakespeare Memorial Theatre at Stratford between 1948 and 1956, turning what was a provincial theatre into a major international company that attracted star players to the great roles. Strong and authoritative physically, his considerable stage success was remarkable for someone who once described his face as 'a currant bun, pudgy and inexpressive.'

Quayle was faced with a uniquely demanding schedule of eight shows a week. Isla Blair, who played Regan, recalls the qualities of his Lear:

> He was a very powerful king: people were worried about getting on the wrong side of him, so they were always walking on eggshells around him. But he wasn't particularly blustery, he was someone who gave the impression of being a very good ruler, who was as fair as he could have been. The mistake he made was dividing up his kingdom, and letting the girls have it.
>
> His madness was more a matter of bewilderment at the way life's events had overtaken him, rather than being insane. It was like someone at the beginning of Alzheimer's, rather than somebody who was going mad. It was not just that he was afraid of forgetting words, but that he was going into a dark tunnel. You felt that he fell from a great height. He wasn't just a frail old man, but someone who was powerful: when he walked into a room people shut up, which was why his fall was so agonising. I found him quite wonderful, and totally moving.

Toby Robertson gave the play an Ancient Britain setting on a simple, straw-covered stage, but also included aspects of a Renaissance court. Blair had mixed feelings about his directing: 'He could be wonderful, but sometimes he would go off on wings of thought, and was completely incoherent, and you wondered what he was saying had to do with *King Lear*. But at other times he would do things that were rather brilliant.'

*Anthony Quayle played King Lear again in 1989 for his own touring company Compass (see page 135).*

# Eric Porter
## *Jonathan Miller*

*Jonathan Miller's second stage production of* King Lear *was at the Old Vic in 1989, with Eric Porter taking the title-role for the third time.*

After directing Michael Hordern in two television versions of the play, Jonathan Miller directed it again at the Old Vic, where he was in his second season as artistic director. His choice of actor to play Lear was Eric Porter, who had already played the role twice, at the Bristol Old Vic and Stratford.

This production was significantly different from Miller's previous three with Hordern. Gemma Jones, playing Goneril, recalled: 'He was obviously very familiar with the text, but he came to it totally fresh, thinking on his feet and ready to react to the chemistry of a new cast.' One new departure was his decision to have much older sons and daughters for Gloucester and Lear. 'It seemed to me to be about middle-aged children becoming impatient with elderly parents,' he says. 'I suppose that was the result of having grown to that age myself – I wanted to see what would happen if you really had the older daughters that age.'

'Jonathan leaves a lot of room for the actors to experiment,' Jones recalled.

> He doesn't overwhelm you with suggestions unless you get stuck. He gently encouraged us, and then polished the edges – and he would improvise moments himself for us, as he is very good at playing women. Although he's an intellectual in every sense of the word, he doesn't let that overwhelm his direction; he works out of a spontaneity that isn't necessarily book-bound. Being a psychologist, he would naturally analyse the characters, but in a domestic way, rather than just quoting Jung and Freud at us.

Miller saw part of his role as reminding actors of things they knew but had forgotten. 'I've learned about directing through watching people. As a doctor I was trained to pick up on minute nuances of human behaviour; I was trained to observe the negligible because precisely that detail might tell the whole story.'

As at Nottingham, Miller again made clear to the cast his views about what he called 'RSC and National Theatre verse-speaking'. 'He doesn't like actors to get weighed down in dogmas about the verse,' Jones observed. 'Instead he is very open to the diverse styles of his group of actors, which is always very eclectic. He is not at all dictatorial about it – his sole concern is that we should get the meaning of the words across to the audience.' In that connection he told Porter 'not to over-dignify the part, not to have any of that versification. He was pleased with that idea, and yielded to it.' In working with the notion of madness, he had Porter constantly playing with himself, and almost revealing his genitals. 'This is what old mad people do,' he said. "It's a very ugly thing, madness: there's nothing pretty or prophetic about it.' There was, inevitably, a good deal of discussion about the nature of senility and madness, and about Alzheimer's disease in relation to Lear.

One of Miller's continuing concerns was to make Goneril and Regan recognisable human beings. He suggested Goneril might have had some psychological trauma which made her behave the way she did. Jones observed:

I remember him saying to me during one scene, 'I think Goneril has got a migraine.' Her travail was making her ill, and her actions immediately became clear. He had Albany portrayed as an intellectual with his head permanently buried in his books, which must have driven Goneril crazy too. So he made the characters into people who could sit around a kitchen table and eat Weetabix as well as commit murder and behave in the most extraordinary manner.

To highlight the references to beggars and homelessness, Miller filled the hovel with sleeping figures, like those who could then be found under nearby Waterloo Bridge. Another innovation was to have the blinding take place offstage, leaving the horror to the audience's imagination. Only two characters, Regan and a servant, were left on stage while it took place unseen. Frances de la Tour underlined Regan's sadism, reacting ecstatically while calmly giving Cornwall instructions ('One side will mock another – th'other too.'). The servant, who would shortly intervene against Cornwall's action, was all but vomiting with nausea.

Miller wanted the set to be pared down to its simplest form. He set the beginning of the play on the apron stage before a high, blackened brick wall, with the stage boxes taken out and bricked up. As the action progressed the wall would fly up, only to reveal another one behind. Gradually the stage area increased in size; by the end it extended as far as the back wall of the theatre, the space literally and symbolically expanding Lear's horizons. For the storm scene he was keen to avoid a Wagnerian effect, so designer

Richard Hudson created sheets of black silk suspended from the flies, with electric fans above and below creating the effect of billowing storm clouds.

There was disagreement over the best period for the costumes, as Hudson remembered: 'We were originally thinking of setting it in the 1930s, with the men in suits and the women looking like glamorous film stars. I thought this would work well, particularly when you got the contrast with the down-and-outs in the hovel.' But Porter was unhappy with this idea, and wanted some kind of period costume. Eventually the solution was to dress the actors in what Hudson called 'pseudo-Afghan robes'. He used Eisenstein's film *Ivan the Terrible* as a reference point for some of the costumes, including those for Goneril and Regan.

Among the critics, Paul Taylor picked out Porter's playing of madness. 'His magnificent Lear is all the more moving because it contains so little self-pity. Madness seems to release in this king a wily sense of absurdity and a prankish intellectual adventurousness.' But Michael Billington had reservations: 'As a portrait of a testy aristocrat, it is superb: what it lacks is that gift of self-revelation that is the benchmark of great acting.' Yet John Gross felt Porter had caught Lear's complexity well: 'He is equally convincing in his testiness, his anxiety that nobody should miss the point, his old man's humour, and his capacity for suffering.'

According to Hudson: '*King Lear* turned out to be the most successful show we did at the Old Vic, and proved immensely popular with audiences. I know a lot of people who regard it as the best *Lear* they have ever seen.'

*Jonathan Miller was to direct his third stage production of* King Lear *in Stratford, Ontario in 2002 (see page 203).*

# Alan Howard
## *Peter Hall*

*Alan Howard played Lear in Peter Hall's 1997 production of* King Lear, *staged during the final repertory season of Hall's company at the Old Vic.*

> The Folio has the real feel of an acting text. It's clearer, harder, tougher, richer, and more compulsive as a piece of theatre, and therefore more exciting to work on. It conveys a Sophoclean – almost a post-Beckett – recognition of the awful meaninglessness and randomness of life.

Peter Hall decided to use the Folio edition for this production, to rely on a version which many contend represents Shakespeare's second thoughts about the play. In his view Shakespeare 'realised that he had over-egged the pudding' in the Quarto edition, and the changes that were made subsequently, deleting static soliloquies and chorus-like conversations, produced a darker play. Controversially, this meant losing the mock-trial scene in which Lear arraigns an imagined Goneril and Regan, a scene normally included in modern productions.

The changes made for the Folio edition meant that, among many others, an invasion by the French army becomes a non-warring rescue party; Goneril and Regan's cruelty is seen to have more provocation; and there's a shift in Edgar's identity as the saviour of the kingdom. It also results in a less despairing tone to Lear's dying speech, leaving it more open as to whether he believes Cordelia still lives. It also omits one of the most arresting philosophical thoughts, Albany's 'Humanity must perforce prey on itself / Like monsters of the deep.'

Hall's reference to Beckett was no coincidence. He had just directed the same company in *Waiting for Godot*, in which members of the Lear ensemble had played three of the principal parts: Alan Howard (Lear) had been Vladimir, Greg Hicks (Edgar) had played Lucky, and Denis Quilley (Gloucester) was Pozzo. For many who came to both productions there were unmistakeable echoes between the two plays, not least in the case of Quilley's blinded Gloucester, which came hard on the heels of his blind Pozzo.

Surprisingly, this was Hall's first production of the play. In the 1970s he had tried to persuade Gielgud to play the part again, and for the present production he had originally wanted Ian Holm as his Lear. Like Holm, Howard was an actor of immense experience with the RSC; he was now playing his sixth Shakespearean king. He was determined to present an imperious, majestic Lear at the beginning, rather than the more homespun one of some recent productions. 'There has got to be somewhere for Lear to fall from,' he argued. 'That is why it is so important, in the opening scenes, to create an image that is potent and Olympian. The division of the kingdom may be ludicrous, but the audience has to sense that this man was once a good king, beloved by his subjects.'

His traditional approach to the role fitted in with the style of Hall's production. As he always did when directing Shakespeare, Hall placed great emphasis on exemplary verse-speaking, and making the text crystal-clear. His was a relatively old-fashioned, straightforward production, without any over-arching concept or gimmicks. The actors were dressed in formal Jacobean velvet and silk costumes, and played on a virtually bare stage, although the backdrop split from time to time to reveal mists, shrubs or barren trees.

In exploring the text with Hall during rehearsals, Howard became fascinated by what he described as the play's 'slippage'. 'I mean that the meaning slips all over the place,' he explained. 'One person says one thing and someone else says something completely different about an event that is alleged to have taken place. So who is one to believe?' He cites as an example Lear's one hundred knights. 'They are usually played as louts who make Goneril's life intolerable. But where is the justification for that? If

Shakespeare had wanted scenes of knights smashing up the place, he would have written them. He didn't. Their loutishness is an invention of Goneril – which puts Lear in a better light.' This was important, he felt, since 'You must have a hero whom the audience can admire.'

Howard's vocal delivery had often been criticised, making him seem a mannered actor over-reliant on verbal tricks. Charles Spencer pointed out:

> He can pilot his way through yards of blank verse with extraordinary skill and clarity, and he can range, apparently effortlessly, from hooting musicality to great growls of anger and despair. The effect, however, is outmoded. Howard puts one in mind of the old-style actor-laddie, giving a demonstration of the voice beautiful, and these days we value racked sincerity above polished expertise.

Several critics reacted unfavourably to this aspect of his Lear. 'He seems to sing rather than live the role,' wrote Benedict Nightingale; John Peter thought his voice 'sounds like a priestly incantation, a metallic ring, barely human'; Robert Butler suggested there was 'more melody in "Blow winds" and "Reason not the need" than in some blockbuster musicals'. Bruce Smith felt: 'The effect of Hall's vocal coaching and Howard's mannered delivery was absolutely stultifying. It was like hearing a technically perfect rendition of the notes in a late Beethoven quartet that lacked any emotional presence whatsoever.' But David Murray dissented: 'From Alan Howard's king one might have expected baroque vocal effects, but no: he is eloquent and quietly intense, never extravagant.'

Some critics liked the rest of his performance, though with qualified praise: 'Howard grows in stature and accomplishment as the evening wears on,' Spencer wrote. 'In the thrillingly staged storm sequence he beautifully shows self-pity turning into human sympathy, as well as poignantly capturing the terror of madness.' But he concluded: 'If this is finally a very good rather than a great Lear, it's because Howard never quite suggests that it has been torn from his very soul.' Michael Billington concurred: 'Lear is a role that requires, though not necessarily literally, a degree of self-exposure … Howard's remains as yet a striking feat of impersonation rather than a piece of self-revelation.'

The critics praised the strong quality of the ensemble acting, with Alan Dobie's Fool receiving particular acclaim. With his shock of white hair and beard, Dobie played him as a vaudevillian in a comical, conical hat, an old man who was a kind of parody Lear. Even as Lear is confronting madness, he displayed his ball-juggling skills, while also commenting on Lear's folly. Billington thought him the best Fool he had seen.

# 8

# In the Round

## Paul Shelley
### Sam Walters

*King Lear was performed in 1982 in the Room at the Orange Tree, a pub
theatre in Richmond in west London. Directed by the theatre's founder and
artistic director Sam Walters, it starred Paul Shelley as Lear.*

> There were no costumes as such because there was no money. The crown
> was virtually the only prop, so you really heard the play. That was
> fantastically exciting.

Paul Shelley was an unusually young Lear, being still not quite forty.
Already familiar with the tragedy – he had been Edmund alongside
Donald Sinden's Lear at Stratford six years earlier – he welcomed the
change of venue, and a chance to work with Sam Walters in a very
different way.

> I remember the excitement of coming from the big stage in Stratford to
> the smaller one in Richmond, where the words were the thing. Sam is a
> very inclusive director, he's not Stalinist at all, so coming to the Orange
> Tree was a breath of fresh air, because your opinions and feelings were
> listened to more than they were at the RSC. They listened a bit there, but
> they usually had their productions ready beforehand.

The theatre was then a small room above the pub, with room for just
eighty people to sit on the former church pews placed on all four sides, and
no curtains on the windows. Walters was keen to find out whether it was
possible to stage such a massive play in such a restricted space.

> Many people said our theatre in the round was ideal for Shakespeare,
> but it seemed an enormous challenge to do such a wonderfully rich play
> as *King Lear* there. We didn't have designers then, so there was no great

concept going on. It was a very bare production: we did it very simply, so the acting and the text were all there was.

With no money for costumes, the actors were simply dressed in sweaters and slacks, while for the storm scene the men wore wellington boots. When they were offstage they remained visible on the sidelines; exits and entrances were through the theatre's kitchen or the door at the top of the stairs. Sometimes the restricted space could be problematic, as Walters remembers: 'It was difficult in some scenes having everyone on stage. One night the actor playing Cornwall was standing in front of a member of the audience, and a hand went out and simply moved him.'

Describing himself as 'a bit of a textual purist', Walters preferred not to cut lines, although he made an exception for the Fool's strange 'This prophecy Merlin shall make' speech. He was helped by being able to see the cuts made for Sinden's *Lear*, as Shelley had kept his edited copy; this showed that Gloucester's speech 'So distribution should undo excess' had been omitted.

'It's great socialist stuff,' Walters suggests,

and it was seeing that and other cuts that made me realise what one misses when taking chunks out of a play. Hence our determination to cut nothing except that Fool speech. When the play is cut it tends to be the philosophy and the reflections that go. You can't cut the story, the action, because you've got to move from A to B, but you can cut somebody thinking about something. So I thought, if we've done nothing else, we've done virtually the whole text. It was still only three hours long, and I don't think we galloped.

He preferred to create the production with the actors during rehearsals rather than come in with a concept. An early decision was to avoid having an ancient Lear. 'I didn't think he was old at all, and certainly not four score years and upward,' Shelley says. 'So we just ignored that. If he's not vigorous the play doesn't work, he's just a daft bugger who they should get rid of. So there was no senile dementia, but a lot of anger. I played him as a naughty, very wilful man, as someone who was corrupted by power and wanted a break.'

One obvious difficulty in such a small space was the storm. Walters remembers their solution: 'Paul said that if the storm is anything like how Shakespeare describes it, then it's impossible to act with. So the sense of their being battered by a storm was done physically. We did it without any sound effects, just using the actors' bodies. They held hands, and pulled against each other in different directions. It created a rather effective storm that was silent. I was very pleased with it.' The fight between Edgar and Edmund was another problem, and that too was done in a stylised way.

Shelley remembers having difficulties with certain scenes: 'I found the one where Lear wakes up a bit sentimental, and I tried to play against that. However you do the scene, it shouldn't be sentimental, it's got to be straight. I don't think Lear is ever pathetic, and that scene can sound pathetic if you're not careful.' His problem with the dead Cordelia scene was of a different order. 'It affected me much more than I thought it would. I was often in floods of tears, and yet I had to continue speaking.'

The production played to full and enthusiastic houses throughout its four-week run. The *Financial Times* commended Walters' production for 'shunning traditional costumes or props, and concentrating rather on tough and heartfelt interpretation'. For Shelley it was a memorable experience: 'I loved playing Lear, it's a great, great role. If somebody asked me to do it again, I couldn't say no. As long as you've got your marbles it would be incredibly difficult to turn it down.'

# Clive Swift
## *Peter Cheeseman*

*In 1986 Clive Swift played King Lear in the New Victoria in Newcastle-under-Lyme, Staffordshire, directed by the theatre's artistic director Peter Cheeseman.*

When Clive Swift received the phone call about the offer to play Lear, the circumstances appeared less than auspicious.

> Peter said that they were due to begin rehearsing *King Lear* on Monday, but that local luminary Freddie Jones had been compelled to drop out. Asking if I would be interested in taking over, he added: 'Before you say anything I should tell you that your Goneril will be older than you, your Gloucester is an amateur who will be giving his first professional performance, and your Fool has only 30 per cent hearing.'

Swift had spent ten years with the RSC, during which among many other parts, including Falstaff and Parolles, he had played Oswald in the Scofield/Brook production of *King Lear*. Despite the obvious drawbacks to Peter Cheeseman's offer he accepted it with alacrity, seeing a once-in-a-lifetime opportunity to play a tragic hero. 'I thought fifty might be just the right age at which to intimate Lear's fourscore years and upward, and yet have the stamina to fuel his passion.'

The New Victoria – known as the 'New Vic' – had only just opened in August that year. The first purpose-built theatre-in-the-round in Europe, as the main civic theatre in the Potteries it had replaced the Victoria, an abandoned cinema in nearby Stoke-on-Trent which had been converted into a theatre in 1962 by Cheeseman, Alan Ayckbourn and Stephen Joseph. There Cheeseman had staged a series of musical documentaries based on local events, using reported reminiscences of those involved. Like the Victoria, the New Vic was a theatre-in-the-round, but one that could seat an audience of 600 rather than 400. The relatively intimate theatre meant the production focused on *King Lear* as a family drama, while the restricted space meant that Lear's hundred knights had to be reduced to just two.

Bearded, small and stocky, celebrated for his trademark baggy jumpers – and known affectionately as 'The Old Man of the Sea' – Cheeseman later outlined his directing style: 'I am not a director who likes to have strong concepts,' he explained. 'I have always been nervous and antipathetic about themed ways of looking at productions. I suppose I am very puritanical in terms of my approach to the text.' He had directed the play twice in the old theatre, in 1964 and 1978. This time he spent the first week discussing those productions, and the play in general. 'The cast didn't utter a word of the text, and I became frustrated and rattled,' Swift recalls. 'After ten days, during which we still hadn't got on our feet, I said I hadn't come here to *read* King Lear, to which Peter replied that actors performed well from nervous adrenalin. But Lear was a big challenge, and I had no intention of winging him.'

The sixteen-strong cast were relatively inexperienced, and had to work under repertory conditions, which meant several of the leading actors had to miss rehearsals in order to appear in matinees and pre-performance breaks of another play. The company only got on to the stage for the first time on the morning of the first night, when the technical rehearsal took place. Swift remembers the occasion: 'As I made my speeches there were chickens clucking and horses neighing. I asked what was going on, and Peter said "I'm trying out the sound effects," and I said, "But I can't fight against all that." Then we had a dress-rehearsal in the afternoon, and opened cold to the critics that evening.'

Swift found working in the round in the relatively spacious auditorium 'vocally taxing'. But he was helped by an unexpected discovery: 'I found that I could still remember a lot of Lear's tirades, though only as an imitation of Scofield, so I had the task of unlearning his sound.' He was pleased with one touch: shortly before Lear goes off to sleep in Act 3 he made him have a slight stroke, which slurred his speech for a few lines. 'As he is then absent from the stage for quite a time, giving the actor a much-needed rest, I imagined that time would heal the impairment before he was seen again.'

But in general he was critical of his interpretation of Lear, feeling that while he had attempted to climb the mountain he had missed the peak, and that his director had offered no great insights into Lear's psychology. 'My mistake was to choose early on to rationalise Lear's intolerable behaviour by suggesting incipient senility. This is not Shakespeare's point; Lear is the very worst of fathers. He doesn't know his children, which is why he treats them like automatons, and why he takes their words – including Cordelia's 'Nothing' – at face value. She is his favourite, which is another sign of bad parenting. Freud may have been right in suggesting that unconsciously he desires her.'

John Peter, the only critic from a national paper to review the play, thought it 'a scorchingly effective production: it is clear and strong, and shows you exactly how to unfold pity and grandeur with minimal means.' Of Swift's Lear he wrote: 'A small, battered man whose every joint speaks of pain, Swift's is a major performance in a minor key, unforgettable in its subtle simplicity.'

# John Shrapnel
## *Andrew Hilton*

*In 2012 John Shrapnel played Lear at the Tobacco Factory in Bristol, under the direction of Andrew Hilton.*

I'm not a concept director, but if anyone throws the word traditional at me, I lash out. I can't bear that description.

Andrew Hilton has been putting on Shakespeare in Bristol since the start of the millennium. His large-cast, unflashy, stripped-back productions, staged in the old Wills cigarette factory in the Bedminster area of the city, have been widely and consistently praised, especially for their clarity. 'People come to us and say, "I can understand Shakespeare now." I want them to listen to the play as if it was a modern one, so I insist during rehearsals that every member of the cast understands every single word. There's no point whatsoever for actors to stand on the stage and speak the incomprehensible.'

John Shrapnel sees *King Lear* as a play for all time. 'It's a play about seeing – or not seeing – clearly, and its extreme cruelty, which could be taken from any of today's headlines, still touches us and makes us wonder if there is any redemptive quality in mankind.' He has an extensive knowledge of the play, having previously appeared as the Gentleman, Cornwall, Albany, Kent, Edgar and Gloucester in previous productions on stage, television and radio, and been able to observe up close how actors as diverse as John Gielgud, Eric Porter, Michael Hordern, Pete Postlethwaite and Timothy West handled the role. 'The general landscape of the play was familiar to me,' he says. 'I'd seen it from various angles having played those other parts. But you can never see the story from Lear's point of view unless you are actually going on his incredible journey.' Apart from the productions in which he has been involved, he has seen the play many times. 'To miss a *King Lear* would be like going to the Accademia in Florence and not bothering to take a look at Michelangelo's David.'

The intimate nature of the Tobacco Factory stage influenced his playing of the part.

> The orchestration of the play and how I pitched it was very much defined by the building. It's a hermetically closed venue, like a boxing ring: you're surrounded on four sides, so there's no escape. You're playing to people who are less than six feet away; you can see their knees as you walk towards them. So you've got to be careful how much you let go, and when you do so. If the audience are frightened or deafened, if they are blown backwards by you early on, you've nowhere to go back to.

The scholar Stanley Wells, who thought the production 'admirably clear and intelligent', described the setting and costume design in the *Stage*:

> The audience sat in tiers on all sides of a roughly rectangular acting area. The trunks of four birch trees defined but did not delimit the area of the main acting space. Stage furniture was simple: a table, a throne, a few chairs, and not much more. Entrances and exits could be made at either end of the space. The well-designed costumes were initially suggestive of the era in which the play was written, rather than attempting to suggest the prehistoric time at which it supposedly took place. As the action continued, however, some modern touches were introduced, as if to help the audience to relate the action to our own times. Apart from a few trappings of royalty, there was little attempt to suggest a courtly setting.

Hilton, an actor for much of his career, suggests that playing in the round presents no special difficulties for his companies.

> We live in the round, and I think the actors find it natural to perform in that kind of space. But it imposes a discipline on me, because I have to monitor the audience's experience, and move the actors around accordingly. It can be difficult to make it work, particularly if you've got a Shakespeare history play and a clump of lords standing about: what the hell do you do with them? But it's always manageable.

The first days rehearsing *Lear* were spent investigating the many questions thrown up by the complex first scene. Hilton identified some of the key ones:

> Who is pre-warned that the kingdom is to be divided? What does each character know – if anything – about Lear's darker purpose? What do Goneril and Regan think of Lear's demand that they express their love for him? Are they resentful, embarrassed, or is it all in a day's work? Is Goneril put out that as the eldest child she is not to inherit the whole kingdom, as would have been the case under the English constitution in 1606?

He and the company also examined the reason for Goneril and Regan's actions. 'With some productions they're just witches, who are just being gratuitously nasty to their father. We didn't see them – as they are often played – as cold-hearted schemers, at least not until late in the play, when they find themselves in competition for Edmund's love. In the early scenes they are reacting to the impossible reality into which Lear has thrust them.'

This discussion led on to a consideration of the behaviour of Lear's knights. Was it as riotous as Goneril suggests, or is she making it up, in order to have a reason for getting rid of them? The text provides no evidence either way, but Hilton believes this is not the point: 'I think the real issue is that she has been given half of the kingdom and then it's effectively been taken away from her. Her supremacy has been usurped. Lear is living in her house and ruling the roost, his knights are there and he is in control of them. Irrespective of how they behave, that situation in itself is intolerable.'

Before rehearsals began he and Shrapnel spent many hours discussing the play, and agreeing on substantial cuts to the text. Edgar's speeches as Poor Tom inevitably came under the microscope, as Hilton recalls:

> In cutting his lines I was not just worrying about the difficulty in understanding them. I wanted to take out those asides where Edgar says he is only playing at being a madman. I think he inhabits Poor Tom in a much more profound way, and one that reflects his own inner state. When he starts his speech he first thinks of being a beggar, but that doesn't seem to answer the psychological need, so he goes further and becomes a mad Bedlam beggar. He talks about them sticking thorns in their skin. So we gave him the clever artificial skin that there is now, and on stage he stuck thorns into his flesh. This self-harming reflects the degree of his self-loathing and unhappiness. I thought it was important to show that he is re-making himself through adopting those personas.

He and Shrapnel had previously acted in a production of *Timon of Athens*, and got on extremely well. Shrapnel underlined the importance of trusting your director.

> Andrew has a priest-like calm, he knows his stuff, and he knew *King Lear* inside out. If he has a strong instinct about a particular aspect or scene, he's not going to impose that on you, but let you find it yourself, which is very gratifying. There were a number of things on which we didn't agree wholeheartedly, but mostly we saw the character in the same way. There was only one moment where there was a tussle, where somebody had to give way. I did, and in retrospect I think he was right.

He remembers a particularly challenging section being from the moment Lear finds Kent in the stocks to his 'O, reason not the need!' speech.

You've been speaking non-stop for perhaps twenty minutes, and you then have to fire yourself off into the storm. It's a question of control, to be able to move intellectually through it and also have enough breath. It took me a long time to find out how to do it, and I couldn't replicate it each time: I would get too excited early on, or not have enough energy, or be slightly distracted. It's a beautiful piece of writing, but extremely difficult to do.

Like most actors, he found the later scenes less problematic. He remembers the reconciliation with Cordelia being 'an utter joy to play, one of the most moving an actor can ever take part in'. For the final scene, he and Hilton discussed how to convey Lear's anguish as he enters carrying his daughter's body.

It's got to be some big, muscular expression; you want to make it important for the audience. We decided I should play it so that Lear was effectively saying, 'All I expect from you who are witnessing this sight is that you should howl, and the fact that you don't makes you men of stones.' If the play has gone along on the right tracks, then whatever you do will work, but I found it strangely satisfying to do it in that way.

Among the critics, Michael Billington complained about the lack of a concept, but most of them applauded Hilton's staging. 'The production is more radical in its apparent conventionality than many a highly conceptual re-working,' Tom Phillips suggested. Jane Edwardes concurred: 'There are no gimmicks here; instead, all that counts is the actors and their words. Every word sounds as if it had been written yesterday.' Shrapnel's performance was also acclaimed: 'This is the most moving Lear I have seen since Richard Eyre's National Theatre production with Ian Holm,' John Campbell wrote. 'When Shrapnel's gorgeous voice bids us "Howl, howl, howl!" I felt like obeying him, and my tears started then.' Mark Kidel judged that: 'He plays the twists and turns of an ego's voyage into annihilation with sensitivity and a nuanced expressive range that makes the man's descent into hell totally believable.'

Hilton was fully satisfied with Shrapnel's work. 'I thought John's perfor-mance was terrific. He had a great ferocity, but I felt he covered the whole ground of Lear's character, from the terrifying beginning to the sweetness and tenderness at the end.' Shrapnel himself reflects warmly on the experience:

It's a huge journey to make, and a big mountain to climb. But it's extraordinarily rewarding to be there, let alone feel you've made some little dent in it. It came a bit close on the heels of playing Gloucester alongside Pete Postlethwaite's Lear. But actually I didn't think of him at all while I was playing the part. I was quite proud of my performance, but the satisfaction and pride was tempered by the knowledge that there were some scenes I couldn't touch, that there was still so far to go.

# 9

# For the Royal Shakespeare Company 2

## John Wood
### *Nicholas Hytner*

*In 1990 John Wood played Lear at Stratford, with Nicholas Hytner directing.*

King Lear is a role that invariably takes its toll on an actor vocally and physically. In John Wood's case it seems to have been particularly disturbing psychologically. During the previews at Stratford he confessed to the journalist Michael Owen: 'The play has such an effect I find I have nightmares, and I wake up crying. It puts you on wild swings that go from euphoria to deep, deep melancholy.'

He also found playing Lear physically shattering, but decided to see this in a positive light while he was performing.

> Now we are playing it I wake feeling about eighty the next morning. I do get seriously tired, but in a way I don't mind. I like to arrive at the theatre feeling tired with a tired voice. You go on stage fighting your own body as well as Lear's enemies. It suits me better than turning up showered, shaved and in full voice.

Age sixty, lean and long-limbed, a ferociously intelligent actor with a dark, bass voice, Wood was then at his zenith as an interpreter of Shakespeare. Having directed and starred in a student production of *Richard III*, he later repeated the role for the RSC. He had been a fine Brutus in *Julius Caesar*, and two years before taking on Lear had been acclaimed for his Prospero in Nicholas Hytner's production of *The Tempest*; Irving Wardle wrote that he 'lit up the text like an electric storm', while Michael Billington called his Prospero 'the best I had ever seen'.

Looking back twenty-five years, Hytner saw Lear as the inevitable next step for Wood:

There was a wildness and originality to John's imagination; an innate power in his presence; an unparalleled intellect; and a ruthless lack of sentimentality. He seemed unlikely to deliver a predictable Lear, or a magnificent ruin. He was too alive, furiously unpredictable, his intelligence too palpable to embrace easy pathos. He also had a voice that had more registers to it, that was more effortlessly expressive, than that of most other actors.

As a director he has become convinced of what he sees as two irreconcilable truths:

> The great tragedies have been warped by a now ancient romantic critical tradition, still lurking to pounce in English-speaking rehearsal rooms, though less so in the rest of Europe. I don't see what Lear achieves through suffering, or what he learns. He is as possessive of Cordelia at the end as he was at the beginning. The cage in which he wants to sing with her is an image of hell. His destructiveness and self-destructiveness feel to me like a bleak but universal perception of the potential disaster that is the curse of every parent/child bond, as the potential of the opposite is its blessing. Lear's exceptional vanity and emotional illiteracy unleash a catastrophe that has no redeeming feature. It's a brutal play which offers no consolation.
>
> On the other hand audiences still crave consolation. If you don't give it to them, you are in some way cheating them of something that may be less to do with the plays and the world they come from than with their performance history, and a lazy reluctance to detach them from their history, or at least to challenge it. But you are nevertheless denying something that is an ineradicable part of them. I didn't solve this conundrum in 1990: my production was abstract to a fault, and not concrete enough. It failed to provide a coherent world. I would want to know who the poor naked wretches are, where they come from, why they are there. I'd want to know what world it is that gets turned upside down by a civil war, what world it is where Oswald rises to the top and Kent gets put in the stocks.

Well-known for his fresh interpretations of Shakespeare, Hytner chose, unfashionably, to use the Folio text, though he retained the mock-trial scene that is excluded from it. At the time he explained his preference for a partially modern-dress production: 'We didn't want it to be in a world rooted in history. *King Lear* has to do with a real father, a real family and real households. You establish those and expand from there. It starts with a father who screws up his daughters. If after that you get a sniff of cosmic disorder, then that's okay.'

Wood described his approach to creating Lear: 'I can't prepare too much in advance. I have to work on my feet. The imagination works a lot slower in the bath than it does in the rehearsal room, when you can get the odd flash of lightning.' Hytner recalls their good relationship in rehearsal:

> I loved his fierce intelligence as we explored the play. He challenged every preconception. There was nobody like him for knowing what possibilities the text offered; he had a way of coming at a line sideways, finding a completely plausible but new reading. We were basically at one about the play and how we wanted to approach it. John was not a sentimental actor, and we both felt dubious about the idea of the tragic hero ennobled and achieving wisdom through suffering. Hamlet by the end has achieved something, whereas I don't think Lear has.

One striking feature of the production was designer David Fielding's clinical set. This consisted of a revolving, open-ended cube, a box-like cell placed upstage which presented a succession of interiors and exteriors: the palace, the heath, the hovel. It suggested a cold, clinical place in which the conflicts of two dysfunctional families were played out. In the storm scene the box swivelled to show Lear and the Fool staggering through a bright, antiseptic hell, reflecting metaphorically the idea that both the world of the play and Lear's state of mind were spinning out of control.

Wood was an intense, neurotic and unstable Lear from the start, delighting in the opening scene in manipulating those dependent upon him. Already tottery and forgetful, he came across as a senile old bully prone to abrupt mood swings between anger and geniality, of the kind that is often a characteristic of old people. Nowhere was this more vividly demonstrated than in his curse on Goneril, as Hytner remembers: 'It was indistinguishable from love. He made a false exit and then came thundering back, and as he cursed her he took her in his arms, and embraced her with real paternal passion. The curse and the desire to embrace her were one and the same thing. That was what was terrifying about his performance.'

There were many other original touches. On being commanded to speak by Lear, an overtly rebellious Cordelia headed for the door, then stopped and faced him, steeling herself before articulating the fatal words, 'Nothing, my lord'. In banishing Kent, Lear hurled him to the floor, but then, apparently shocked at his own violence, allotted him five days' respite, and stroked his head in doing so. Immediately after the blinding of Gloucester, from which the servants turned away in horror, Regan delivered her line 'How dost my lord?' to Gloucester rather than to her wounded husband, suggesting a momentary flash of guilt. And in the final scene Lear's howls were heard offstage before he brought in his daughter's body.

Rather than present Goneril and Regan as embodiments of evil from the beginning, Hytner's reading followed Peter Brook in suggesting more justification than usual to their point of view. It suggested that both of them needed their father's love, that their speeches in the opening scene were not seen as insincere by Lear, who chuckled with delight at them. But

Lear's towering rage, together with certain hints of incestuous desire in the way he kissed all three, served to burst open their repressed frustration, and compel them to oppose him. In one chilling moment Goneril arrived at Regan's house with a wheelchair and two attendant nurses, as if to have him certified as mad.

By a curious coincidence both Hytner and Kenneth Branagh, whose touring production with Richard Briers as Lear opened in the same year, had cast actresses as the Fool, Emma Thompson for the tour, Linda Kerr Scott at Stratford. Small and stick-thin, with a knock-kneed walk and a Glasgow accent, half-pixie and half ventriloquist's doll, Kerr Scott was an acrobatic, ageless and androgynous Fool. Hytner recalls their relationship:

> Linda had a real gift for embodying one of those scraps of humanity that became professional fools. She adored Lear, as a dog adores his owner. But the adoration was not returned; Lear was too vain and self-convinced. At one point he picked her up and hung her by her coat on the back of a door, because he wanted her to shut up. She looked as if she was used to it, and cowered as a dog would cower.

Wood's original performance attracted a mixed response from the critics. Michael Billington wrote of 'an immensely intelligent production with a brilliantly idiosyncratic performance from Mr Wood', suggesting that 'no actor has ever brought out better King Lear's emotional anarchy' and that he 'has the uncensored capacity of the very old to switch in a second from intemperate rage to sweet tenderness'. Hailing him as the best since Scofield, he noted that 'Wood's Lear exists in a permanent state of schizophrenia … It is a performance that destroys the barrier between madness and sanity: this Lear occupies both territories at once.' Michael Coveney thought the intensity of his descent into madness made him unforgettable. 'Most Lears explode with anger at the start then find a way of making the rest of the play work in a sort of temperamental unravelling – Wood used that first scene to unlock his passage to his natural habitat of insanity.'

For director Michael Grandage:

> It was the first time I'd ever seen an actor being utterly unsentimental in the part – not just in the emotional trajectory, but in the musicality of the journey. He had great vocal prowess, but he never milked an audience with his voice, it was never anything that was about beauty, sentimentality. There was a hard edge to it, and as a result it was very moving.

Adrian Noble also praised his work: 'As an actor he was so passionate and intense, and very emotionally volatile, and he brought all that to his performance of Lear.'

While other critics admired his intelligence and authority, several thought his performance too technical and self-regarding, and so lacking in emotional depth. Charles Spencer observed: 'It's a technique that shows off the actor's virtuosity rather than illuminates the role.' Paul Taylor accused him of 'vocal narcissism', suggesting he offered 'a master-class in how to avoid sounding natural', and that he gave 'the impression of listening to himself'. John Gross had a different criticism, stating: 'There is little sense of hubris on the one hand, of concentrated evil on the other.' Jack Tinker wrote harshly that 'he knocked on the door of greatness, and was not admitted'. There were also concerns about Linda Kerr Scott's Fool, whose squeaky voice and monotonous Scots delivery sometimes made her indistinct, and whose comic capering prevented her having the kind of emotional relationship with Lear which emphasised her role as Lear's conscience.

Summing up in 1990 how he saw the challenge *King Lear* presented, Hytner said: 'There you are with a knapsack on your back, and 99.9 per cent of the play is towering above you. You realise you are just strolling in the foothills. Or you are peering nervously over the crater wall, watching the sulphur bubbling, and you can't get down there.' Today he makes it clear why he never wants to direct the play again. 'I don't find anyone in it invigorating, and I wouldn't know where to start. I don't even like seeing *King Lear*. Unfortunately my friends are now reaching the age when they want to play the part.'

*John Wood's performance gained him the Evening Standard Award for Best Actor.*

# Robert Stephens
## *Adrian Noble*

*In 1993 Adrian Noble directed his second production of* King Lear *at Stratford, this time starring Robert Stephens. The production subsequently moved to the Barbican in London.*

Adrian Noble had more than one reason for choosing Robert Stephens to play Lear in his second production of the play. 'I did it again because of Robert. I thought he was an amazing actor, a great, great actor, and after his triumph with Falstaff two years before I wanted to see what he would do with Lear. At sixty-two he was of course the right age, but I knew he didn't have long to live.'

The journey was to prove not just a challenge to Stephens' acting ability, but a severe test of his physical, mental and emotional stamina. Already beset by ill-health, with problems affecting his liver and kidneys, he developed a serious foot infection during rehearsals, which meant he could hardly walk. He was taken to hospital, the opening was postponed, and he missed several previews, his part being taken by his understudy Christopher

Robbie. During the London run he was ill again, and missed a further fifteen performances. 'On the right night he was unsurpassable, absolutely untouchable,' Noble says. 'But he couldn't manage that more than twice a week.' Simon Russell Beale, playing Edgar, recalled: 'When Robert was on form the second half was mesmerising. He was actually dying, and I think he knew whereof he spoke.'

Because of these various problems he had difficulty in rising, and had to use a chair to help himself up. On some nights his acting was wayward in the extreme: entire phrases were often inaudible, and he slurred or swallowed words. Many lines were fluffed or re-written, making them nonsensical, and sending the metre haywire. His courage in the face of his physical handicaps is remembered by David Calder, who played Kent:

> It was either genius or awful. When he could remember the lines he could be absolutely brilliant. At other times we were on the verge of taking the audience home to breakfast. Often he would ask me during the storm scene what he said next. But he was working under extreme pressure. He would go off to hospital now and then to have pints of liquid drained from his liver. When there was a quick change before the 'Birds i' the cage' scene with Cordelia, he'd have a fag or a can of Guinness in the wings. Once he was sick in a bucket, then went straight back on stage. He was an astounding trouper, and very courageous.

In contrast to most actors, and indeed to Noble's view of the part, Stephens was convinced that you could play King Lear more fully than you could Hamlet. 'There is so much about Hamlet, so many elements and contradictions, so many complexities, that he is unplayable. You can give an edited opinion of him, which is what the best actors do. King Lear goes on a clearly defined journey.' He liked to decide how to play a part before rehearsals started, and then persuade the director of the validity of his ideas. In discussing Lear in lengthy meetings with Noble, whom he described as 'an immensely patient and considerate director', he claimed that he compelled him to agree with his interpretation. Noble, however, disputes this somewhat one-sided notion: 'It didn't seem like that to me. We just got on with working in the normal way. In terms of the basic architecture of the play I trusted him and he trusted me. But then I don't micro-manage actors; I think that's rather impertinent.'

Stephens later outlined his approach to the problems the play throws up.

> I try to play Lear in broad strokes and I discover new things about the part every time I act it. You see different colours and elements – it's like an enormous kaleidoscope. If you pace it carefully you can score it better. Within two minutes of appearing on stage, Lear flies into one of his fearful rages, and then you have to find the vocal power to roar against the storm. There's always a danger of hitting it too high, too soon, and

then you run out of gas. But if you can orchestrate it properly, you don't have to thunder all of it.

In rehearsals Noble concentrated on the domestic element. He thought the story of the three sisters a brilliantly drawn portrait:

> Goneril has to fight all the way to get anything, as the older sibling always does. Regan gets the bike three years earlier than Goneril. And we learn a lot about them through the men they marry. I think Goneril got out fast and married a very respectable senior aristocrat. Regan was always the crazy one, and married the crazy boy with the Harley-Davidson, who was sniffing coke and taking drugs. Then Cordelia comes along and is doted upon. It's a difficult part, because she is virtuous, which is not very highly rated as a quality. But she behaves exactly according to character. When she says 'Nothing', she thinks she's got it absolutely right, and Dad will understand. But she misjudges him, just as he misjudges her. It's a perfectly observed family. If you just follow that, everything works.

Avoiding a totally modern setting as well as a Stonehenge one, he set the play in a timeless world, with an abstract backdrop marked by changing colours and images. 'It was a world that probably related to Europe some 150 years earlier, with people wearing greatcoats, where people still hunted, where the motor vehicle hadn't taken over the world. But neither the designer Anthony Ward nor I would be able to place it within fifty years of a particular date.' The map of the kingdom papered the stage floor, on which the white-faced Fool – elegantly dressed in a waistcoat and buckled shoes – painted the red lines to mark the division of the kingdom.

While concentrating on the family aspects, Noble also emphasised the cosmic by having a huge moon suspended over the stage. After the blinding of Gloucester it cracked open, pouring forth sand and creating a harsh Beckettian landscape, with Gloucester staring sightlessly at it. 'It seemed to me an exquisitely painful image, with the moon's very strong connection with the eye, suggesting the milk of human kindness had vanished.'

From his earlier production with Gambon and Sher he retained the controversial accidental killing of the Fool by Lear. 'But we didn't create the same intensity of relationship as we did with Michael and Tony: there was a big age-gap between Robert and Ian Hughes, so it was hard to get the same kind of intimacy. He was still a professional comic, but not in the same kind of patter, double-act way.' Noble also repeated Edgar's dramatic re-entry into the play, when as Poor Tom he bursts out from below and wrecks the stage, which then becomes the basis of the hovel.

Simon Russell Beale's Edgar started as a bookish, bespectacled, frightened scholar, but became an unusually violent and possessed Poor Tom. Traumatised by the blinding of his father, in revenge he smashed Oswald's eyes while killing him with a pikestaff, and tried to gouge out

Edmund's eyes and strangle him after their duel. 'I started off as a swot, as someone who wouldn't hurt a fly,' Russell Beale recalls.

> I thought he had been brutalised by his experience, as well as having learned something from it. But it's still a puzzle to me why he doesn't say, 'Dad, it's me,' before the end of the play. I constructed reasons for that, to do with him allowing Gloucester to learn from his experience. Someone suggested that Edgar might hate his father, with very good reason. That had never occurred to me. I needed more of those lateral thoughts, because I don't think I really cracked Edgar.

Stephens later explained: 'I never milked Lear for sympathy, nor suggested that he was anything much more than a fond and foolish old man.' He was, he stated, 'less interested in the tyranny and rage of the man than in his comic potential and his spiritual journey after the storm'. In fact his Lear was a powerful, majestic king, capable of terrifying violence, as when he threatened Goneril with his riding-whip, and delivered the curse on her. Noble recalled: 'He did do all those opening scenes without any problem. He had this extraordinary facility with language, and the rage, the extravagance of language, just flowed out of him like a volcano. He could do the whole part, fulfil all the aspects of Lear's character.'

Irving Wardle concluded: 'No production since Peter Brook's thirty years ago revealed the play's dimensions so fully.' However, other critics were concerned about the opening scene, in which Stephens behaved in a jovial manner, beaming at everyone, treating the love test as a game, and hugging Goneril and Regan. There was, they felt, too much geniality, with the court laughing politely, and even applauding Cordelia's 'Nothing'. Charles Spencer noted: 'In banishing Cordelia he is a jovial old buffer with a quick temper, not a monster of blind, authoritarian self-will.' John Peter similarly wrote: 'He plays Lear as an amiable old codger at the start, which makes Goneril and Regan's treatment of him harsh.'

But his final scenes were much admired for their simplicity, and reduced some in the audience to tears. The academic Peter Holland observed: 'One would have had to be men of stone not to be wrenchingly moved by Stephens' Lear. If this Lear did not make one weep, no performance ever would.' However, Stephens was not strong enough to carry the dead Cordelia on in his arms, so she was brought in by three soldiers. In Lear's final moments he pulled her corpse along as he crawled across the stage, focusing on an empty space on the line 'Look there, look there', in a way that for Spencer made it 'almost unbearable to watch'.

Reflecting on its continuing appeal, Noble suggests:

> The play has the attraction of a fairy story that's both profound and simple. An old man who was the king had no sons and divided his kingdom in three, they all started quarrelling, and he went mad. I think

those fairy stories echo quite deep within our civilisation; they won't go away. Also the subject matter of family, of familiar relationships, is very attractive to audiences, because they deal in an extreme way with the fissures that happen in many families.

This notion was confirmed by Stephens' own experience of the play's impact on theatre-goers. 'People seem to find their own family situation reflected in the play. They come to the stage door after the performance and tell me how much Lear reminds them of their dead father, and how much more tolerant they feel they ought to have been towards them.' Another audience member who linked the story to his own situation was the RSC's president, Prince Charles. After seeing the production he remarked: 'There is one thing I've learned from this play: don't abdicate!'

Immediately after the end of the London run Stephens went into hospital for a liver transplant. Within a year he was dead.

# Nigel Hawthorne
## *Yukio Ninagawa*

*The RSC* King Lear *in 1999, a co-production with the Saitama Arts Foundation in Japan directed by Yukio Ninagawa, had Nigel Hawthorne in the title-role. The production ran for ten weeks in Tokyo, played in London at the Barbican for four weeks, and ended up in Stratford in 2000.*

There on the stage was one of the most chilling sights I've ever seen in my fifty years as an actor. At that moment I felt real terror.

When Nigel Hawthorne first saw the theatre at the Saitama Arts Centre he was horrified. Rehearsals there had not yet begun, but to him and the company it seemed as if the Japanese creative team were already well into the technical rehearsal.

The scenery was up, and ready for the first night; it was lit; the huge stage crew was standing by, all dressed in black; the music had been composed and recorded; the sound effects were ready. It was as though Ninagawa was saying: 'All right. You've come over here to do *King Lear*. We're all ready for you. Get up there and do it!' I would have been very surprised if not every single member of the company felt as I did.

This theatrical clash of two very different cultures was to have a profound effect on what turned out to be Hawthorne's farewell to the stage. The problems were many and considerable, the seeds being sown from the moment the ambitious project was launched.

As an experienced stage and screen actor, Hawthorne had been asked
to take on the part once before, shortly after he had finished playing the
title-role in Alan Bennett's *The Madness of George III* at the National
Theatre. The play had distinct echoes of *King Lear*, and included a funny
but poignant scene in which the recovering George is found reading the
text. He then compels his doctor and two politicians to play the reconciliation scene with him, casting himself as Lear. At the end he mimics a
Wolfit-style curtain call, declaring: 'Pray you now forget and forgive; I am
old and foolish.'

Not surprisingly, Hawthorne felt 'it might not be wise to attempt in
quick succession two kings who went potty'. But he declined the offer for
other reasons as well. He felt there were too many inconsistencies in *King
Lear*, too many problems, and that the exertion of playing such a massive
role for a long period was too daunting. However, by 1998, when the RSC
offered him the part, he felt the moment was right, that he should grasp
the opportunity before it was too late. Now approaching seventy, he would
have a whole year to prepare before rehearsals started. But even then he had
anxieties, wondering if he could cope with the stress involved, and fearing
he would be compared to all those actors from Donald Wolfit to Ian Holm
who had succeeded in the part before him.

He and Ninagawa met in London to discuss ideas about the production.
The director had come to England to stage a production of *Hamlet* in
Japanese. He had previously directed Japanese versions of *Macbeth* and
*The Tempest* in the UK, and had committed himself to stage the entire
Shakespeare canon in Tokyo. The first three productions in this ambitious
project – *Romeo and Juliet*, *Twelfth Night* and *Richard III* – had been
played in Japanese; *King Lear* was to be the first to be performed in English.

Hawthorne was impressed with his *Hamlet*, with Ninagawa's striking
visual imagination, and his ability to keep the narrative clear and unclut-
tered. Hamlet was being played by Hiroyuki Sanada, a martial-arts expert.
Struck by his vulnerability, Hawthorne suggested Sanada might make a
suitable Fool, seeing him as 'the perfect bridge between East and West'.
Ninagawa promised to consider the idea, which Hawthorne found encouraging. 'He seemed open to ideas, and extremely likeable. I had a feeling we
would get on well together.'

However, problems soon arose. A fundamental one was that Ninagawa
spoke little English and Hawthorne even less Japanese, so their conversation had to be conducted through an interpreter. Subsequently pages
of suggestions and ideas spelt out in the simplest possible terms were
exchanged between them by letter or fax. Hawthorne was understandably
nervous about this method of communication.

In preparing his interpretation of the role he wanted to avoid playing
Lear as a despised tyrant. He saw no evidence in the text for such a notion,
preferring the idea that the king was a respected but volatile old man
suffering from a form of senile dementia. Since several of his friends had

Alzheimer's disease, he was familiar with the symptoms: 'I know how the moods and sufferings of this distressing complaint fluctuate: bewilderment changes in a flash to anger, to self-pity, to forgetfulness and repetition. Lucidity comes and goes. I began to find places where I could work these into my performance.'

He was also clear about the style of his performance.

> I wasn't going to boom. I'm not a 'boomy' sort of actor anyway. I've sat through an awful lot of boomers, when I've prayed for Gloucester to come on again because I've been so bored by the Lear. All that ranting and raving may show you that the actor is very good at holding the stage, but you find out very little about the man he's supposed to be playing.

After reading the play at the Barbican, the company flew to Japan and, after the initial shock of their introduction to the theatre, set about rehearsals. Here the inherent defects in the set-up came to the fore. Throughout this time Hawthorne had not a single note from Ninagawa, nor any discussion with him about Lear's character.

> Having trained as an artist, Ninagawa enjoyed tinkering with the set, the props and the lights. He was like an opera director: he expected you to know the arias. My finished performance as the king was supposed to have travelled with me from London in my luggage. His job was to create the right mood, shunt you around, and make you look good.

A further problem was that David Hunt, the RSC's associate director also involved with rehearsals, was of limited help. 'He had a good mind and was well informed over textual matters, yet he was less clued up when it came to interpretation. Every time I went to him with a problem about the king's emotional state he couldn't enlighten me; all he could do was explain the meaning of the text.' Hunt in his turn felt that Ninagawa was excluding him, and that the creative team were making decisions among themselves in their own language. The working script had Japanese on one side and English on the other. Most of the time, while the actors were speaking their lines in English, Ninagawa was following them in Japanese. Communication was additionally hampered by the fact that discussions about staging, and his instructions on movement, posture and vocal pitch, had to be conducted via the interpreter.

Hawthorne claimed that when he made suggestions, for the first few days he met resistance and even hostility from his fellow-actors, who felt the ideas should come from the director. It was clear to him that Sanada, who had had to learn English from scratch, was struggling with the Fool, which he was playing as a capering kabuki entertainer. 'He was quite the nicest, most generous actor I've ever worked with, he was doing sterling work, and his whole attitude was inspiring. But his English was poor, and sometimes it was difficult to follow what he was saying.'

The set, inspired by the classical Japanese form of *noh* theatre, was a virtually empty space. However, a problem soon arose over Ninagawa's idea for the storm scene. He had decided that in addition to the wind, rain, lightning, thunder effects and music, a number of 'rocks' should be dropped from the flies, reflecting the line 'Crack Nature's moulds, all germens spill at once'. These were huge lumps of wood covered in lead foil, which crashed on to the stage. Hawthorne was understandably concerned: 'Sanada, Christopher Benjamin as Kent and I approached the scene with more than the usual trepidation. I knew that if one of the stage hands was incorrectly cued, or wasn't paying attention, just one of those rocks was heavy enough to crush the living daylights out of me.' When the actors complained to Ninagawa that the rocks were dangerous, his only concession was to reduce their number.

Hawthorne's surviving script is covered with detailed annotations of the text, reflecting his ideas about Lear's moods and intentions. Some of his notes to himself have also survived, reflecting the care he took with his performance. These three examples are characteristic:

> *Act 1, Scene 4* Delight at seeing the Fool. When he gets abusive, be hurt rather than angry – like a spurned lover. Then forgive him, and hug him. It's a very tactile relationship. Watch him for guidance. A pupil with his teacher – Lear the pupil.
>
> *Act 4, Scene 6* Dover. Think Beckett. Find the silences. Just sit, watch and listen. When Gloucester has difficulty pulling off Lear's boots, laugh with him: two old men united on the pebbled beach. Embrace him suddenly and unexpectedly. Comfort him like an older brother. Cry with him about what life has done to them both.
>
> *Act 5, Scene 3* Carry Cordelia on to display her to the assembled crowd. The absurdity of asking a group of soldiers for a looking glass. Then see the feather on the ground. Time stands still as Lear holds it beneath her nostrils, knowing as we all know that there's no point. When Albany says of Lear 'He knows not what he says,' Albany is wrong. Lear knows exactly what he's saying. He knows his sanity comes and goes. He knows that Cordelia is dead.

Although the play was received ecstatically on the first night, Hawthorne knew it would be different in London. 'We were floundering about rather like a ship without a rudder, and there was still a great deal of work to be done.' He was heartened when, during a brief visit to Japan, the RSC's artistic director Adrian Noble offered him a couple of simple but helpful notes. 'In the first scene don't move around. Show your authority. Make them do what you want them to do.' For the scene on Dover cliff he suggested: 'Don't stand over Gloucester, go and sit next to him. Don't be afraid to put your arm round him.'

Noble later pinpointed the problem:

Nigel never really found the shape of the role, the journey that each interpreter needs must make. And Ninagawa just didn't know how to help him. Their approach to acting was fundamentally different. Consequently Nigel felt and looked overwhelmed by the role, like a man wearing clothes that were several sizes too big for him. He felt that Ninagawa was primarily interested in the visuals of the show, which were pretty remarkable but, arguably, rendered the language superfluous. Unsurprisingly, he became increasingly frustrated.

Hawthorne's partner Trevor Bentham provided him with a valuable critique: 'He felt I was straining and shouting, probably through insecurity, trying too hard, and had to establish myself as the leading man, not just a good company member. In other words, play the king.' He took this advice the very next night, setting himself more apart, and felt that it transformed the first scene. He discovered that this helped him with his concept of Alzheimer's. 'I found moments where I could legitimately pause, as though I had forgotten what I was about to say, hesitate over people's names, and have the sudden squally rages subside as quickly as they'd arrive.'

At the Barbican the critical response was overwhelmingly negative, with most reviewers believing he was too benign an actor to succeed in the role. Charles Spencer thought 'he seemed curiously detached from the proceedings, and of Lear's rage there is virtually no sign at all ... When he calls on the darkness and the devils he might just as well be ordering a nice cup of tea.' Michael Billington described him as 'a minimalist, not a megawatt actor' who 'lacks the necessary temperamental and vocal range'. Paul Taylor wrote: 'The touching aspects of the role he once again beautifully encompasses. It is the Titanic ego, caring passion and sense of Lear as a force of nature that is missing.' Benedict Nightingale decided: 'His rages are little more than piques ... We're left with a poignant, warm-hearted, occasionally even comical Lear, not a majestic savage burning on his invisible wheel of fire.'

The Sunday papers were generally kinder: John Gross described Hawthorne as 'a subtle and intelligent actor ... his reading of the part is moving and finely detailed ... I have seldom seen a Lear who makes you so aware of the frustrations of old age.' John Peter praised 'a hauntingly but savagely beautiful production' which reinforced 'the uncomfortable Shakespearean vision of a world where you are left without the consolation or guidance of a moral order ... The great achievement of director and designer is to have created a world that is both fifteenth-century Japanese and pre-Christian English.'

The audience reaction was in complete contrast to that of the daily critics. The run was booked out, the company received sustained cheers at their curtain calls, while Hawthorne himself received scores of supportive letters. Many said it was the first time they had understood the play or been moved by it; others said the press had got it wrong. The same thing happened in Stratford, with the theatre sold out for every performance, and more letters of support pouring in. But for Hawthorne the critics' reaction 'hurt like a deep knife wound, and I shall never be able to erase it from my mind'.

While recognising that it was part of an actor's job to take criticism, on the occasion of the final performance he felt sad that 'after fifty years as an actor, what should have been something special had been sullied'. In defence of his performance he concluded: 'I can only say that it was carefully considered, and I believed that even if the way I had chosen to see this old man may perhaps have been different to the norm, it was consistent and truthful, and I knew what I was doing.'

The much-loved actor died the following year.

# 10

## At the Globe

### Julian Glover
#### *Barry Kyle*

*In 2001* King Lear *was staged at Shakespeare's Globe on London's Bankside, with Julian Glover playing the king, and Barry Kyle directing.*

Looking back on his performance, Julian Glover recalls the difficulties facing an actor playing in a theatre where spectators were encouraged to become 'spectactors'.

'It was the early days of the Globe, and the audience was still into the idea of chucking things at the actors, and saying "Ho, ho, ho" and such like, and laughing at silly things and shouting back.' During the matinees the noise could be excessive.

> Vocally one had to be more alive then, as you could see the audience – and also hear the babies crying! One afternoon all the riverboats went down to the mouth of the Thames tooting their horns, and two hours later they came back. Helicopters would sometimes hover, which was very frustrating: the Globe is very good acoustically because of all that wood, but at those moments you couldn't bring your voice down as you normally could.

For director Barry Kyle the problems were of a different order.

> It's a difficult place for a director to work in, and a lot of them don't want to work there. I was very aware of its many limitations. You have both your arms chopped off and then somebody says, 'Now direct.' You can't change the stage, there's no scenic evolution, you can't light anything, you can't alter the dynamic. It's fundamentally about the relationship between the actor and the audience.

Then there was the theatre's policy of original practice, whereby all aspects of the production were supposed to be done exactly as they were in Shakespeare's time.

> It would be a bit unfair to compare it with militant Islam in the current political climate, but it's a bit like the Sunni wars with the Shias, whereby the original practice is the only way to go. It was particularly those people involved with the massive empires of the costumes and the music, who were very outspoken in defence of their areas. So for example a costume couldn't be in blue because they didn't have much blue dye in London at that time, it was such a rarity.

In fact the actor Mark Rylance, the theatre's artistic director, had suggested directors need no longer be constrained by original Shakespearean practices in new productions. So Kyle and his designer Hayden Griffin were able to change the permanent stage for the first time, covering it with a temporary set of bare wooden planks, which concealed the fake marbling and the *trompe-l'oeil* effects, creating a more intimate, less courtly atmosphere. They also introduced another innovation, putting a post up in the yard in the middle of the standing audience. Several significant passages were spoken by actors who climbed on to it, as Edmund did for his bastardy speech. 'My thought was that Edmund was one of the groundlings, in among that audience with ordinary people,' Kyle explained.

Having co-directed Donald Sinden's 1976 Lear in conjunction with Trevor Nunn and John Barton, and also staged a production in Czech in Prague in 1991–2, Kyle had considerable experience of working on the play. 'I feel it's the most Chekhovian of Shakespeare's texts, in that it's dependent on the full spectrum of characters. *Macbeth* doesn't succeed or fail on the quality of Ross and Macduff, whereas in *Lear* all the characters completely matter.'

He was especially keen to explore the question of the missing mothers.

> It's a theme that fascinates me all through Shakespeare. It's partly caused by the difficulty of the boy actors being asked to play mature women, but turned, as ever by Shakespeare's genius, from a practical obstacle into an artistic possibility. He creates this question, Where's the mother? The daughters never talk about theirs. In a play about bastardy it's not apparent they were all from the same mother. So I cast three women who could not possibly have had the same mother. Patricia Kerrigan, as Goneril, was a redhead who I based on Queen Elizabeth; I think Shakespeare was re-cycling something about a powerful woman. Felicity Dean was a blonde Regan, while Tonia Chauvet as Cordelia was a mixture of French and Irish, and clearly a very different ethnicity from the others. We also don't know anything about Edgar's mother, while we hear all too much about Edmund's mother, by which Gloucester reveals his own folly.

In preparing to play the king Glover, then aged 66, deliberately limited his research.

> Like most actors, I read about other Lears. But I'm not a great researcher. I think you can be slightly put off course by knowing too much about what other people have done. You want to know how their performances went down, and their general approaches, but not too much detail. I didn't read the original story, or the Nahum Tate version. I just sank into a miasma of Lear without being academic about it.

In rehearsal the cast went through a series of exercises, including working on other texts from Shakespeare, and speaking the sonnets. 'These exercises were very helpful in getting everyone used to the language, and learning to observe the rhythm of the verse, which is so important. But I saw no need to go into the back story, into questions such as why Lear has such young daughters. I don't think these matters affect what he is.'

He felt Kyle's staging of the storm scene worked well, with he and John McEnery's Fool struggling across the stage yoked together by a rope: 'The effects were wonderfully organised by Barry. It was done with drums and human voices: the whole of the cast went up to the top of the theatre and became winds.' He also appreciated the novel idea of carrying in the dead Cordelia on his back. 'I thought it would be very bad for my voice, but it was the reverse, it absolutely opened up all the chambers, and I got a fantastic foghorn voice out of it. At the end she was taken off me. That completely solved the problem.'

Directors have come up with many different ideas of how to handle the Fool's disappearance from the action, or suggest his subsequent fate. Kyle's decision provided a startling theatrical image immediately before the interval. As Poor Tom exited through the main doors upstage, the audience saw John McEnery's corpse hanging in the doorway; he has committed suicide because he can no longer bear Lear's suffering.

Kyle was clear about the nature of Edgar's absorption in his feigned role.

> Whenever Poor Tom began to talk about who he was seeing, there was never any doubt that he was having genuine visions of a schizophrenic nature, and that some of these were to do with the devil, and were to be completely feared. It clearly goes beyond being a disguise. This is not Rosalind dressing up in trousers in the Forest of Arden, it is somebody who like Hamlet enters into a disguise, and the disguise becomes a pathway to psychosis. He puts on the antic disposition, and then can't get it off, which is what happens to Edgar. They both assume they will be able to drop in and out of it, but discover they can't.

He was very pleased with Glover's performance. 'Julian brought this straight-backed, power-house quality to the role. He had a fantastic command, and he allowed himself to go through areas of experience that are shattering. Every inch a king is what I would say about his Lear.' However, Glover himself saw both positives and negatives in his playing.

> I think I generally succeeded in presenting a man with a once-strong mind who is very old, finding at the very last his centre as a human being. All his life he has been distracted by all those things he has had to do, sending people to prison, fighting battles, all those kind of things. When he gets rid of all that, he finds a wonderful empathy, not just for other people, but for himself. I don't think he ever liked himself very much, but I think at the end he thinks he's all right, and he's learned the power of forgiveness.

Yet he also had considerable criticisms of his performance.

> Afterwards there was always 'Oh I messed that bit up!' You know inside when you've done that, even if it's not obvious to anyone else. I suppose most people playing the great parts like Lear feel these reservations. It was a good, interesting piece of hard work, but I thought quite a bit of what I did was rather superficial, though I tried not to make it so. Some of it was a bit generalised.

The critics' reviews were equally mixed. Charles Spencer decided that 'Julian Glover is not the loudest, the maddest or the most terrifying Lear I have ever seen, but his performance cannot be faulted for its sheer, unshowy humanity'; Maddy Costa felt that 'his humdrum Lear isn't an authoritative king nor a particularly piteous fool'. In Heather Neill's view: 'His performance is well crafted rather than moving. His clear verse-speaking serves the production well, clarity being its virtue.' According to Susannah Clapp, 'Julian Glover's Lear is capable and forceful, but the journey he travels – from bluff and confident captain of the ship to being dishevelled in a nightie – is not seriously disturbing.'

The production was variously praised for its rigour, clarity and intelligence, but criticised for being undistinguished, unsophisticated and lightweight. Benedict Nightingale wrote: 'There's plenty of justifiable laughter in Barry Kyle's revival, but also a troubling lack of intensity ... Maybe such informal contact between actor and audience is less friendly to tragedy than comedy.' Other critics tended to agree. Costa observed: 'Many of Shakespeare's plays can withstand the Globe's pantomime atmosphere, but *King Lear* isn't one of them. There's something distinctly unpleasant about spotting two tipsy people flirting across the aisle while Gloucester stumbles about with his eyes gouged out.' Spencer wrote: 'The fidgety, beer-swilling teenagers in the yard were a distraction, but even worse was the American lady who commented loudly on the action as if watching a baseball game. "Take 'em both!" she screamed, when Edmund pondered the merits of his two mistresses.'

For Kyle there were magic moments during the run.

The nature/art balance which is fundamental to the plays of Shakespeare is reconfigured at the Globe. Every moment the wind is moving, the light is changing, you hear people, you smell the river, and you hear the world of London. Sometimes I got an uncanny sense, just for five seconds, of being transported: it's 1606, you're there now, the river's over there, the sky's up there, those words are being said, that's Lear, that's the Fool. It was a pretty extraordinary experience.

# David Calder
## *Dominic Dromgoole*

*In 2008 King Lear was played at the Globe by David Calder, in a production directed by the Globe's artistic director Dominic Dromgoole.*

In preparing to stage his production, Dominic Dromgoole laid out his stall.

I've always wanted to do *King Lear*, I've always been passionate about it, always drawn more wisdom and insight and understanding from the world of that play than I have from any other. There has been a lot of over-gilt and over-decorated energy in the last few productions. So it will be wonderful to present it as simply and as cleanly and plainly as possible, to make it about the human beings and the human voices and the human mind.

Six years on he emphasises the essential qualities to be expected in any production at Shakespeare's Globe. 'Our theatrical language is no set, no lighting, no sound, deeply human, a sense of humour, a love of language, an electric speed of understanding language, a deep desire for storytelling rather than ideas, and a mad hunger for flesh and word rather than for idea and concept.'
He likes to emphasise the Globe stage's flexibility.

We always put part of the set into the audience in some way. Partly it's because when they built the stage they put the pillars in the wrong place, so you don't have a point of command where you can be still and talk to the whole audience. Extending it out into the courtyard increases the dynamic, when in one instant you have an intense close-up with an individual who's only inches away from you, and in the next you can be quite epic against a big backdrop telling a larger historical story. That movement between the intimate and the epic is at the heart of a lot of Shakespeare's plays, and it's at the heart of the Globe.

His chosen Lear was David Calder, an experienced Shakespearean actor
who had played Kent in support of Robert Stephens' Lear. 'David has
got Shakespeare chops, which not many people have. He's got them in
spades. He has a strange, extra level of intuition, the ability to hover and
listen to the language and find a very high, light, fine place. That's quite
rare.'
    Calder was uncertain whether the tragedy would work in this setting.

I'd always had the idea that the play was better suited to more of a
living-room space, like the Cottesloe or the Almeida. The Globe just
seemed a vast space which wouldn't help me. I thought it would all
be a bit 'togaish' in its costuming, and I was fearful of it just being
a tourist attraction. But it's a much-changed theatre now. There's a
problem with what's called the 'shelf', with that great canopy, and
those dead spots. But I came to realise it was a remarkably good place
to do *King Lear*. Everything that I thought was going to be negative
had its own strange magic, of concentration and listening. There was
nowhere to hide.

He decided to learn his part before rehearsals began. 'It's not something
I usually do, but there were so many things I wanted to think about in
playing it, I couldn't do it if I hadn't learned its music beforehand. And I
know the curse of spending your time in rehearsal in a memory game, as
opposed to playing the part. I'd seen this with other actors, so I acquired a
lot of the performance before the rehearsals.'
    Testing his ideas out with his director, he found they were broadly in
accord. Dromgoole was keen to approach the play with an open mind.

I try never to come to any play thinking, This is what the play is, and this
is why it matters. You read and read and read, and you develop instincts
and a sense of rhythm. During rehearsals you try to bring some instincts
into the room, but not too many decisions about what the journey is.
Then you can observe it as you go along. David, like all great actors, left
more than enough from his initial work on Lear to react to the energy
the others brought to rehearsals.

He decided to use a conflation of the Quarto and the Folio editions, then
cut the resulting text back to about the same length as the Folio. Speed, he
felt, was of the essence, so he excised much of the early exposition, though
he only slightly trimmed Poor Tom's lines. 'You have to take it at a lick in
this theatre, because the audience are standing or sitting on uncomfortable
benches. You have to play it fast: there's no time or need for self-indulgence,
and one scene has to flow very easily into another. If you don't move very
quickly through the language, people get very frustrated.'
    Calder took this requirement on board.

'I have had no larger experience in the theatre.'

*1. Paul Scofield, with Alan Webb as Gloucester, Stratford, 1962*

'I'm at the age now to completely understand Lear's plight, and to empathise with it.'

2. *Frank Langella, Chicester Festival Theatre, 2013*

'The strain was destroying me, and I wondered how I was going to shake it off.'

*3. Brian Cox, National Theatre, 1990*

'My satisfaction and pride were tempered by the knowledge that there were some scenes I couldn't touch.'

4. *John Shrapnel, Tobacco Factory, 2012*

'There can't be a set of scenes anywhere in dramatic literature of such depth and wonder.'

*5. Tim Pigott-Smith, with Richard O'Callaghan as the Fool, West Yorkshire Playhouse, 2011*

'It's not the sort of role a non-white actor gets to play every day.'
6. *Joseph Marcell, Shakespeare's Globe, 2014*

'The Shakespearean rhythms have never meant much to me. I prefer my own rhythms.'

*7. Derek Jacobi, Donmar Warehouse, 2010*

'Lear is a fabulous role, encompassing everything from tragedy
to comedy.'

*8. Jonathan Pryce, with Phoebe Fox as Cordelia, Almeida, 2012*

One thing we all learned very quickly was to forget the pauses, and just open your mouth and get on with it, without rushing it. You have to do that: you're holding an audience in the open air, sometimes it's cold, sometimes it's raining, sometimes it's too hot, so you have to think how to hold their concentration. So as somebody exited, the next scene started. That really made it roll along, and we got it in under three hours.

His approach was not to probe too much into Lear's motivation.

I'd come to a point with Shakespeare where I felt there was too much of an attempt to try to make it all make sense. That's often not the way poetry and the mechanics of plays work. Sometimes you don't know what you're talking about with Shakespeare, you just say it. With *King Lear* you can really play that to your advantage. You do what it says in the text, without asking yourself, Why is he saying this, why is he sane there and mad there? I discovered that if you simply play it as it unfolds, the wildness and the craziness and the pain pour out.

He found little use for the many books and essays written about the play.

I know that Lear is a great play. I read academics who say this is the greatest play ever written, but I haven't the first idea what that means. Are they just saying this because they feel they should? What is extreme about it is that the redemption almost doesn't work. It goes right to the edge of total despair – there's no hope, and only just a glimmer of redemption at the end. The modernity of the play is staggering. That's what makes it a gigantic tragedy, seen through the journey of this unlikeable man, whom you begin to love because of his human frailty.

Dromgoole brought the actors closer to the audience by creating a bridge leading from the stage to an octagonal space in the middle of the courtyard, where some of the mad scenes could take place. 'It didn't feel like, Oh look at the people being a bit mad over there. It became a glorious act of sharing. It also provided thinking space, where Lear could invite the audience into his privacy. Because his private thoughts and his public persona are so distinct from each other and so far apart, it seemed good to accentuate that.'

For Calder this was a considerable asset.

It enabled me to have contact with individual members of the audience, to take them through Lear's journey, to refer to them and ask for their help. That came to fruition when I brought on the dead Cordelia. I made it a demand of the audience, to which they don't respond, so *they* are the men of stones. I've always found that line slightly melodramatic. I've always wondered, Who is he talking to? Why doesn't he just talk to the audience and make this demand of them? I did it very quietly, to enormous effect.

In his direction Dromgoole was at pains to draw out the humour in the tragedy.

> Shakespeare's plays are nothing if not fantastically humorous. He would be utterly horrified by the way we segregate his plays into rigid boxes of tragedy, comedy, history, Roman, whereas these elements can co-exist in the course of a single scene. With *Lear* a Jacobean audience would have found the set-up with the Fool, as well as a lot of the language, extraordinarily funny. It's that strain of English humour, in a *Waiting for Godot* sort of way, which is jagged non-sequiturs. You get it with Pinter and with Beckett; you could even call it Pythonesque. There's a beautiful absurdity about it. If there's no laughter, it's not the play.

In casting the Fool he avoided making him a contemporary of Lear, choosing an actor, Danny Lee Wynter, who was thirty-five years younger than Calder.

> Having the Fool as an old man is simply a directorial trick. It's become a commonplace over the last thirty years, but it's nonsense. He's called a boy throughout, so he's meant to be a young man. In Shakespeare's day he was played by the same actor who played Cordelia. When she goes off the Fool comes on, and when he goes off she comes on again. And their relationships with Lear are very similar. His stuff is full of sorrow, mixed with a desire to needle and aggravate Lear, and at the same time there is a huge tenderness for Lear, whom he reveres as a father.

Calder highlighted the need to get the nature of their relationship clear.

> I felt it was very important to show how much Lear is reliant on the Fool, who uses these joke tricks to get him to face up to things; but he's not listening properly, he's not hearing him. The Fool loves him so much he just wants to hit him over the head. It's possible for the actor playing the Fool to be so frustrated with Lear's blindness about the consequence of his decisions and actions that he can end up appearing to hate him, which I think is entirely wrong.

In staging the storm Dromgoole decided to have the drums, the wind machine and the thunder-sheets, and the stage hands who worked them, in full view of the audience. Calder was not entirely convinced by the idea,

> but you have to go along with doing it in an Elizabethan way, because it's the Globe. I certainly don't like the way the storm is sometimes internalised in Lear's mind, because that's not the music of it. You have

to engage with it – he's imperious, and then he crumbles, and he's at the mercy of the storm. But sustaining it vocally in the open air was difficult. It sometimes felt like we were playing in *Lear in Vietnam*, with the helicopters flying overhead; at one point three Chinooks flew low over the theatre.

He spoke of what is required of the actor in the Dover cliff scene.

Although Lear is mentally extremely disturbed, you have to play it with some rational thought of great sense. The more open and natural it is, the better his emotions bubble and burst and come out. He's bouncing off walls, but not once does he not make sense. He's firing on all synapses, but they're not joining up, the circuits aren't quite going in the right places. As every pain and every sensation happens to him, he articulates it. It's quicksilver stuff, and a wonderful scene.

Dromgoole emphasises the huge demands the play makes on the director as well as the lead actor. 'It's a very painful play to do, it's very exacting, you get fairly shredded absorbing it eight hours a day, six days a week, for six weeks.' He was full of admiration for Calder's performance:

It had great clarity, a sense of the spirit, which is very hard to define in our secular age. The idea of a spiritual opening up and awakening and a greater degree of aliveness is crucial to the journey of the play. David was not frightened of exposing it. But he allied that to a sharply critical understanding of the movement of the play.

Paul Copley, playing Kent, was also impressed: 'David's Lear was never self-pitying. I thought it was a very clear depiction, and one where he could make you weep in sympathy. I knew there were times when he was terrified, but he would just take a deep breath in the wings and go out there.'

The critics too praised his performance. Charles Spencer observed: 'Calder discovers a humanity, vulnerability and spiritual beauty in the role that is as moving as any I have seen.' Lyn Gardner praised his 'magnificent, broken Lear', and picked out 'some genuine five-star moments: Lear and Edgar hugging each other in recognition of a shared pain; Lear's sudden flash of understanding of his own vulnerability in the cry, "I would not be mad".' Paul Taylor noted his virtues:

This stocky, superb actor has the gift of fusing thought and dangerously molten passion. Here he delivers a magnificent performance, mercurially swift in tracking the king's erratic switches of feeling, and his perplexing shuttles between reason and madness. Unforced and unafraid of finding subtly quiet notes, he communicates the humour, the release into anarchic insight, and the final spiritual grace in the part.

Dromgoole's work was generally liked. Lisa Childs commended 'a classic staging supported by music, song and traditional sound effects which perfectly complement the setting'. Spencer wrote: 'His outstanding production is direct and fast-paced: it discovers a surprising amount of humour within this savage text, and penetrates to the heart of this darkest and deepest of Shakespearean tragedies.' He was impressed by the concentration of the audience. 'In the Globe's early days Shakespeare sometimes seemed to be turned into a pantomime, with much tedious barracking from the groundlings. Here, those standing in the yard watched this most demanding of plays with rapt attention and stillness, as if Shakespeare were addressing us directly across a gap of four centuries.'

One of those 'groundlings' had vivid memories of the production.

I stood with my head pressed up against the stage for three hours, totally engrossed. This was the first time I'd seen the play performed in the open air, with none of the crutches of lighting and recorded sound afforded to indoor spaces. It was devastating in its pureness and apparent simplicity. Although I'd admired the performances of many actors playing Lear, this was the first time I'd truly been carried away into the world of the play, and I remember finding the king's descent into madness all the more harrowing because of this.

*This was Bill Buckhurst, who five years later was to direct the next* King Lear *at the Globe.*

# Joseph Marcell
## *Bill Buckhurst*

*In 2014, for the Globe's touring production of* King Lear, *the king was played by Joseph Marcell, with Bill Buckhurst directing.*

Lear is such a complex character, he covers so much, you need a performer who can go to the extremes of rage and vulnerability. The scope and energy needed is enormous, and it doesn't come naturally to every actor. You need someone old enough to have the gravitas to play the part, but also the vitality and the energy needed to sustain it.

Bill Buckhurst's choice to play Lear was a bold one. Born in St Lucia, and now sixty-six, Joseph Marcell achieved worldwide fame playing Geoffrey the family butler in *The Fresh Prince of Bel-Air*, the hugely successful American television series. Less well-known is his distinguished Shakespearean career, which included being one of the first black Othellos, and several productions with the RSC. Although colour-blind casting was becoming more widespread, would audiences accept him as Lear?

'You get to a certain age and that's the part you want to play,' Marcell says, straight after playing a *Lear* matinee at the Globe. 'It's not the sort of role a non-white actor gets to play every day, so it demands a degree of suspension of disbelief from the audience. One has to commend the Globe and Dominic Dromgoole for taking the risk.' Having played Kent fairly recently in a production in San Diego directed by Adrian Noble, the play was still fresh in his mind. 'It's a matter of drawing on all the productions you have seen, but exorcising the ghosts of actors who have played the part before.'

His experience as Lear was very different from that of Julian Glover and David Calder. This was a stripped-back touring production, with a set simple and flexible enough to fit into a wide variety of playing areas. It consisted of a couple of trestles and a stool, two wooden structures at the back housing the props and costumes and, for scenes such as the storm, a curtain that could be drawn right across the stage. The actors sometimes changed their costumes in full view of the audience, and were often seen at the edge of the action waiting for their next entrance. 'I found all this very liberating, because you just have to tell the story,' Buckhurst says. 'You don't have the luxury of fancy lighting and sound effects. It's all about the actors and their inventiveness.'

The tour was a gruelling one. During 2013, and again the following year, the play was staged both indoors and in the open air, in parks, fields and theatres. They ranged from the Master's Garden in Corpus Christi College, Cambridge, to the middle of a field at Hodson Priory in Nottinghamshire, from a rough fit-up in a Brighton park to the Georgian theatre in Richmond in Yorkshire, from the quadrangle of the Bodleian Library in Oxford to the edge of a cliff in St Ives in Cornwall. Audiences numbered between 200 and 600, and 1,500 at the Globe, with the company sometimes playing two performances a day.

As the tour progressed Marcell found he preferred working out of doors. 'There's a kind of immediacy and shared experience there compared with the formality of a theatre. Of course there are aeroplanes, cars, motor bikes, helicopters, pigeons, music. Yet because we're all in it together there's a concentration that's just unbreakable. There's a link between us and the audience that's hard to get in an enclosed space.'

The actors establish that link from the start, coming on stage to set up the props, then mingling with the audience before returning to the stage to perform a song as they don their costumes. 'It starts a very important relationship early on,' Buckhurst says. 'We're saying to the audience, We're in a shared light, and you're going to be as much a part of the story as we are.' While many of the actors engage individuals in the audience in conversation, Marcell, as befits his character, keeps a certain distance. 'I try to be a kind of *maitre d'*, who doesn't give any special favours. So I simply say, Welcome, or, Good to see you. Once somebody offered me a polo mint, but I said I really shouldn't. But it's a good way of getting into the play.'

Buckhurst stresses the qualities Marcell brings to the work.

> You need someone who is able to adapt, to have the energy to play in all these diverse spaces. Joe is incredibly fit, technically brilliant, and fantastic with the verse. He's also extremely diligent as an actor. Now that we've revived the show for a second year with a somewhat different cast, it's been lovely to re-visit and reappraise the text. Joe is constantly working to uncover new things, wanting notes and feedback the whole time.

With just eight actors playing twenty-eight parts, much doubling and even tripling of parts was required. Alex Mugnaioni for instance played Edgar, Cornwall and Burgundy; Daniel Pirrie was cast as Edmund, Oswald and France; John Stahl took on Gloucester, Albany and the Doctor. Sometimes an actor had to leave a scene and return immediately as another character. Where there was no time to change costume backstage, the switch between characters was effected by a simple change of headgear or the addition of a cloak. Once, to the amusement of the audience, when Edmund and Oswald were in the same scene, Pirrie dashed from side to side of the stage to keep the conversation with Goneril flowing. 'I was worried the doubling would be confusing for people who didn't know the play,' Buckhurst says. 'But apparently it isn't.'

The most striking pairing, and one that has a historical precedent, was that of Cordelia and the Fool, both played here with great warmth and youthfulness by Bethan Cullinane. 'There's some debate about whether they were played by the same actor in Shakespeare's time, but I think it makes perfect sense,' Buckhurst says.

> It's a completely different dynamic than the usual one between Lear and the Fool, but no less touching. You have a young person wise beyond their years, and their relationship develops in a lovely way. It also works well at the end, with Lear's line 'And my poor fool is hanged.' In his muddled brain he sees the similarity between the two characters, the closeness he has with both of them.

His vision of Lear's character was of a still-vigorous warrior king.

> You get the sense that he's been quashing rebellions left right and centre, that he's been on the back of a horse flourishing his sword and leading the charge. I don't think he gained power by signing treaties and shaking hands. His world is a very violent one, and it needs someone who terrifies people, follows through with his word, and keeps things under his control. So he's perhaps not naturally paternal.

This, he argues, helps to explain the behaviour of Goneril and Regan, whom he was keen not to portray as totally inhuman.

> Perhaps they have acted the way they do because of how Lear has treated them. We are seeing them at extreme moments, when they are being pushed into corners. They're used to this very male environment; some of the language Goneril uses is militaristic and tough. So once they are given a sniff of power, they don't want to let go of it – in fact they want more. So there's an element of a chip off the old block.

He and the actresses playing Goneril and Regan on both tours spent time exploring the sisters' back story.

> What's going on in that first scene? Why are they ingratiating themselves with Lear? What is that dynamic about? You have to engage in those kinds of conversations to have the bedrock you need for the rest of the play. I found that a stimulating exercise, filling in the gaps without going too far. Sometimes you can dig too much, and you just have to go with what you're given, and trust it.

Marcell was happy to fall in with his idea of Lear. 'I have seen many productions, but never seen Lear played as a warrior king,' he says.

> I've only seen him as a tired old man who may have *been* a warrior. But even in his last moments you can tell he's a man who's been splashed with blood. The thing that kept him young was the responsibility of his position; that's where his vitality comes from. We try to make it so that he spends the whole play fighting his old age, not giving in to it.

He finds it difficult coping with Lear's impetuosity.

> His mind is like quicksilver, he's constantly changing direction, switching from one idea to the next. That's often hard for me to chart. Even when he's railing, he changes the subject as he's shouting, as he's reprimanding the fates and the gods. Sometimes the verse gets very complex, so that paying attention to the line endings when you're going through a highly emotional speech can be difficult. But Shakespeare tells you how he wants it spoken by the way the verse is set out.

Although the Globe has excellent resources for the actors to draw on, he was wary of making use of them initially.

> What was important was to find his character, how he held himself, how he behaved, how he saw himself. The moment I was able to see all that, and work on the text and the meaning of the words with the Globe

associate Giles Block, I became comfortable about reading all those books like *The Wheel of Fire*, and the notes in the Arden edition. But those are just the flourishes, they're not the substance and foundation of what you're doing. The substance is what Shakespeare has written, how you can absorb it and make it yours. The moment you get a unity between what you're trying to create, how the director sees it, and what Shakespeare wants, then you can read that material.

Both tours have involved visits to other countries, including Austria, Malta, Turkey, and finally America, ending in California. Marcell expresses pride in the fact that the tour has followed in the footsteps of another famous *King Lear* production. 'We're doing about a third of the route that one of the really great, unsung, non-white actors, Ira Aldridge, took when he played Lear.'

Buckhurst suggests the play speaks to many different cultures.

In Turkey we played it in a fifth-century church, with surtitles projected on to a dome above the stage. It was a vast, cavernous space, and the words just echoed round it. The audience were very reverential, very quiet; I think they found it very hard-hitting and moving. In such a male-dominated society, they perhaps identified at a deeper level with Lear than people might do in the UK.

The company often had to battle against the elements. An electric storm in Austria halted the play for 20 minutes. At St Ives the rain was so fierce that three-quarters of the audience left, leaving the actors to carry on manfully. Marcell recalled a memorable performance in Cambridge: 'During our final performance at Corpus Christi College the sky opened. We had thunder, lightning and rain, but the most wonderful thing about it was that it came at the most apposite time, when Lear was on the heath. We all got soaked of course, but it was magical.' In Portsmouth there was a different kind of interruption. When Marcell spoke Lear's line 'Can anyone tell me who I am?' someone in the audience shouted out 'Geoffrey!'

The reviews on the tour were mostly warm and welcoming. According to the *Hunts Post*: 'Joseph Marcell is a lithe and magnificent King Lear, able to evoke both horror at his venom when he banishes one daughter and curses the other, and pity for his plight when he loses everything.' The *Cambridge News* critic wrote: 'He commands the stage, tyrannical in his treatment of Cordelia, doddering and convincing in long johns as he flounders about blinded by mania, and touching as he sinks into heavy, confused despair.' A critic of the Brighton performance, however, was less positive: 'As he struts around his court and demands like a spoilt child to hear his daughters' gilded proclamations of love, Marcell has all the regal vanity required to precede the king's fall from grace, but when this violent tumble arrives it feels oddly cushioned. Even in the throes of despair, this king retains a vestige of royal vanity, ultimately robbing the tragedy of its gutting intensity.'

Buckhurst himself was unstinting in his praise: 'The qualities Joe brings to the role are wonderful. I find his performance incredibly moving, and the reconciliation scene heartbreaking. He brings a tough, kingly quality to those first scenes, but then his natural vulnerability and openness and kindness come to the fore in the second half.' Dromgoole concurred: 'Joe is quite magnificent. He has massive reserves of spleen, which for a deeply genial man is quite surprising. And he's one of the best speakers of verse in the world.'

# 11

# On the Road

## Timothy West
### *Toby Robertson*

*For the first of his three Lears, Timothy West played the part for Prospect Theatre Company, under its artistic director Toby Robertson. The production opened at the Assembly Hall during the 1971 Edinburgh Festival. It subsequently visited Venice and Australia, toured the UK, and finished at the Aldwych in London.*

> I think it makes sense if Lear is a man physically and mentally in a good state to continue ruling the country. If he's simply too old for it, it's just a story about a man in retirement who has some very unkind daughters, and then it's not such a considerable play.

Timothy West believes Lear was not in a good mental state when he says he is 'four score and upward', so that his words about his age can be discounted. As he started work on the Prospect production, he thought of the king as being between sixty and sixty-five, but decided to play him at the beginning with considerable energy. This made practical sense, as he himself was only thirty-seven. John Shrapnel, playing Edgar, recalls: 'It was astonishing that he could play the part at that age, but then he has an ageless quality. He aged up a little, but I don't think it struck any of us from the read-through onwards that he had anything he needed to compensate for.'

'I'm not really attracted by power, although I've played a lot of very powerful people,' West says. 'But I always go for their foibles, which is perhaps the most interesting thing about them.' In exploring Lear's foibles he had to decide about the nature of his madness, and for this he sought medical advice. He spoke to a specialist, who told him Lear showed the classic symptoms of artero-sclerosis rather than senile dementia: a hardening of the arteries producing a psychoneurosis, alternating periods of lucidity and delusion, the latter becoming gradually more frequent, and fits of extreme anger. The specialist talked about Lear's reference to *hysterico passio*, a disease which caused women to imagine their womb was racing around inside them, and one that could also afflict men. 'He was pretty right, though not uniformly,' West says. 'Although it didn't answer all the problems, and was only a theory, it gave me a grounding, and an authority for Lear's behaviour.'

Like most actors he found the opening of the play difficult to fathom.

Shakespeare's first scenes are always slightly difficult, and this one is particularly problematic. I think there's too much information in it, but there is also a misunderstanding about how he intends to divide the kingdom, whether Cordelia should indeed be getting a third share, because she's already betrothed to France or Burgundy. When Gloucester and Kent come on at the beginning, why they aren't talking about the third share?

Toby Robertson, he says, didn't favour much textual analysis, or discussions about the meaning of words, or the value of the versification.

He was not an over-analytical director, but he had enormous flair and was very invigorating, and we worked together very well. There was no hesitation, no hedging, no compromise; you simply had to dive in at the deep end. If it worked in a general way that was wonderful, and you could do the fine tuning later, and if it didn't you saw exactly *why* it didn't, and then it was back to the drawing board. There was no question of 'Let's just see how it's going and develop this a bit,' or 'You might just hold back on that.'

John Shrapnel offers a similar view of their director: 'Toby was a showman, a huge enthusiast, and begetter of Prospect. I don't think he was a subtle director, but he was an extremely competent one, and a populist.'

In order to put the focus on the actors and the text, Robertson created a simple, stark production, with a bare stage, and the actors sitting at the side when not involved in a scene. There was a bright, constant light from the 70 lamps hanging from the ceiling, and snatches of music composed by Carl Davis which set the tone of the scenes. The actors all wore light oatmeal woollen costumes, so that with Lear's three daughters dressed in similar fashion there was no pre-judging of their characters.

During the Edinburgh run West wrote to his actress wife Prunella Scales, who had given him some notes:

I've taken your notes to heart, and introduced them into the performance stealthily, one by one. People are generally enthusiastic, in spite of the fact that it's a pretty gruelling experience for them all, in that baking hot auditorium with no air-conditioning and megawatts of lighting only a few feet from their heads. For us, seven performances a week in these conditions feels like a lot. I've been prescribed salt pills, just as if we were in India.

The pressure on him was slightly eased during the tour, when *King Lear* was staged in repertory with *Love's Labour's Lost*, in which he played Holofernes.

The play went down well with the Edinburgh audience. West found the part emotionally and physically exhausting: 'I've done a lot of Shakespearean parts – Iago, Macbeth, Shylock, Prospero, Claudius, Enobarbus – but Lear is the most challenging of all. There's usually a physical reaction to such a major role, in that you're tired most of the day. Once you get to the theatre you're fine.' He apparently had no vocal problems, even with the storm scene, which was created by means of percussion. 'That scene is the most difficult one, emotionally, dynamically and technically, but I seemed to manage it. I think the audience has to take a slight breath there, and think: "It will be over soon and we will get back to the story."'

For the final scene he insisted on carrying Cordelia on in his arms.

I don't believe in dragging her on by the scruff of the neck. You don't know whether the man sent to intercept the order to kill Cordelia will bring her back alive, or whether he has been too late. And then you hear this awful noise: 'Howl, howl, howl, howl!' So it's got to be a pretty big moment technically and dynamically.

The production was commended by the critics as a clear, intelligent rendering of the text, qualities seen as Prospect's particular strengths. Irving Wardle described it as 'full of intelligence, invention, and human observation … It takes Lear a long time to crack, and when he cracks he takes his common sense with him into madness, achieving a series of emotional shocks far beyond the scope of direct pathos or rhetoric.' Another critic suggested that the actor's 'stocky body, bowed shoulders, the head thrust forward, the incipient decay, were reminiscent of the failing Winston Churchill'.

West himself, as actors sometimes do, had an anxiety dream after the first night, in which the whole of the next morning's edition of the *Daily Telegraph* was given over to a critical notice of his Lear. When he awoke in the morning he went straight out and bought a copy of the paper. 'The review certainly wasn't a rave, but it wasn't as bad as all that.'

# Timothy West
## *Stephen Unwin*

*In 2002 Timothy West played Lear for the English Touring Theatre, in a co-production with Malvern Theatres, directed by Stephen Unwin. After a UK tour it had a five-week run at the Old Vic.*

Although he was extremely familiar with the role of King Lear, there seemed little danger that Timothy West would merely repeat his earlier interpretation. 'I retained a lot of the same feeling about the part. I'd thought a lot about different areas of the play, because in the previous years I had seen it a number of times. I thought back over my previous performance, and considered where I could do better.'

*King Lear* is director Stephen Unwin's favourite Shakespeare play. 'That and *Measure for Measure*,' he says,

> because they're the most social and political documents written in drama. *Lear* is a very political play, in which Shakespeare puts a spotlight on the poor naked wretches and the excluded. Every step of the play is full of social insight. You see the way in which a well-organised and well-structured society collapses. It charts brilliantly the way that things go wrong. It's meticulously realistic.

The author of valuable books on Brecht, he describes his austere production as 'the most Brechtian I've ever done', acknowledging the work of the Berliner Ensemble as an influence.

> I was very interested in Edgar becoming a wandering prophet, a Leveller if you like. He's also a mad Jesuit. Those moments like the 'Poor naked wretches' speech seem incredibly important, where the social order, all the things that have been accepted, are in a process of change. Those are the real learning points for both Gloucester and Lear. But I don't buy the Jan Kott idea that so influenced Peter Brook's production, of there being a parallel with the Theatre of the Absurd, especially Beckett's *Endgame*. I think the play doesn't show that human beings are utterly vile. Some of the characters reach a point of despair in which the world seems to have no meaning, but that isn't true of the whole society. Nor do I think the Stalin-parallel idea works: you don't want a Lear already mad or totally angry and brutal at the beginning, you want to show the process of change. Lear has to have somewhere to go.

Unwin had directed West as Falstaff in *Henry IV*, which also toured, but had not seen his Lear:

> I felt he would be ideal for the part. He's prepared to play someone really unpleasant, someone very difficult to deal with; he got that brilliantly. He's an excellent verse speaker, and although he has a powerful presence on stage, he's able to show a fantastic vulnerability, which you need for the last quarter. He's a fine, socially observant actor, not a barnstorming show-off. He's a strong figure, but not macho; he's got this bullish force, but he's also psychologically lethal. And he's one of the few actors with

his kind of profile who is prepared to go out and tour a good play for not very much money. He's incredibly dedicated.

In keeping with the tone of the production, as well as his own preference, West made his Lear more human than regal. 'My own ability is always to play the man rather than the king,' he explains. 'I can't do kingliness, but I can play a man who is caught up in being a king.' In exploring again the complex opening scene, he sought to explain the basis of Lear's decision to divide his kingdom.

> I think he wants to give the best part of it to Cordelia, but rather than ride over his other two daughters he comes up with this ridiculous game of their declaring their love for him. He thinks Cordelia will make a much better and more genuine declaration than the other two, but her refusal to play the game blows his plans apart. So he takes out on her his frustration, and his awareness of how foolish he's been. It's good psychology on Shakespeare's part: we often take out our rage at our own mistakes on other people.

Unwin recalls the early scenes:

> Tim played him at the beginning as a bad-tempered, unpredictable king. Some people thought his performance was too domestic in scale. But you need to see the psychological connections between these people. He made him a perfectly good leader, but one who was grumpy and wanted to move on and have a better time, who was fed up with it all and wanted to retire. He was blisteringly powerful in banishing Kent, and when he was cursing his daughters he caught a sense of saying terrible things to people you love, knowing that you shouldn't, but doing it anyway. When he got to 'O, reason not the need!' it was heartbreaking: it had a real sense of rising panic, and trying to keep that down.

As many other actors have done, West struggled with the storm scene. 'I don't think we could quite express it fully enough,' Unwin admits. 'But I don't know how you can make it convincing in the modern theatre. We had some wonderful lighting effects and some rain and sound effects. But we kept having to pull the volume back; Tim is such a subtle actor that he can't just do a technical event, it has to be very felt.'

The company's aim was 'to bring quality theatre to as many people as possible throughout the country'. Unwin prepared a version of the text that he felt would allow the actors to approach the play with a fresh and open mind. He cut it extensively, especially Poor Tom's lines: 'I think a small amount of flibbertigibbet goes a long way.' He took out most of the punctuation marks, removed elisions where they made no difference to the metre, and omitted the stage directions entirely. 'A Shakespearean text littered with *Exeunt* or *Tuckets* or *Enter the king with train* and so on, can all too easily feel like a kind of Elizabethan theme park. I believe we should discover Shakespeare's dramatic demands from his words, not from what modern editors think.'

West pinpoints the strengths of Unwin's work:

> Stephen is frightfully good on text, and on the emotional content of the play. He has a sense of the dynamism and the whole shape of a dramatic spectacle. The production was very simply staged, because with a touring theatre you can't take a lot of stuff with you in a pantechnicon. It was just a floor and some costumes, and that's all to the good, it keeps the play moving.

Unwin set the play between the reformation and the Civil War, which is being anticipated.

> The social forces which are unleashed are the same sort of forces. It was nothing to do with the golden age of Queen Elizabeth, but a much darker period. The women were in furs, the peasants were quite Brueghel-like, and you really saw the difference, it was very vivid. I got very caught up by the atmosphere of that period, and the huge social distinctions.

He underlines the challenge of touring the UK for three months:

> Although it was simple what we were presenting, it was quite sophisticated and finished, the lighting was very delicate, and that kind of aesthetic requires as much control as anything else to make it work. In every theatre you get a different relationship with the audience, and a different acoustic, all of which is hard. So it was good to settle it down in the Old Vic at the end of the tour.

West recalls the changing attitudes to certain features of the play.

> When we were doing it in Edinburgh in 1971, there was almost universal sympathy for Lear being allowed his one hundred knights: 'Poor old guy, he's used to having them.' By my time of this production it was: 'Why does he need all these knights? I can't even get someone to do my garden!' Of course you can't consider that when you're acting, but it's in your mind. Also you can't help getting more aware over the years of the 'Poor naked wretches' aspect, and how increasingly true that is. That section gained more and more weight in relation to homelessness.

The critics variously labelled the production traditional, unpretentious, conventional, but above all else extremely clear. Charles Spencer wrote: 'Unwin's production may ultimately lack the shuddering impact of a truly great *King Lear*, but there are many unshowy moments that penetrate right to its heart.' Alan Bird was also qualified in his praise: 'Stephen Unwin's production brings to the fore the warmth and vulnerability of King Lear, but lacks the passion and rage to make this tragedy sting.'

Some felt West's low-key king lacked majesty, and that he failed to cope with the storm. But for Benedict Nightingale he gave 'a rich yet intricate performance,' while Michael Billington wrote: 'The production elicits from Timothy West – whom I have always regarded as an actor of robustly Johnsonian common sense – a fine performance of self-revealing vulnerability.' Brian Clover was one of several who praised his handling of the later scenes: 'West comes into his own when Lear's awful descent into despair and ultimate wisdom begins. As these scenes accumulate he finds progressively more depth and pathos in the role, so that when the play reaches its conclusion the emotion is almost unbearable.'

Although West doubts he will play Lear again, should he do so there are areas where he would try to develop new ideas.

> The play has so much in it, and so much to be added to it, one could go on thinking about it for ever. I've never been totally happy about the first scene. If I was directing it or playing the part again, I could see a way in which I would make it easier and more logical, and give the audience a kind of authority about what was going on. But as far as acts four and five go, you can't plan anything, you just have to let those scenes happen to you, they're so wonderfully simple. The only way you can get them wrong is by trying to have control of them.

By the time the company arrived at the Old Vic he felt very positive about the production, not least its appeal to a younger audience. During the run he observed: 'We have groups of schoolchildren in who expect Shakespeare to be boring and unintelligible because of the way that it's all too often taught at school, but they very quickly get gripped by the story.' Unwin underlined the importance of clarity for such audiences:

> It's a word that gets used about my work quite a lot. I always take it as a badge of pride, but you realise it can also be regarded as worthily clear. But the story should be absolutely clear every step of the way. On the tour most people hadn't seen *King Lear* before, so that was always my duty to them.

# Anthony Quayle
## *Don Taylor*

*In 1986 Anthony Quayle played King Lear for his touring company Compass, in a production directed by Don Taylor which toured the UK.*

Anthony Quayle set up Compass in 1984 in order to bring Shakespeare to the provinces, where he believed audiences were starved of the plays; Aberdeen, for instance, had not seen a production of *King Lear* for thirty-five years. The Compass production toured for nine weeks around the UK, playing almost exclusively in the large, beautiful Frank Matcham theatres, some of them having 2,000 seats.

Quayle was now seventy-four, and his reviews were very positive. Paul Copley, who played the Fool, recalls a traditionally mounted production. 'Tony's Lear was big, full-blooded, an old proscenium-arch kind of performance. Some of his sharp-tongued insults really hit home, but he didn't get the more pathetic, sympathetic moments.' Copley used his own Yorkshire accent for his Fool, while the style of his jester's cap was suggested by Quayle. 'He had a little Jack Russell that he really doted on. So my cap was a dog's head, with the snout raised and the ears flapping. His idea was that the Fool would be like his dog, faithful and loyal but a little snappy.'

The set consisted of four moveable megaliths, while the costumes ranged from Elizabethan to punk. Copley recalls an incident when they were playing in Blackpool. 'We opened the second half with "Blow winds and crack your cheeks". Before we began a man announced the winner of a lucky dip for a bottle of whisky, ending with: "And now on with the show!" By this time Tony and I were shaking with laughter in the wings. Then the curtain went up and we had to pretend to be weeping in the storm.'

The director was the playwright Don Taylor, who worked extensively in television as well as theatre. Co-artistic director of Compass, he nearly lost one key member of the company before rehearsals began. Kate O'Mara was given the unusual choice of playing Goneril or Regan. 'The deciding factor for me in choosing which of the two sisters to play came with Goneril's speech "Milk-liver'd man!", in which she contemptuously berates her husband Albany for his lack of manhood. I thought that exactly summed up her character, that she is in fact more masculine than he is, and goes on to make preparations for war.' To her dismay, when they reached that point in rehearsal Taylor suggested the speech be cut. Only after she threatened to leave the production was it restored.

By the end of the tour Quayle had become ill. It turned out to be his last stage role: two years later he died of liver cancer, and Compass was taken over by Tim Pigott-Smith.

# Richard Briers
## *Kenneth Branagh*

*In 1990 Richard Briers played King Lear for Kenneth Branagh's Renaissance Theatre Company, with Branagh directing. The production visited Japan,*

*Eastern Europe and Portugal; played in big cities in America; toured exten-*
*sively in the UK; played at the Edinburgh Festival; and ended up at the*
*Dominion theatre in London.*

Looking back twenty-five years, Kenneth Branagh remembers why he cast
Richard Briers as Lear: 'As an actor he had a great desire and appetite for
the leading classical roles, which his career had not always given him the
opportunity to play. He was hungry to tackle Lear, but not as some grim
obligation involving a terrible effort. I thought he was an obvious and
exciting choice.'

Known for years as a highly skilled comic actor on stage and television,
Briers had recently unexpectedly triumphed as Malvolio in Branagh's
Renaissance production of *Twelfth Night*. Not only had he brought out the
comic possibilities of the role, he had also conveyed in considerable depth
the pompous steward's pathos and vulnerability. 'I had a great rapport with
Richard during that production,' Branagh says.

> The relationship between the director and the leading actor in these great
> plays of Shakespeare must be very strong, either with a great rapport
> or some great tension or friction, in order to get the best out of each
> other and the great work of art. Richard was very direct, there was no
> tiptoeing around fragile egos in either direction. So I knew we could
> discuss Lear openly and extensively.

He also felt Briers' consummate skills as a comic actor could be put to good
use.

> In working with him on *Twelfth Night* I had the opportunity to see the
> brilliant humour and comedic skill he had at his disposal. I think that's
> a pre-requisite for a great performance in Shakespeare: it's an ability you
> must have in order to extract the humour. Shakespeare certainly runs
> humour through all the darkest material: it's a cynical, bitter and hard
> humour, but it's there.

The challenge for a director of *Lear*, he suggests, is to link the domestic
core with the epic events shaking the outside world. 'How to make it
clear that Lear's stubbornness and Gloucester's gullibility lead to national
catastrophe, how the individual human folly causes mass suffering, how
the banality of a row around the kitchen table can unleash such profound
consequences – your task is to show how all this connects.'

He and Briers met regularly for eighteen months before rehearsals, to
talk about the play and the problems of the role. They read the text aloud
in order to make basic decisions, such as whether and where cuts should
be made, and which scenes were particularly difficult and needed to be
worked on. They considered the cause of the fragility in Lear's family, and

the question of madness: does Lear actually go mad, and what is meant by that, what does it mean for him and for other people, and what is Lear's particular fear of madness?

They also discussed the matter of age, its effect on Lear's faculties, and how that would be expressed. 'Richard was then fifty-six, so we considered whether he should play older,' Branagh says. 'We also wondered whether taking a detailed look at mental illness would benefit his approach to the part. Should he pad up or grey up, or try to slow down in the way that people feel that people of a certain age do? In fact we plumped for a vigorous approach, with no additional playing of age.' He also declined to have any overall concept for the production.

The costumes designed by Jenny Tiramani were deliberately colour coded: scarlet costumes for the main players, with the French dressed in blue, and the Fool in black and white. The flexible set consisted of a simple circle in dull red, set within a steel drum, with a pockmarked grey wall at the back. With the tour in mind, and conscious that many audience members would not be hearing their first language, Branagh cut some of the Poor Tom scenes, as well as certain parts of the scene on Dover cliff between Lear and Gloucester.

As director Branagh was keen to combine the intimate family aspect of the play with the epic. In creating the scene on the heath he wanted to show the insignificance of Lear, the Fool and Poor Tom in the face of the forces of nature. To help create this effect, he insisted on having a rain rig, which went with the company on tour. 'We used it in a slightly abstract way,' he explains. 'There was real rain, but Richard didn't have to be in it the whole time, and carry a cold all round the world. For me there was never enough rain or noise in the storm, but Richard always wanted it pulled back.'

He cast himself as Edgar, a part he found challenging:

One has to consider the circumstances under which he makes the extraordinary decision to believe Edmund's story about their father, to leave the court, then pass himself off as a beggar, and finally attach himself to his father. There are complex motivations here. I did enjoy playing the part, I loved his heart and his intelligence. But I didn't feel I was a very good Edgar.

He feels this was due in part to his dual role as actor/director. 'I didn't have enough focus, and I was watching everyone else way too much.' Later he described himself as 'the worst Edgar that's ever been on stage'.

Emma Thompson's Fool was a highly original characterisation. Dressed in a dark shroud, displaying a white, skull-like face and a twisted body – one critic described her as 'a skull on a bent pair of tweezers' – she was a hunched, spider-like cripple, bent almost double as she hobbled about. She moved with increasing deformity, finally disappearing down into the space from which Poor Tom had emerged. She would like to have played Cordelia as well as the Fool. 'They make such a wonderful double, and they are the only two characters who tell Lear the truth,' she confessed later. She also underlined the power of the play:

> I had a great time playing the Fool, and after my character had died, I would listen to the play in my dressing-room and love every performance. It's an extraordinary feat of poetic and humanitarian imagination. It contains more love and hate, more redemption and blackness, than any other play. There's nothing sentimental about it, it's terribly harsh, and yet for all its horrors, the power of love comes singing out at the end. A natural balance reasserts itself, and one feels renewed hope for the human condition.

Branagh felt fully justified in casting her.

> Whoever plays the Fool needs to have an excellent rapport with Lear, whether it's a sparring or loving or challenging one. Richard and Emma got on very well, and she based her performance on her adoration and deep-seated love for Lear, for which she accessed that which she felt for Richard. She has great mimetic skill, and played the Fool as a damaged, rather broken, androgynous character. The pathos in her performance was profound, and heart-breaking. She also has great comic ability, so all those interchanges in the double-act between her and Richard, bitter though they might be, had the possibility, particularly with Richard's comic skill, to be really laugh-out-loud funny.

In America the play opened in the Mark Taper Forum in Los Angeles, then moved on to Chicago and New York.

> Playing it in America with this young English company was interesting, because we had lots of dialogue about how to do Shakespeare with local actors, who were very kind and supportive of the show. We talked about English style and English accents, and the mellifluous tones of the Shakespearean voice that might be associated with English productions, in contrast to the wonderful hard R of the American approach.

The critic Richard Christiansen wrote: 'This *King Lear* is played with clarity, force and passion ... Branagh's staging seems to have connected to the heart of the play's story, so that, with the aid of urgent drumbeats that punctuate the scenes, its upheavals of social order and turmoils of nature are played with crackling intensity.' He thought Thompson's Fool 'extraordinary ... a mocking and haunting commentator on Lear's tragedy', and also praised Briers' performance:

> The production has the benefit of a ripened, knowing and wisely apportioned portrayal of Lear by Richard Briers. As his pride and his power

are brutally taken from him, he moves believably from an outraged king to a homeless madman, and finally to a dying, distorted shadow of his former self, stripped of all his earthly goods and ready now for the sweet release of death. This is an acting obstacle course of mammoth challenges, and Briers navigates it with barely a stumble.

Branagh believes the production developed significantly during the tour, and that the company learned more about the play from the differing reactions it had in cultures as diverse as those of Japan and Portugal. He recalls one particular performance in Zagreb in Croatia:

> We had got through fifty performances, which I think is a key stage in Shakespeare productions, when a performance has really gelled in some meaningful way. That evening Richard was absolutely transcendent. The company all applauded as he came off, there was talk of it in the wings; everyone realised something extraordinary was happening. You felt it in the audience too: there was a lengthy standing ovation. He had somehow channelled the role so that the poetic resonance of the whole play was released and enhanced and deepened.

Briers himself observed: 'Lear is a colossus of emotion and verse, a huge bloody symphony. It takes you fifty times to get control of it. I felt there were only a couple of performances when I seemed to hit something special. I felt I had got close to it but, infuriatingly, I never knew how or why!'

In the UK they played in many different venues, from a tent in Norwich to the vast, 2,500-seat Dominion in London. It was a severe test of Briers' stamina and range, and Branagh felt he rose to the challenge. 'He could play the chamber moments as effectively as the epic ones, and hold an audience like the Dominion as well as the intimate spaces. It was an amazing actorly gymnastic workout to take Lear round the world in such a variety of theatres.'

For the English critics, Benedict Nightingale noted a production which combined 'a rough, raw world, reflecting elemental conflicts' with an eighteenth-century Hogarthian look, when 'cruelty and a certain harshness was accepted, and you had to be fit to survive'. Others found much to praise: Milton Shulman, noting Briers' 'fierce petulant outrage at the start', wrote that he 'rises to the part both vocally and spiritually'. Unusually, for the final scene he entered backwards, dragging Cordelia's body. Lyn Gardner was struck by 'his piercing cry at Cordelia's death, like a doomed animal caught in a trap'.

Branagh himself spoke glowingly of Briers' performance:

> There's a theory that no actor will ever fully correspond to all the qualities and characteristics that Lear requires. With Hamlet there's no character angle, you just have to somehow bring all of yourself to it.

With Lear there are particular requirements: the humour that Richard had, the tremendous energy, the probing intelligence, the humanity, the pathos. He also brought to the part a tremendous masculinity as Lear the former soldier, and, having two daughters himself, a keen emotional intelligence about family life. He was willing to go with all those colours; he wanted to explore every dimension. I think he was very successful in his ambition to approach a complete Lear. He measured up wonderfully well.

# 12

# In Wales and Scotland

## Nicol Williamson
### *Terry Hands*

*In 2001 Terry Hands, artistic director of Clwyd Theatr Cymru in Mold, North Wales, directed a production of* King Lear *with Nicol Williamson in the title-role.*

> Nicol always took risks. Some were well-judged, some weren't. He could reduce the company to tears in rehearsal, and the audience in performance. On his night he equalled Paul Scofield.

Although Terry Hands rated Nicol Williamson highly as an actor, his decision to bring him to his theatre to play King Lear was a brave one. Once regarded as the most exciting and dangerous actor of his generation, Williamson dazzled audiences with his versatility, and his ability to play older characters convincingly. But he had later become notorious for his temperamental outbursts, his falling out with colleagues, and his tendency to miss performances, or even walk offstage during them. Yet Hands felt the risk was worth taking. 'I had watched Nicol's work for decades, his Hamlet, Macbeth, Coriolanus, as well as his films,' he explains. 'He was a big, powerful, unconventional, aggressive actor, slightly mad, a dominant figure in any situation, with a superb voice. I felt it was his time to take on Lear.'

Now sixty-three, the actor's unconventional approach to creating a part was graphically illustrated before rehearsals began. He and Hands spent a week exploring the text in detail in a village on the island of Rhodes, where Williamson was living. 'Academic analysis didn't interest him,' Hands remembers. 'Instead he simply *was* Lear throughout the day. Whether in bars, shops, during interminable lunches, or on walks, he blustered, confronted, dominated, insulted, ate, drank and showed extraordinary, if wayward, generosity. By the end of the week we both knew the direction his Lear would take.'

Despite his two decades with the Royal Shakespeare Company, and his years in charge of Clwyd Theatr Cymru, Hands had not previously directed *King Lear*. It is, he feels, 'that most terrifying of all Shakespeare's journeys – Lear's progress through madness to redemption while two families and an entire kingdom go to ruin. It covers relationships, families, politics, truth and lies, kindness and cruelty, the tension between young and old, the delicate line between madness and sanity, and the mystery of what it is to be a human being.' Comparing audiences' responses to Shakespeare's two greatest plays, he observes: '*Hamlet* is shorter, funnier, and you leave the theatre feeling perhaps just a little smarter than when you walked in. *King Lear* is deeper, richer, and you leave the theatre hoping against hope that you never grow old – particularly if you have daughters.'

He used the Folio text, cutting only repetitions and the occasional Elizabethan word-play. Rehearsals confirmed his belief that Williamson would rise to the challenge. 'We rehearsed as we usually do at Clwyd. The actors learnt their lines before rehearsals, we stood up and talked to each other. Once a week we explored Shakespeare's sonnets. Nicol contributed to all aspects of the work. He gave everything, every day.' He and Williamson decided to emphasise Lear's kingly, patriarchal qualities. 'We talked about Edward I. Might he have been Shakespeare's inspiration? The great warrior-king who had united the kingdom, now presiding over its division?'

While he accepts the idea that the same actor may originally have played both Cordelia and the Fool, 'the only two truth-tellers in the play', he dismisses it as irrelevant.

> The Fool is conventional, licensed to tell the truth, employed to remind Lear of his mortality – part confidant, part dog. As such he can be stroked or whipped, and in a play that explores hatred in detail, he gives love. As Lear finally collapses into the storm of his madness, so the Fool drifts away. He is no longer necessary, or noticed.

Among the critics, Charles Spencer praised the director's work. 'Terry Hands, a great Shakespearean director, gets excellent work from many of his supporting company, in a lean, lucid production that is Beckettian in its final bleakness.' But he found Williamson's performance disappointingly inadequate:

> He is vocally underpowered, with an accent that veers bizarrely between English actor-laddie plumminess, New York, and his native Scotland. He also has a far-from-confident grasp of his lines, and a cloth ear when it comes to the rhythm of Shakespeare's poetry. Again and again great speeches are gabbled, stammered, or ruined by false emphases. None of this would matter so much if you felt that Williamson was digging

deep into the role and into himself. But this is a depressingly superficial reading in which the king's fear of madness, his wild rage and his painful growth into full humanity, seem to have been applied from without rather than torn from within.

In contrast Michael Coveney, while acknowledging its flaws, was won over by Nicolson's performance: 'His Lear was all over the place, but full of brilliance and great shafts of pathos. Many of the speeches were cut to shreds and delivered in the wrong order. But it really didn't matter, because you just knew you were in the presence of true greatness. The performance was fretted with moments of gold dust and heartbreak.' Michael Kelligan praised the quality of his acting in the later scenes: 'Nicol Williamson's powerful Lear finds his greatest degree of sensitive playing in the second part of the play. His forgiveness and reconciliation with Cordelia and his tenderness over her dying body demonstrate Williamson's great ability to engage with the audience.'

Terry Hands believes his gamble paid off. '*King Lear* is an orchestral piece, in which all the instruments are given their full value. The company responded as an ensemble, inspired by Nicol's performance.'

# David Hayman
## *Dominic Hill*

*In 2012 Dominic Hill directed* King Lear *at the Glasgow Citizens' theatre, where he was artistic director. The title-role was played by David Hayman.*

Compared to *Hamlet, King Lear* is so much about the world, about all of society, about the haves and the have-nots. Over the last few years it's seemed to me incredibly important. It's a very public play.

In staging his production in Glasgow, Dominic Hill was determined to emphasise the political elements of Shakespeare's great work. 'I can't see the point of doing the play unless it reflects the world we live in,' he says. 'What interests me is that it's so much about a sense of social awareness and social justice, about how rulers should behave, and the importance of responsibility and leadership. It has an extraordinary humanity, and it feels phenomenally relevant.'

In order to emphasise this view, Dominic Hill hired eighteen drama students to act as a kind of Chorus, a brooding underclass of vagabonds who help create the atmosphere and tell the story. 'The stage was occupied round the edges by a group of homeless people,' he explains. 'The play began with them looking in on the first scene. Then they gradually invaded the space as Lear came down to their level. And at the end they occupied it, the dispossessed and the poor, with Edgar being one of them. There was a sense that they were taking over.'

He set the action in a non-specific, hard-edged contemporary world, with the men in suits and fur coats and hats, operating in Tom Piper's design of an abstract modern world of black walls and metal-framed perspex. 'If you're doing the play in a contemporary way, you've got to find a world in which an autocratic ruler is a believable thing. I wasn't saying it was any particular country, but it had shades of those Eastern European dictatorships of the 1980s, like the Ceausescu regime in Romania.'

David Hayman was an experienced Shakespearean actor, whose previous roles in his early years at the Citizens included Hamlet (twice), Troilus, Petruchio and Lady Macbeth (in an all-male production); he had also played hard men such as the gangster Al Capone and the reformed murderer Jimmy Boyle. Hill explained his choice: 'I felt David would bring to the part what I wanted to bring to the production, which was a vitality, a front-footedness, and at times a brutality, which would suit a twenty-first-century *Lear*.'

Hayman, aged sixty-two, played him as the very opposite of senile. 'He wasn't a doddering old man that people could take advantage of, but someone who at the start had all his faculties about him,' he says.

> He played games with his daughters as an exercise in and an abuse of power, and it was a sign of his arrogance that he didn't have an inkling how they would react. I wanted him to have a masculinity that still worked. He was a very vital physical warrior, who still wanted women, and caroused with his soldiers into the wee small hours. I think that made his fall from grace, his hurtling into insanity, all the more telling.

In rehearsals he found Hill's method very much to his taste.

> I loved its free-wheeling nature, the creative, non-judgemental atmosphere, which is what rehearsals should always have. Dominic is very laid back as a director, very open, but he's also very intelligent; he knows what he wants, and is very subtle in how he gets it. He gives you a free hand to try something if you want to come at it from left field. If a director becomes judgemental you eventually stop coming up with ideas. The word 'No' should not be in their vocabulary: 'Maybe' or 'That's interesting' or 'Let's try it' are fine, but never 'No'. That way your creative juices are cut off at source, and they stop flowing.

Hill created the storm on an almost bare stage, littered with the carcases of old pianos. The homeless chorus played on their strings to produce composer Paddy Cuneen's abstract music that mixed with the thunder and lightning. For Hayman it was a thrilling experience: 'You have to steel yourself to get through it, to have enough breath to rage at the heavens. But it was very exciting, one of those moments when the adrenalin is pumping and you're on a high.'

Hill gave his production some unexpected touches, such as Cordelia being clearly pregnant on her return from France. 'I thought it would accentuate the idea that in a less cruel world she would be the symbol of goodness prevailing: she would carry on, she could be the future.' Its violence was underlined by Gloucester being blinded in one eye by Cornwall's corkscrew, and in the other by Regan's stiletto heel, and by Kent shooting himself in the mouth at the end. And in an echo of the Gambon/Sher production, Hill had the Fool killed during the mock-trial scene: 'In his rage Lear mixed people up, and brained him against a chair. It was quite dark and shocking, but I think effective.'

Although Shakespeare, apart from the English history plays, is widely performed in Scotland, *King Lear* is rarely staged. According to Hayman 'the production set the heather on fire'. The critic Mark Brown certainly thought so, describing it as one 'which could stand beside the best in this year of the World Shakespeare Festival'. As an ageing Stalinist dictator, he wrote, 'Hayman inhabits the role as if it were a familiar bespoke suit'; his final scenes were 'an achievement of shuddering anguish and contagious pathos'. Mark Fisher was less impressed: 'Hayman brings out the violence of Lear's language, but we feel little sympathy when he is cast out into the wilderness to rage some more. Only towards the end, when his madness is externalised and he seems to enter an asylum, do we connect emotionally with this man who has lost everything.'

Hayman is keen to re-visit the role some time. 'When you're dealing with a classic as dense as *King Lear* there are so many journeys you can take through that labyrinth of story, you can only capture a certain percentage of it.' In Hill's opinion: 'David brought great vigour to the role. He had the energy and the ability to catch the dangerous edge of a despot, to be active and terrifying at the beginning, but also to be incredibly moving at the end. It was a very strong arc, and a powerful performance.'

# 13

# Young Audiences, Young Players

## Tony Church
### *Buzz Goodbody*

*In 1974 Buzz Goodbody directed an adaptation of the play originally entitled simply* Lear. *Created for school audiences, it had Tony Church playing the king. It was staged in Stratford's smaller theatre The Other Place, of which Goodbody was the artistic director. It also played in The Place in London, and toured extensively in the UK and the US, including a run in New York.*

In December 1973 Buzz Goodbody sent a memo to the RSC's artistic director Trevor Nunn, arguing for a 'studio/second auditorium' operating on a near-invisible budget, using RSC actors already on contract, and aimed at an audience of locals ('notoriously hostile to us'), factory workers from Coventry and Birmingham, and schoolchildren. This was The Other Place, its name derived from Hamlet's remark 'If your messenger find him not there, seek him i' th'other place yourself'. Seen as an alternative venue to the main theatre, Goodbody saw it as a first step towards breaking down the economic and social barriers between the RSC and the public that helped finance the company.

Her memo set out her vision for The Other Place:

Its first aim is to offer good theatre cheaply. Its second aim is to work as members of a classical company in a small theatre where we can challenge our own traditions of proscenium theatre. Its third aim is to put on shows with a specifically local character, hopefully building an audience that hitherto thought the RSC were out of touch. Its fourth aim is to do specific educational projects for local schools, thus reaching out to a new, younger audience. Its fifth aim is to create a forum where the audience can come into closer contact with the Company.

The first woman to join the RSC's directorial team, Goodbody had previously run Theatregoround, the company's outreach programme, which toured small-scale productions to schools, factories and church halls, with minimal casts, props and sets. Her productions of *King John* for Theatregoround and, on the main stage, *As You Like It*, had been controversial and attacked by the critics, in part because of their startling modern cultural references.

A member of the Communist Party, Goodbody described herself as 'a Marxist-Socialist revolutionary'. She made her political intentions clear: 'To me working on a production is a political act. One of the sad things about much work on Shakespeare is that it springs from a mildly left, incredibly hegemonic order over the arts which has a very distinct bourgeois ideology behind it. That is unfair. I would like to see good Shakespearean productions done by Marxists.' A committed feminist – she had started the first feminist theatre company, the Women's Street Theatre Group – she examined the emotional centre of *King Lear*, putting the emphasis on personal relationships and families, a focus that the small space demanded.

She initially adapted the play for A-level students, re-titling it *Lear*. She cut the text drastically, resulting in a running time of just over two hours instead of the usual three or more. The cast was reduced to ten actors, with France, Albany and Cornwall all disappearing, so that it fell to Goneril and Regan to put out Gloucester's eyes. The intimacy of the space demanded a production style that was simple and unadorned, allowing the actors to address the audience directly, and interact with them. Each performance was followed by a short discussion between the cast and the audience, an innovative feature for the time.

Goodbody's particular interest was in the poor and the needy who are revealed to Lear when he encounters Poor Tom. She prefaced the play with a controversial prologue spoken by Lear and Edgar, which highlighted the play's themes. It juxtaposed contemporary and seventeenth-century attitudes towards poverty, old age and law enforcement, drawn from an anthology that offered similarly provocative material to schools. The actors protested, arguing that these ideas were self-evident in the production, and the prologue was dropped after a few performances.

Some of Goodbody's rehearsal techniques were unconventional. Tony Church was a distinguished character actor and one of the founders of the RSC. He had played Cornwall in the Scofield/Brook production, and during his career was to play Lear five times. In one exercise with the actresses playing his daughters, he was asked to shut his eyes and explore their bodies with his hands, and describe what he felt as their father. Another exercise influenced his ideas about the back story:

> Buzz told me to lie down while she sat by my head and talked me into a dream state, where first of all Kent, my second in command, saved me from being killed in battle. Next Gloucester, my chief minister, got me

out of an appalling political fix. I went on to dream about the mothers of my three daughters. I'm certain the girls all had different mothers who had all died in childbirth.

The conditions at The Other Place, a former makeshift rehearsal room and storage space, were decidedly primitive. The first audiences had to sit on mattresses, which were later replaced by hard wooden seats and eventually padded benches. With tickets costing just 70p, there was no foyer, bar, bookstall or reserved seating, and no showers for the actors, some of whom had to make entrances through the toilets. Actors and audience were in close proximity, and with no air conditioning the temperature was uncomfortably hot.

Yet research indicated that young people responded extremely positively to such productions, rating The Other Place 'the best of what the Royal Shakespeare Company does'. They liked the intimate, informal atmosphere and its rough-and-ready setting; many claimed that the small theatre helped to foster and broaden their knowledge and experience of drama. The productions sometimes had an overwhelming impact on them. The critic John Peter, who praised Goodbody's ability to capture the sense of Lear's 'ruined greatness', reported: 'During the scene of Lear's reunion with Cordelia three teenagers sitting near me wept openly and unashamedly.'

The critics were predictably split about the production. The *Sunday Times* thought it' short on comic grandeur', combining 'harrowing force' with occasional 'lapses of bizarre vulgarity'. But *The Times* called the production 'the most dispassionate re-examination of the play since Peter Brook's 1962 version', praising the spectacle Goodbody had achieved with 'a few banners on a bare floor'. The *Daily Telegraph* said of Tony Church: 'He may be too solid and sensible an actor (remembering all his dukes and earls for this company in the 1960s) to persuade us of Lear's madness or majesty. But his voice, among so many which are apt to be inaudible, is always a pleasure; and his grief at Cordelia's death is most moving.' The play attracted positive reviews in New York, and the text was later used in an Australian production by the Queensland Theatre Company, starring Warren Mitchell as Lear.

Goodbody's next production was an acclaimed *Hamlet*, but four days after the production opened for previews she committed suicide. Trevor Nunn, who took over the supervision of *Hamlet* during its run, said of her small-scale *Lear*: 'What was interesting about it was that, although it had a lot of impact, it was still fundamentally a big theatre production spoken quietly.' But he acknowledged the influence of her work on his own acclaimed 1976 chamber production of *Macbeth*, starring Judi Dench and Ian McKellen. Many other directors, including Bill Alexander, John Barton and Deborah Warner, also credit her directorial style as an important inspiration for their work.

# Richard Haddon Haines
## *Cicely Berry*

*In 1988 the Royal Shakespeare Company's head of voice Cicely Berry staged a production of* King Lear *in The Other Place. With Richard Haddon Haines playing Lear, it later moved to the Almeida theatre in London.*

> It was an extraordinary opportunity for me, as I had never done a production for the RSC.

More than a quarter of a century on, Cicely Berry looks back with satisfaction at her innovative work at The Other Place. This was a chance to test her long-held belief that 'we cannot understand Shakespeare fully until we inhabit the language in our bodies as well as our minds'. Like Buzz Goodbody, she was challenging the RSC's production methods, which she believed flawed because they excluded the actors' creative input in rehearsal.

'So much is decided before rehearsals begin – all the choices about time and place, sets and costumes – that the way language is used simply has to fit in with all those things.' Her aim was to reverse the process, starting without any directorial concept, and exploring language first and in more depth than is usually possible. 'I wanted to approach the play by speaking it first, listening to the movement and texture of the language before coming to conclusions about character, place and relationships.'

The production was initiated by the RSC's education department: designed for a schools' audience, the project included practical workshops for the students. Invited to choose a Shakespeare play, Berry settled on *King Lear*: 'It was an ambitious choice, and I felt slightly nervous about it. But I felt it offered wonderful opportunities for the actors to make discoveries. The language of the play is so incredibly expressive and rich; it's the most imaginative piece of work Shakespeare wrote. I also think it's more accessible to young people than the much more complex *A Midsummer Night's Dream*.'

During rehearsals she set up various exercises to help the actors with the language. The bulk of the time was spent on the storm, which she saw as the centre of the production. 'The play is about people meeting on the heath, not just about one central character,' she said. Lear was played by the South African actor Richard Haddon Haines. In one exercise, as he began his 'Blow winds' speech the actors surrounded him and, sometimes shouting, sometimes whispering, threw his words back at him. As the exercise got rougher they threw light objects at him, to represent twigs and leaves disturbed by the storm. The idea was to make the story palpable to the actor by a combination of the noise and the words in his head.

Katie Mitchell, who was Berry's assistant director, recalled:

Richard Haddon Haines would read the first two speeches several times, and each time Cicely would give tasks to the rest of the actors e.g. repeat out loud any words that catch your imagination; mine the images in the speeches; run around the space repeating words that are violent. Afterwards we would discuss the language together ... Although this method of working gave all the actors a shared understanding of the violence and physicality of Lear's language, it also threw into relief the fact that the storm needs to be a concrete force with which Lear was in conflict.

At the Almeida the storm scene was dealt with in spectacular fashion: the stone platform of the opening scenes split apart to become rocky boulders that the characters clambered over. The critics were impressed with the production, particularly the language. 'The words, simply spoken, explode like words in a combustion chamber,' wrote John Peter. Irving Wardle observed: 'Throughout the show, abrupt descents from sustained tone to conversational expression set the words on fire'. Michael Billington suggested the production proved that 'understanding what you are saying is the key that unlocks Shakespearean word-music. "Was this well spoken?" inquires Lear. Indeed it was.'

Berry feels the success of the production proved her point: 'It made people realise this was a proper way of working on language. After that it was taken seriously as part of the RSC rehearsal process.'

*For her production Cicely Berry was nominated as Best Director in the Evening Standard Awards.*

# Timothy West
## *Alan Stanford*

*Timothy West played King Lear for the second time in 1992 in the Tivoli theatre in Dublin, in a production by the actor/director Alan Stanford for his Second Age Theatre Company.*

For many performances in the small Tivoli theatre, especially the matinees, around 80 per cent of the audience were schoolchildren. 'Irish children don't do a lot of Shakespeare, so it was a bit of an eye-opener for them,' Timothy West recalled. 'It was a good production, very fast, and cleverly cut, so that it could be clearly understood by a young audience. There was no time for complicated sub-text to be brought out. The children were thrilled by the play, and mostly behaved very well.'

Alan Stanford was the founder and artistic director of Second Age, which had a responsibility to cater for schools audiences in Ireland. An experienced actor, he was best known for his work at the Gate in Dublin, and would later direct himself as Lear. 'I couldn't find a natural Lear in Dublin,' he says. 'I had seen Tim's Lear for Prospect, and thought he could do better than that. He was too young then; I felt Lear must be at least fifty.'

He underlined the value of the part for an actor:

> *King Lear* is certainly the greatest play ever written, but no actor can catch every aspect of the part. I believe certain parts are more educative than others. Playing Lear is going to be your PhD in acting. It teaches you what you should and can do. You're on a perpetual journey where the directions change all the time. As an actor you're shoved and harried in every direction, and it's a matter of keeping control. When you finish that journey you end up knowing a hell of a lot.

West was now fifty-eight. Returning to the role after twenty years, he wrote to his wife Prunella Scales during rehearsals, pondering on his greater suitability for the part: 'I feel I already know more about the play than last time. In 1971 the boys were only tiny; now they're of an age when both they and I must harbour occasional thoughts of the nuisance I may be to them in my dotage.' Suggesting he might now be 'a more selfish, certainly a more intolerant person than I was twenty years ago', he felt that 'the first two acts seem to be the better for it'. He also observed: 'Perhaps the most worthwhile aspect of the exercise is that very few people in Dublin have ever seen the play before. Very little Shakespeare is done here.'

Stanford recalled his attitude in rehearsal: 'Tim's a real actor, with an incredibly open mind. He was open to my line of thinking, and a joy to work with. He's been playing old men all his life, while still remaining a boy, and he's never lost his enthusiasm for discovery. His attitude was, Where are we going to go with this?' West liked Stanford's method, telling his wife: 'Alan's directing it very well, I think. He's good on text, sound on the psychological development, knows his theatre, and has a refreshingly low boredom threshold.'

Among the Irish cast, the Fool was played by Bosco Hogan. 'He and Tim had a wonderful rapport from day one,' Stanford says.

> He was the conscience on Lear's shoulder, and he had a great delicacy of touch. It was a joy having them examine new ideas together. Tim would put forward a proposition which would be tested by Bosco, for instance in the waiting for the horses scene, with its link with *Waiting for Godot*. That scene is pure Beckett, and they *were* Gogo and Didi.

West drew a comparison between Hogan's version of the Fool and that of Ronnie Stevens in the Prospect production: 'With Ronnie you knew very well that he had abdicated from some kind of life, had dedicated himself to Lear, but was unhappy about it. With Bosco – a very wonderful, poetic

Irish actor – you felt perhaps he was having a sabbatical from writing some wonderful book, a treatise about something, and was just looking in on Lear.'

The theatre had a thrust stage, deeper than it was wide, with excellent acoustics. The set was a simple one, based on Stanford's vision. 'The play needs to be done on a barren stage,' he says. 'In recent times there have been too many special effects or complicated design ideas. The simpler and purer it is the better. You can't embellish the play, you have to strip it down. You don't try to help Shakespeare, you try to serve him.' West approved of the set, but was less than happy with the costumes. They only appeared at the last moment, which meant adjustments had to be made to accommodate what the actors had been doing for three weeks in rehearsal. The designer drew his inspiration from Kurosawa's celebrated film *Ran*, a re-telling of the *King Lear* story, which prompted Bosco Hogan to dub the Dublin production 'Also Ran'.

One anxiety during performances was the digital wrist watches in the audience. Lear's speech over the dead Cordelia, 'Thou'llt come no more; never, never, never, never, never', usually came at exactly 11 o'clock. To avoid the quietest moment in the play being drowned out, if the performance was running a little late West would slow down the early part of the scene to get the chimes of the watches in the speech, and if they were a little ahead he would speed it up so that they didn't go off during Edgar's final speech. As he observed: 'You shouldn't really have to think about that, should you, when you're playing King Lear?'

His performance greatly pleased Stanford:

> It was streets ahead of his first Lear, partly because he had reached a much greater understanding of himself. He was magnificent. Vocally he had no fears with the storm, and he captured all the passion and anger required. He made the 'Poor naked wretches' speech real; you saw an epiphany happening. In the scene on Dover cliff he captured a man released, not mad; the shackles of being Lear had fallen away. It was like a man coming out of his cell and discovering sunlight, and he played it with such pity for Gloucester. With the 'Birds i the cage' scene you felt the outpouring of love. But I thought he never quite cracked the opening scene, never summoned up a belief in his own majesty. He played the actor's game of authority, rather than believing he is all-powerful when he gives an order: he was *hoping* he would be obeyed, not *knowing* he would be.

West was delighted with the favourable response to the production. But he questioned the value for school children of being part of such an overwhelmingly young audience, arguing that they shouldn't be coming to the theatre simply to get help with their exams. 'It should also be an introduction to theatre-going, and that means seeing what it's like to sit for two and a half hours watching a play surrounded by adults whom you don't know.' Stanford had hoped for more mixed audiences, but felt the production had made an important impact. 'Tim's Lear had a big influence on young people. It was talked about for years afterwards, with people saying they had started going to the theatre because of seeing it.'

# Nonso Anozie
## *Declan Donellan*

*In 2002 Declan Donellan directed a production of the play for the RSC at the Swan theatre in Stratford, with a young cast headed by Nonso Anozie as King Lear. The production transferred to the Young Vic theatre in London, then toured in Spain, Italy and France.*

> I do think *King Lear* is about young people as well as the old. We get so involved with Lear and Gloucester, we sometimes don't look at what's happening to the younger characters.

The question of youth was at the heart of Declan Donellan's unusual production of *King Lear*, which he staged with a cast of 16 young actors fresh out of drama school. It was the first production under the banner of the newly formed RSC Academy, initiated by the theatre's artistic director Adrian Noble. Its aim was to give the actors intensive training in Shakespeare, and the chance to rehearse in depth and perform one of the plays. 'We held long and intensive auditions,' Donellan explains. 'Then we had a rehearsal period that was much longer than normal, with more work than usual on voice and the verse.'

As Lear he cast Nonso Anozie, a physically impressive young actor of Nigerian descent, aged twenty-three and standing six-foot six, and the only black actor in the cast. 'I thought Anozie was naturally brilliant; he went on to play Othello in our Cheek by Jowl production two years later, and has done very well since. He had the weight and the power you need for the part, which is important. He was like an oak tree.'

Donellan's inventive and irreverent productions, staged in partnership with Nick Ormerod for their Cheek by Jowl company, have included *Macbeth, The Winter's Tale, A Midsummer Night's Dream, Measure for Measure* and *The Tempest*, as well as celebrated all-male productions of *As You Like It* and *Twelfth Night*. He had long wanted to direct *King Lear*, drawn to it by its enormous themes.

> It's a very great play, an intense cosmic experience about life and death, the fear and contemplation of death. But it's also about the fact that perhaps there is nothing. The great theme of nothing rolls across the play like an enormous, dangerous cannon-ball on board a ship in a storm. It

brings us into contention with the idea that there might be no love, just oblivion, a cold void, which is an absolutely terrifying idea.

He brushes aside the question of whether there is any redemption in the play.

> A play is not about having redemption or not, it's about sharing with the audience an intense experience, asking them first of all to feel, and then perhaps to question. It's not the business of a play or an artist to bring us redemption; the idea is grotesque. It's for an artist to suggest a world of experience, and then we respond to it. It would be absolutely appalling if we started to think of Shakespeare as a redemptive writer, as if he was writing a terrible self-help book. It's a pretty bleak and unredemptive world in Lear. But I don't think for one instant Shakespeare is saying that's what the world is like, I think he's saying, *Is* this what the world is like?

Donellan's stripped-back production in the Swan was set in a modern world, the formal opening having the actors in Edwardian evening dress, the later scenes revealing a post-holocaust world, in which the hitherto bare stage was filled with upended furniture and a rusting tin bath. To emphasise his view that Lear is also about young people trying to understand their world, Donellan moved Edgar's final lines – ending 'The eldest hath borne most; we that are young / Shall never see so much, nor live so long' – to the beginning of the play, making it a prologue, and the rest of the play a flashback.

As always, he preferred to make use of the actors' ideas rather than start by imposing his own:

> You leave yourself open to what is provided by the actors in rehearsal, and then guide and discipline it. I see what's coming from them, and then use it; I'm absolutely dependent on their impulse. We had an American actor Edward Hogg playing the Fool, who was extremely good. He was rather thin and small, and he had his own dynamic with Anozie. It was complex and it was worked through, but it wasn't something that came as a result of my pre-conceived vision.

On stage he made no attempt to encourage the young actors to age up. 'Age was just a detail. Although Anozie was only twenty-three, you just had to believe that he was the father of those daughters. People do have imaginations. Of course you didn't have that recognition of those two old men in the Dover cliff scene, but you got other things.'

Anozie's arrogant, impulsive and self-adoring Lear was praised for his gravitas, though for some he remained even in his suffering a figure more to fear than to pity. The *Sunday Times* critic wrote of the storm scene that it was 'all the more harrowing for Lear's almost childlike fury and the way he declines into petulant, smiling madness'. Michael Billington welcomed a production that 'bursts with energy and innovation', one that 'strips the play of barnacled tradition and allows youth its head'.

For Donellan the play feels revolutionary, and always modern. 'Every time you read *King Lear* it's different. It also has the feeling of being written effortlessly, which is extraordinary. It's quite brilliant.'

# Paul Copley
## *Tim Crouch*

*In 2012 Tim Crouch directed a shortened version of* King Lear *as part of an RSC educational project. The production starred Paul Copley as Lear, and played in America as well as around the UK.*

'People said you can't do *King Lear* for eight-year-olds,' director Tim Crouch remembered.

> But it was invigorating to put it in front of an audience who had no prior knowledge or experience of it, and see them react spontaneously to the story. It was a complex challenge, but I think we succeeded in giving clarity to the colours and journey of the play. The young audiences certainly connected to it very quickly.

In 2012 he directed an 80-minute, stripped-down version of *King Lear* for the RSC's 'Young People's Shakespeare Project'. The production was aimed at bringing a live performance to children aged eight upwards, to families, and to young audiences with the least access to Shakespeare. It was seen in scores of schools and theatres around the UK, the venues ranging from school canteens to mainstream city theatres. The eight-strong company also took the play to America, where it was performed in Ohio and New York, and filmed for distribution to all New York City schools.

Paul Copley, who played Lear, recalled: 'It seemed to work really well, the eccentric granddad who was a bit of trouble, the various rivalries, the family squabbles which turned into something darker and deeper. The young kids in the UK were enthralled, and by the time we got to America you could hear a pin drop most of the time.'

Tim Crouch has no doubt about the play's greatness:

> For me *King Lear* is the play of all plays, because it has that profound streak of humanity in it, the revelation for Lear about how we are in the world. The Dover cliff scene is as near perfect an identification of what art can do in terms of taking someone to a point safely, and then have them discover something about themselves. And to hear Shakespeare

talking about injustice and privilege and wealth, and about reducing someone to the thing itself, is just mind-blowing.

With the young audiences in mind he decided to domesticate the play, and focus on the family relationships. Out went France, the battles, the politics – including the 'Poor naked wretches' speech – and much of the philosophy. He shortened some of Lear's longer speeches, including 'Blow winds', and cut Lear's curse on Goneril. 'The danger is that for a young audience Shakespeare can repeat himself. If you're moving a story along quickly, what you need to get from that scene is that he rejects Goneril emphatically. The true horror of condemning your child to sterility might not have the impact with eight-year-olds that it would have with adults.'

With only eight actors involved doubling was inevitable, including Edgar and Cornwall, and Gloucester and a Soldier. Most strikingly, Kent was conflated with the Fool: the actor took over the Fool's lines but kept Kent's persona. 'How do you square the circle of the Fool to a young audience who have no notion of an Elizabethan Fool?' Crouch asks. 'Both he and Kent have similar roles in pricking Lear's conscience, in trying to get him to see clearly. Then there's the unresolved mystery of the Fool's disappearance, and Kent's transformation into Caius. It was a way of resolving those difficulties.'

In casting Paul Copley as Lear he wanted to avoid having a raging, tyrannical king.

> Quite early on I had this image of a father losing his grip on his family as much as a monarch losing his grip on his country. In Paul I sensed a kind of vibrating delicacy, and a gentleness. He's a quality actor who has access to a twinkly domesticity, as well as to many other things. And even though he was bound by quite a domestic setting, he still managed to reach the emotional heights without our having to go into a mythical epic.

Since there was only a short rehearsal period, Crouch had to arrive on the first day with the text already radically cut to 80 minutes, and many decisions already made, including design ones. His basic idea was to set the play during the seven days between Christmas and the New Year.

> We talked a lot in rehearsal about families, about the patriarchs who at Christmas think their powers should be dominant, whereas the younger generation are organising everything, and trying to give grandfather a sense of authority which he no longer has. It's a time when emotions are much more extreme, when deep-seated resentments bubble to the surface, when inappropriate gifts are given, and the family falls out.

As the audience arrives a Christmas party is taking place: the actors are playing party games such as charades, and taking photos of each other, ad-libbing to themselves, but not to the audience. Lear arrives wearing a paper crown, and enters into the spirit of the occasion as a kind of genial Father Christmas, giving out presents. 'We wanted to keep it as light as possible, to keep his sense of playfulness until the moment when he turns,' Crouch explains.

> We wanted to be pulling back the bow for as long as we could, so you didn't know when the arrow was going to fly. I didn't want to telegraph the end of the play at the beginning. I didn't want the kids to think they were going to see a great Shakespearean tragedy, because that would present a block, and they would come with preconceptions.

Given the variety of venues the company were to play in, the set had to be simple. The basic floor covering was a rich-looking Persian carpet, which was gradually peeled back after the opening scene. The rest of the play was set not in a mythical heathland, but in an urban wilderness, complete with double yellow lines, and a drain in which Edgar found a set of dirty clothes to use for his Poor Tom disguise. The production had an unusual, ironic musical score using Christmas songs: the storm was accompanied by 'Let it Snow', the hovel scene had 'Silent Night' in the background, while during Gloucester's blinding 'Jingle Bells' was played. Crouch steered clear of showing the horrific deed naturalistically. 'You're in dangerous territory with violence and a young audience. I wanted to suggest what was happening by just having a knife raised, leaving them to complete the image in their minds.'

He also preferred not to be explicit about dementia.

> We needed to think about it to some degree, as part of the spur for Lear's irrationality in rejecting Cordelia. He doesn't think, his mind is not right at that time. But I didn't want Paul to play a man who was demented, because dementia comes in much more subtle hues. You either drop into cliché, which is past the stage of subtlety, or you keep this side of it, and let the audience try and work out how much this is an ageing process, and how much the character of a man still in his prime. The big discussion with Paul was Lear's culpability, deciding how aware he was of what he was doing, and how much of it was a discovery after the fact.

He used colour-blind casting, with a mixture of black, Asian and white actors.

> I wanted to disturb and challenge stereotypes. I was happy to have a black Gloucester, an Asian Edgar and a white Edmund, and not give a damn what colour their skin was. We were working in an art-form, and an art-form is in the realms of possibility, so you need to push what's

possible. I think it's imperative that if you're making work for a young audience, you show them a model of the world around them. Even if they are mono-cultural Warwickshire kids, I think it's incumbent on you to show them a diversity, to create an idea of a society that is multi-cultural.

Paul Copley believes the production held the young audiences for 90 per cent of the time.

'The other 10 per cent was in those schools which were less used to live performance. They weren't particularly misbehaving, it's that they weren't used to it, and if they didn't get particularly involved, it got a bit difficult. But that didn't happen very often. Quite a lot of the time the schools we thought would be the most difficult were the most involved.'

Tim Crouch echoes the point.

If you go to a well-heeled school in the UK the kids have been trained how to be a theatre audience, which is never a good thing. What you want as a theatre-maker is to hit an audience stripped of preconceptions, who can have a direct response to what they are seeing, unmediated by an idea about how they should respond. If you go to schools which have no history of this kind of visit, they are often the most remarkable, because they are coming completely fresh to the play. The only precon-ception we might have been battling against was, This might be boring.

The actors came from a range of backgrounds: Paul Copley was a Yorkshireman, Anna Bolton (Goneril) a Geordie, Tyrone Higgins (Gloucester) a Brummie, Matt Sutton (Kent) was from Hull, and Dharmesh Patel (Edgar and Cornwall) came from East London. Crouch was insistent that they keep their own accents. 'I think it would have been reprehensible to ask the company to neutralise their differences. It was a matter of challenging received pronunciation, of showing that the world is much more interesting and diverse than that.'

The actors deliberately made direct contact with the audience. When Edmund pretended he had been wounded by Edgar, Ben Deery came among them and invited someone to slap his face – which they did, to universal glee. When Edgar became Poor Tom he went into the audience and begged, holding out a paper cup. This prompted some in the young audience to see if they could find money to give him; in New York one youngster produced a dollar bill. But some of the reactions were unplanned. In New York, when Lear made his first entrance through the audience, a small child high-fived him. When Edmund wondered aloud which sister he should have, it often prompted the answer 'Both!' or on one occasion, 'The one in red!' And when he kissed one or other of the sisters it prompted hoots of derision, bringing the play momentarily to a stop.

Copley recalled the question and answer sessions:

> The kids would ask where the mother or mothers were. There was also a lot of interest in the rivalry between Edmund and Edgar. They wanted to know why Edmund was disenfranchised, since he was a human being too. That was especially the case in America, while in England it was more a question of, 'You said *bastard*! That's a rude word!'

The company had considerable support from the RSC: a verse specialist attended rehearsals, and there were movement sessions every day. Workshops for schools were run by the education department, and the company were encouraged to contribute ideas. 'We were very well supported,' Copley says. 'With such a heavy touring schedule you need all the help you can get to keep your vocal range going, and to keep it subtle.'

When the play reached the Nuffield in Southampton, Michael Coveney wrote: 'As an introduction to a masterpiece, this is a pretty good, robustly acted edition.' Crouch believes that, for the future of theatre, this kind of production is the most important Shakespeare that the RSC stages.

> If we don't take a young audience super-seriously then we are shooting ourselves in the foot. As audiences they don't lie to you: if they're not with you, you will know it. The sadness is that this kind of work is not treated as critically as work for adult audiences. It's often seen as a secondary thing: actors will often do young people's theatre because it will help them get other parts. They pay lip-service to young people's work, but they don't really mean it, they just see it as a necessary evil.

He remains satisfied with what his production achieved, and messianic about the value of Shakespeare.

> It was lovely when we punctured the rhetoric and the audience felt they were being spoken to. We're introducing an audience, many of whom have never seen or touched Shakespeare, to a strand of their cultural heritage. I wanted them to understand that how we understand human behaviour now is in some way connected to Shakespeare. We mustn't remove Shakespeare from their lives.

# 14

# For the Royal Shakespeare Company 3

## Corin Redgrave
### Bill Alexander

*In 2004 Corin Redgrave played Lear at Stratford, under the direction of Bill Alexander. The production subsequently moved to the Albery theatre (now the Noël Coward) in London.*

On the second day of the Stratford rehearsals, in a letter to Annie Castledine, a friend and experienced director with whom he shared his thoughts about the play, Corin Redgrave wrote:

> I think *King Lear* is a huge moral challenge to audience and actor. What kind of world do we want to live in? Who is responsible for suffering, poverty? Can we put it right? How? I don't find these questions exhilarating yet. Only daunting. There is so much to tell you about this part that it would already fill a notebook or two.

He confessed to doubts and fears as he prepared to take on the formidable role, which he had played in a radio version two years before:

> That feeling of exhilaration with which one launches oneself at a new job is beginning to ebb away, as it always does. Its place will be taken by humility, self-doubt, anxiety. No matter what our experience, we come naked and slightly ashamed into rehearsal, with the awful prospect of having to reach some sort of maturity in eight weeks, knowing that, just as in life, where maturity always seems round the next corner, one will never reach that promised land.

He had another, more personal reason for feeling anxious: 'Driving into Stratford past the Clopton Bridge yesterday, I was haunted by the memory that my father played Lear here fifty-one years ago. At the age of forty-five. Almost twenty years younger than I am.' Perhaps fortunately, all he could remember of Michael Redgrave's performance was his wig and costume, the cursing of his daughters, and his final entry carrying Cordelia.

Earlier he had admitted that the shadow cast by his father discouraged him from attempting the role while he was alive, and that he had recently agonised for a week over asking Michael Boyd, the RSC's artistic director, whether he could attempt the part. He confessed to a nagging self-doubt about whether he was up to it. 'I don't think I'm born to play it. It would be a lucky actor who felt that he was, and probably a rather wrong-headed actor.' He revealed that it was the only Shakespeare play which had reduced him to tears on reading it, and admitted, unfashionably, that he was greatly influenced by Donald Wolfit, whom he felt had the 'inspired self-confidence and simplicity and theatricality' to master the part.

He saw the play as 'modern, topical and relevant, because it so vividly portrays a country divided by an almost impossible fault-line between those who have enough and those who don't. Any attempt I make to build up an idea of Lear the man, Lear the ruler, is still very strongly influenced by that thinking.' This desire to explore the politics of the play resonated with director Bill Alexander who, reflecting on his production ten years later, suggests that *King Lear* is the most political of Shakespeare's tragedies.

> The play seems to me to be a picture of a man who has misunderstood the nature of power, who has not begun to understand that with kingship comes an intense responsibility to look after others under your care. As he moves through his madness, the revelations that come to him are mainly about the missed opportunity of power and authority. What he perceives he could do with that authority – for the needy, the unfortunate, the people whose lives he could have bettered – is part of what drives him mad, as much as if not more than the lack of love shown to him by his eldest daughters. I don't think these ideas came to me because Corin was very political, although that may have subconsciously influenced me. But that was certainly a way in which he would have access to the part, and that was why he was a very good Lear.

He and Redgrave worked along the same lines throughout rehearsals.

> We agreed on the basic idea of Lear as a man who had exercised power in a very unproductive way. A man who was morally, intellectually and spiritually short-sighted. A man who was patriarchal, who believed in automatic love regardless of desert. A man who, if he loved his daughters, loved them more as possessions than through any innate feeling of love. A man who was selfish, and very, very un-selfaware. That ties in with a central Shakespearean theme, of it being the first duty of men to know themselves, to try to understand themselves.

As Redgrave explained to Castledine, he was attracted to a play that could be 'a lesson and a warning to those in power', a play 'that dares to portray a real commonwealth in which "None does offend, none I say, none", a commonwealth that is a divinely inspired vision in the mind of a madman'. As he saw it, Lear experiences 'an ascent through a chaos of grief and pain into a self-understanding, and an understanding of power, government, and the corruption of absolute authority'. Writing not long after the invasion of Iraq, he added: 'I completely agree about the occupiers in Iraq. Perhaps our performance can convey the savagery of unrestrained power.'

Alexander has his own view of the play's political dimension:

> I don't believe that when Shakespeare puts such egalitarian sentiments into the mouths of Lear and Gloucester that there is any kind of proto-socialism there. I think the way of looking at the politics of it is through a very humanitarian analysis of what selfishness is doing to people, in the form of capitalism and the breaking down of old feudal certainties, and specifically the idea that the medieval church put out about the responsibility to share with the poor. I think Shakespeare is much more likely to be reacting against the depredations of wealth and selfishness than seeing any political possibility of egalitarian structures in his society.

The set for his production was a simple one, with scaffolding and a plain, half-destroyed brick wall at the back. 'We're aiming to create parallel worlds: the Victorian married with strange bits of technology,' the designer Tom Piper explained at the time. 'I wanted to include a broken element, to convey a sense of a world that could be in decay or on the edge of industrialisation.' The result was a cold, austere postwar world, set in the early twentieth century, with the actors dressed in glamorous evening dresses, frock coats, wing collars and military uniforms. 'The intention was to evoke the age of revolution, a period of political turmoil in Europe,' Alexander recalls.

He and Redgrave agreed there should be no suggestion that Lear was retiring because he was old and tired: this was a virile, vain Lear, younger than usual, and prone to childish mood swings. The idea was highlighted in performance at his first entry, when Redgrave appeared as a stooped figure, carrying a stick and accompanied by a nurse. Suddenly he straightened up, threw the stick away, and broke into a gleeful cackle at having convinced the court of his infirmity. 'It brought out the joker in him, a quality he shares with the Fool,' Alexander explains. 'He's in full possession of all his faculties; he just wants to get out there and have a good time while he's still up for hunting and fishing and drinking.'

They discussed the fact that, while Othello and Macbeth and Hamlet all have soliloquys, Lear has none. Alexander observes:

> The speech 'Blow winds' isn't a soliloquy, but a monologue. It doesn't have that essence of soliloquy, which is self-examination, and being a

different person by the end of the speech than you were in the beginning. That's vital, even if the movement is only marginal. With soliloquies the character is talking to himself, but through the audience. Lear doesn't have that; he has the Fool instead. I wanted a Fool who was a kind of parallel to him, a man exactly his own age, in order to emphasise that the Fool is his inner soliloquy, his conscience, the more receptive part that he has never developed.

He remembers that Redgrave struggled to handle the storm scene effectively – which may be part of the reason he lost his voice as early as the third week of rehearsal. 'However, it has taught me something,' he told Castledine. 'Having to save my voice, I also had to look for other ways of expressing Lear's anger, rage, longing for vengeance – other, that is, than vocal ways. And that has expanded my expressive vocabulary in some interesting directions.'

During rehearsals he used music as a stimulus to help him find the appropriate emotions for Lear's 'chaos of grief and pain': 'I am searching for the music which most expresses this for me,' he wrote to Castledine. 'During rehearsal I try to find the music which will become for me the theme for what I am acting. I think Lear's music might be Berlioz's *Harold in Italy*, or possibly Smetana's *Má Vlast*. The idea is to find a melody which will reinforce the mood you are creating.'

The production, which used a conflated text, lasted nearly four hours. The critics were divided about Redgrave's Lear. Charles Spencer criticised his lack of rage, seeing 'a man who has never grown up, a spoilt child' played without any 'sense of growing spiritual illumination'. John Gross found the production 'for the most part an impressive affair, marked by energy and clarity'; Redgrave's Lear he thought intelligently conceived, though he felt he failed to scale the heights. Paul Taylor was 'torn between admiration for, and misgivings about, Corin Redgrave's subtle, highly intelligent, but less than emotionally shattering performance', observing: 'Actors who are intellectuals have a problem with this role. This character thinks from the gut. He may become a wise man, but he's by no means a clever one. By-passing the brain is a tricky feat for brainy performers, but to communicate the elemental simplicity of some of the play's greatest moments, it has got to be pulled off.'

The director Bill Buckhurst recalled: 'I found his Lear terribly affecting. It made me engage with the darkness of the play at a deep level. I found it devastating. At the end, when he was trying to revive Cordelia with the kiss of life, it was so desperate.' Alexander summed up in similar terms:

With perhaps the exception of a few moments in the centre of the storm, I thought Corin's was a tremendous, immensely intelligent performance. He certainly got the emotional depths of the part. I believe emotion is in the text, not in the sound of the text; it's in the thought, not in the vocal elaboration of the thought. So I like to say to actors, 'I don't want to know what you're feeling, I want to know what you're thinking, and if I know that, then I will feel with you.' That's great acting. Scofield had that quality, and I think Corin also had it. That's why I loved working with him.

# Ian McKellen
## *Trevor Nunn*

*In 2007, as part of the RSC's Complete Works Festival, Trevor Nunn directed his third production of the play at Stratford, with Ian McKellen playing Lear in the temporary Courtyard theatre. The play then visited Newcastle, and toured to Singapore, Melbourne, Wellington and Auckland. In America it played in New York, Minneapolis and Los Angeles, before returning to the New London theatre in the West End.*

> Our own personal experiences are stirred and awakened by reading *King Lear*. You realise things about families, things about human behaviour, the regrettable aspects of human behaviour, and you perceive them not as academic propositions, but as things you have actually encountered in life, or in public events in your life.

Trevor Nunn once said that you have to stage *King Lear* three times before you get it right. It was now more than thirty years since he had directed Donald Sinden as Lear, and nearly forty since he had staged his first production, with Eric Porter playing the king. In staging the new production, which closed the RSC's Complete Works Festival, he saw the play as 'an investigation of the extremes of human nature, an inquiry into the nature of man', suggesting his life experience since those earlier productions could usefully inform this one: 'Shakespeare engaging with questions about mortality, and what we construct for ourselves either to explain or accept our mortality, speaks very potently to me now,' he observed.

Ian McKellen too was on his third *Lear*. Previously he had played Edgar in the 1973 Actors' Company production, when Robert Eddison had appeared as Lear; and Kent in Deborah Warner's 1990 version at the National Theatre, which had Brian Cox in the title-role. He and Nunn – old friends from university days at Cambridge – had already worked together on acclaimed productions of *Macbeth* and *Othello* (McKellen was Macbeth and Iago), and had vowed that if either of them were to be offered *King Lear* again, they would insist on the other one joining them.

As rehearsals approached McKellen, now sixty-seven, expressed anxiety about one aspect of his part:

It's bothering me that Lear doesn't seem to have any soliloquies, any more than Othello does. It's interesting that in *Othello* the villain is the only one who talks to the audience. No wonder everyone likes Iago. A soliloquy is the most wonderful release an actor can have. There's an immediacy about it, which I think should always contain the possibility of the slight pause, the question mark, the raised eyebrow, inviting the audience to give their response.

It was Nunn's practice with Shakespeare to come to the first rehearsal with his concept fully worked out, enabling him to spend the next weeks working on the detail with the actors. The first step, he suggested, was to uncover the theme. 'If you're a director you must X-ray the play, to find out what its bone structure is and where its vital organs are. A production shouldn't work from the outside, it must proceed from a sense of what the internal structure is, and thereby discover how everything contained in the play is meaningful because it is contiguous to that thematic structure.' He added: 'In the case of *Lear*, it being one of the greatest plays of Shakespeare's maturity, the investigation is not going to be easy, and the wellspring is not going to lie very close to the surface.'

He began by talking about Shakespeare's verse and the iambic pentameter. To show how his verse evolved he asked the actors to read aloud extracts from early drama through to Shakespeare, using the Shepherd's Play from the *Wakefield Cycle*, the early Elizabethan play *Gorboduc*, and then Shakespeare's *Henry VI Part I*. Implicitly rejecting the approach favoured by Peter Hall and John Barton, he advised the actors just to follow the verse and the sense would take care of itself. In his work on the verse he favoured exploring the sonnets, believing their 'highly organised, compressed speech presents every possible language problem, breathing problem and technical problem to the actor'.

After reading and discussing the text, he instituted what he called 'a fun day'. He paired the actors off and asked them to tell fairy stories to each other, encouraging them to listen simultaneously to the other person's story in order to increase their concentration. He then formed them into groups, and made them improvise situations, in which they had to display emotions such as being shipwrecked, missing the last train home, or gate-crashing a party.

One of his acknowledged skills as a director was his ability to develop the smaller parts in rehearsal, a tendency noted on this occasion by David Weston, playing the Gentleman: 'Trevor gives his full attention to even the smallest part and the least important scene, and strives to give them substance. For instance he made it clear that Burgundy and Cordelia were in some sort of romance before the play started, which made his rejection of her when he discovers she has no dowry even crueller.'

As someone who had directed *Hamlet* several times, Nunn mused on Shakespeare's state of mind when he came to write *King Lear* seven years later:

Why was Shakespeare drawn to the subject of madness again? Was there anything going on in his life to explain why? I do feel he's passed from one stage of life to another. I think of that sonnet 'Tired with all these for restful death I cry.' Was the composition of that extraordinary catalogue of life's disappointments in any way contemporaneous with *Lear*? How much despair was Shakespeare in about the world he saw around him?

For McKellen, the fact that the play didn't throw any light on Lear's past was frustrating:

As an actor that won't do: you have to imagine a back story if you're going to believe in a character. I assumed he had two wives, so I wear two wedding rings. One wife gave him the two elder sisters, of a certain character that was visited on them in some way. What happened to her? Maybe she died, maybe she was put to death, or maybe they got divorced? And then there was another wife, perhaps the love of his life, who gave him Cordelia. I assumed that she died in childbirth, and he brought up Cordelia himself, and therefore loves her most.

Like others who had played Lear, he was able to draw on his own family background in trying to capture Lear's disintegration:

As the play proceeds he is less fitted to understanding what's going on and being able to retain his firmness of purpose, because he is old and decrepit. I think we can all relate to that. Before we started rehearsing, my step-mother died at the age of a hundred. I'd seen her decline mentally as well as physically, but not emotionally. Her emotions were in fine fettle; indeed her interest in the world was as alert as it has ever been.

Nunn chose to give the production a Russian-style flavour, setting it round about the time of the Romanov dynasty. The nobles wore Tsarist uniforms, with Lear dressed in scarlet, the others in black and silver, while the daughters wore ball gowns at the start. Lear's knights, played as crazy drunken Cossacks, were decked out in fur hats and greatcoats. The initial grandeur provided a stark contrast to Lear's later appearance on the heath, when McKellen – as he had done when playing Edgar earlier – removed all his clothes, to become 'unaccommodated man.'

Presenting a priest-like, self-important Lear on his first entrance, McKellen arrived at the head of a stately procession to a flourish of organ chords, dressed in gold and blessing the courtiers, who fell to their knees in worship. The opening scene was staged as a family gathering in the royal library, with Lear reading a prepared speech about the division of his kingdom. The idea of setting up a love test for his daughters seems to have come to him on the spur of the moment, and he treats it in a jovial manner, approving smilingly at Goneril's and Regan's efforts to please him, until Cordelia's refusal to do so unleashes his fury.

Since the main Stratford theatre was being re-built, the production was staged in the temporary Courtyard theatre, built down the road next to The Other Place. McKellen's Lear was mostly warmly greeted: Benedict Nightingale thought his performance 'showed the complexity of a humiliated, angry, vulnerable man', Kate Bassett described it as 'psychologically complex, heartrendingly poignant, and free of mannerisms', while Charles Spencer applauded the actor's 'grace, simplicity, and emotional candour'. But although Tim Walker described his performance as 'a breathtaking tour de force', he concluded: 'Not for a moment did I believe I was watching Lear. I was watching McKellen as Lear.'

Spencer thought the production 'one of the most powerful, lucid and moving I have ever seen'. John Peter felt it ranked with Nunn's best work: 'Nunn's genius as a director is in his handling of characters. He can find their deepest urges, secrets and confused ambitions.' But other reviewers were critical of his staging: Paul Taylor thought it 'technically very resourceful, but fussy and unfelt', Susannah Clapp suggested it had 'too many aural effects – dogs, horses, birds', and Bassett wrote: 'The production does have its weaknesses. Nunn's use of swelling orchestral music – like a cinematic soundtrack – is obtrusive and sometimes cheesy.' Tim Pigott-Smith criticised another decision: 'They hanged the Fool in the scene before the blinding. That was a daft thing to do. There's the one scene of insane violence, and before it you put another scene of violence, in which nobody speaks. It was disastrous, and completely undermined the power of the blinding.'

In director Michael Grandage's view, 'Ian McKellen's Lear was semi-successful, but he should have performed it in a small space. He's not a natural big-space performer, and he became a bit too bombastic for my taste.' Perhaps he might do so, for after playing Lear for a year, McKellen suggested he might return to the part one day: 'When it ended I felt some regret as well as relief. I was enjoying it so much I wanted to continue; I felt there was a further distance I could go. You can never mine these parts deeply enough, there are always more jewels to be uncovered.'

*In 2008 a filmed version of the production was made, directed by Trevor Nunn and Chris Hunt.*

# Greg Hicks
## *David Farr*

*Greg Hicks played the king at Stratford in 2010, in a production staged first in the Courtyard theatre, and directed by David Farr. It moved to Newcastle, and in 2011 played in the Roundhouse in London. It then opened the transformed Royal Shakespeare Theatre in Stratford before visiting the Lincoln Centre in New York.*

Lear is a bit like the Pacific Ocean – the more you plummet, the more you find there's another depth to plummet. There was always another thousand feet to go when I played him.

Greg Hicks had severe doubts about his suitability for the part.

I'm not an obvious Lear, and I knew that at the time. I was nearly 57, which technically was quite young for Lear, and my sensibility as an actor made me not an obvious choice. The first time in rehearsal I got up to enter in that opening scene, I took probably the deepest breath I've ever taken. With Leontes in *The Winter's Tale* there's more of a feeling of a journey of reconciliation and spiritual education, whereas Lear is simply unfathomable. So I had a lot of self-doubt. But the more I read about it, the more I understood that most actors who tackle the part felt that way.

He and David Farr already had a strong relationship, having previously worked together when Hicks tackled hugely demanding roles such as Coriolanus, Leontes and Tamburlaine. 'Greg works off self-doubt,' Farr says. 'That's how he is. When you get to know him you realise that's deep in him. I think fundamentally it's rather a useful part of an actor's psyche. But he's fiercely intelligent, and once he starts working all that goes away. He's one of those actors who just needs to start, and not think about it too much.'

As part of his research Hicks watched two film versions of the play, Kurosawa's *Ran* and Peter Brook's re-working of his stage production, with Scofield as Lear. 'I thought Brook's movie masterful, and Scofield had those great qualities of pain and majesty. I used those films as my point of reference.' The many writings on the character he found less useful. 'I read a lot of them, but everybody had such strong things to say about Lear, my head started to explode with possibilities. So I stopped.'

Farr's industrial-style setting in the Courtyard, a barn-like space with a metal and wood structure, was like a semi-derelict warehouse. The production was deliberately anachronistic, mixing sizzling striplights, skewed girders, medieval religious chants and first world war soldiers. 'I surprised myself by deciding to embrace the historical more than I thought I would. My first instinct was to make it modern, but then I thought the play needed a poetic world of its own, a tension between old and new to release its enormity and its extremity.'

He was confident that Hicks would be comfortable with this approach.

The more extreme the situation the more relaxed as an actor he becomes, which is a useful counterpoint. As a director you don't have to reach too hard or with much effort to be in these places with him. I knew the ferocity he was capable of, and that he wasn't afraid of being hostile and unpleasant and unpopular. I also knew he had the physical and vocal and emotional stamina required.

Hicks struggled to get Lear sufficiently aged, despite making use of his ninety-nine-year-old father as a model. 'A lot of his emotional, spiritual and visceral shapes were there. But I had a movement teacher who was constantly on my back in rehearsals, saying I still looked like fifty-seven, instead of eighty something. Frankly after a while I forgot about it, and there were times when I was jumping about when I clearly wasn't that age.'
Unlike other Lears he found the first half easier than the second.

Those earlier scenes with the daughters were rock and roll: I felt I was on fire, I felt in command. But as the play progressed I found it more and more difficult. I certainly never got the last few moments right, including the reconciliation with Cordelia; I couldn't find the unfathomable depth of lines like 'You do me wrong ...'. Also those last scenes all happen in such a telescoped way, there's a problem to keep a narrative line on it. The leap between going to prison and coming back and saying 'Howl! Howl! Howl!' is very difficult to capture, without being sentimental or overdoing it.

His Fool was played by Kathryn Hunter, a bold but easy casting decision for Farr.

She had played a clown a lot in her work with Complicite. I'd long been an admirer; she's a fabulous performer, and totally unique. I thought the gender thing would be fascinating. Kathryn didn't play the part as male or female, but as deliberately androgynous. She was really wonderful, very eerie with a kind of melancholy mischief. At their best Greg and Kathryn produced a tenderness that really was quite beautiful amidst the mayhem. Her sense of loss in relation to him was profound, and was probably one of the hallmarks of the piece.

Hunter herself had a novel take on the Fool's relationship with Lear. 'From the beginning we agreed that it was based on love and kinship. I once played an autistic child who was very verbal. So the whole rhyming/riddle element came from that. Those big truths couched in little songs seemed quite near to a child-like sensibility, so I imagined him about twelve, with a gift of insight.' There was, however, an initial problem.

When we first started rehearsing I found it unbearable, because I had once played Lear, I knew all his lines, and I didn't think I could cope. Then one of the actors said, Why don't you use it, you know him so well, you know what he's thinking. So I did. I just imagined that he had such a high degree of sensitivity that he knew exactly where Lear was coming from. It became a positive thing.

The critics admired her performance: Michael Billington thought her outstanding in her 'sad-eyed, watchful concern', while Charles Spencer described her as 'deeply touching as a tiny Fool whose face is etched with unbearable sorrow at Lear's plight'. Hicks' Lear was mostly liked: Benedict Nightingale decided he was 'stern and scary, so his decline was more disturbing than usual', while Michael Coveney declared it to be 'as total and powerful a performance as was his Coriolanus for the same director'. Charles Spencer was less taken with it, arguing: 'He is a brilliant speaker of Shakespearean verse, but his acting often seems to be all technique and no heart. He lacks grandeur, though not vitriol, in the great scenes of anger, and there is surprisingly little pathos in his anguish.'

There were mixed feelings too about the production. According to Claire Steele: 'David Farr's production is a masterpiece of theatrical fluency … gripping, inventive and assured'; the *Independent on Sunday* critic decided it was 'fantastical, comical and heartbreaking'. But Spencer was again critical, calling it an 'irritating and stubbornly unmoving new production' marked by 'a bumper box of theatrical tricks'. The director Tim Crouch was also unhappy: 'I had not seen an RSC production for over ten years, and nothing much had changed. There were still a lot of supernumaries, a lot of RSC acting, people standing with nothing to say with their legs slightly apart. There were all the classic signifiers – men in great big coats, a wild boar, an abstract heath.'

Farr himself feels he fell short with the Gloucester sub-plot. 'I find that business of the bad brother and the good brother not very interesting. My focus wasn't enough on them. I could have concentrated more on Edmund: it was ridiculous not to, there's so much in his part, and the whole Iago-style plot.' But he was more than happy with Hicks' Lear. 'I think Greg was at his peak in the mad scene on the heath, where he was transcendent. I never felt he was pushing playing irrational, vain or eccentric or any of these words; he was just being.'

Hicks himself concluded: 'It's an impossible play, which is why it's worth attempting. I'd love to have another go at it in a few years. Perhaps when I'm seventy would be a good time?'

# 15

# In Smaller Spaces

## Robert Demeger
### *Deborah Warner*

*In 1985 Deborah Warner staged a production of the play in Edinburgh for her Kick Theatre company, with the king being played by Robert Demeger. It moved to the Almeida theatre in London before embarking on a six-week tour of the former Yugoslavia.*

> We were in reaction against what had gone before. People felt they were being given something incredibly close and deliciously raw, clean and clear and not declaimed.

During the 1985 Edinburgh Fringe festival, Deborah Warner and a group of young actors staged a stripped-down production of *King Lear* in a church hall. The set consisted of three step-ladders against a bare brick back wall; the only props were buckets of water for use during the storm scene, and a cart; the actors all wore neutral white shirts and trousers. The bareness of the production was born of necessity.

> We were about the actor and the text, and nothing else. We didn't have any money, any sets or any breakfast. We were a group that came out of Thatcher's Britain and the cuts to theatre. Kick was run on principles that appealed to actors. We were a true ensemble, and unpaid; people would give up their summer holidays to work on the productions.

She suggests her production had an impact because regional theatres no longer had room for Shakespeare, and a fringe company wouldn't normally put on a big play such as *Lear*. Its iconoclastic nature gained it glowing reviews: John Peter called it 'the keenest and most exhilarating clarification of the text since Peter Brook's production'. It changed the fortunes of Kick Theatre which Warner, aged twenty-one and then a stage manager, had set up five years earlier, with the aim of exploring the classics. By this time she had already staged *Measure for Measure* and *The Tempest*, as well as Büchner's *Wozzeck* and Brecht's *The Good Person of Sichuan*, and after *King Lear* would move on to *Coriolanus*, before Kick was disbanded in 1986, and she moved on to the RSC.

She saw *King Lear* as the ultimate Shakespeare play:

> What it does is take the audience into the interior of themselves. It's a mirror of the desolation of the human spirit, how lost it is, how far we fall in families, and how hard sought are the conditions that prompt personal change. As a young director, I was conscious of the far reach the play required, that there might be older actors playing Lear who would think, This is a very young director; what does she know about what it's like to be over fifty? That was the relationship that I had to it.

It was during her production of *Wozzeck* that she began using a rehearsal method that she still practises today.

> I would make the first week entirely a preparation one. There was no staging as such: we would read the play every day, and I would get all the actors to play parts other than their own. So for *Lear* Robert Demeger would start in a small role, perhaps one of the knights, while the actors playing tiny parts would take on the big roles. I made sure that at the penultimate reading Robert would read the Fool, and the Fool read Lear, so they got closer and closer to the real thing. It's a wonderful way of getting to know the text really well: if someone reads your role with intelligence it gives you a wealth of ideas.

Once the actors resumed their own roles she would ask them to paraphrase their lines, to translate them into modern English. 'I felt that was an essential part of the discipline. At one level it was all about bringing the company together, but it was also about getting them to understand the material, to really excavate and dig deeply.'

Lear was played by Robert Demeger, a former teacher, and at thirty-four the oldest member of the company. He had already played the Duke in *Measure for Measure* and Prospero, and it was he who suggested they tackle *Lear*. 'He was always playing above his age,' Warner recalls.

> He was hugely enthusiastic, and he thought he could manage the part. He was quirky, idiosyncratic, warm-hearted and sensitive. He was one of the first to go naked on the heath; that was his suggestion. Stamina is obviously an issue with the role, but he had huge energy. He also discovered for me Lear's playfulness. There was something

very delicious about having a relatively young actor play the part, and you didn't doubt his age for one moment. He was a very good Lear.

The Fool was played by a young disabled actress, Hilary Townley. Because she was unable to walk she was pushed around in a little cart by Demeger, carried through the heath scene, and then dumped and left in a corner when Lear goes off with Poor Tom. Warner often doubled parts in her productions, again out of necessity, but also in order to give good roles to the women in the company. In *Lear* she had Townley double as the Fool and Cordelia. 'I do think it was ever thus, that they did this in Shakespeare's day. It's very good when you do it, and you don't have to decide whether Lear is referring to the Fool or Cordelia when he says at the end "And my poor fool is hanged", because it's the same person.'

Her characteristically minimalist production required the audience to make full use of their imaginations, especially when it came to the storm scene. 'It began by everybody collectively putting their head in a bucket onstage, so that they were absolutely soaked. Robert was at the top of the step-ladder, with everybody else cowering underneath, and water pouring through on to them. I always thought it was very close to what I imagined they did in Shakespeare's time. It really worked.'

Her austere stagings of Shakespeare were much influenced by the work of Peter Brook.

He was a huge spur for my decision to become a director. The most seminal work of his that I saw was his production of *A Midsummer Night's Dream*, although I was only nine at the time. But later at the Bouffes du Nord in Paris I saw *The Cherry Orchard* and *Ubu Roi*. And his film of *Lear* was an inspiration; it had such immediacy.

Her first version of the play had a significant influence on her production at the National Theatre five years later.

I went there with a little suitcase marked Kick, with things in it that I hugely valued from that time. I think I was closer to the heart of the play with that production than with the later one. Of course the Kick cast weren't as magnificent as the actors at the National, and the subtleties and the complexities of the text probably flew. But I think that first, innocent approach, with young actors passionate to have a go at it, was closer to the engine that makes the play work.

*The production won a Time Out Theatre Award and a Drama Magazine Special Achievement Award. Deborah Warner directed the play again at the National Theatre in 1990 (see page 222).*

# Tom Wilkinson
## *Max Stafford-Clark*

*In 1993 Max Stafford-Clark staged* King Lear *at the Royal Court in London, where he was artistic director. The part of the king was played by Tom Wilkinson.*

> The key thing about a classic is that you have to have something to say about it. I was remarkably cheeky in starting rehearsals not absolutely certain what I wanted to say, and finding out as we went along.

If twenty years later Stafford-Clark was recalling accurately his initial approach to the play, there was certainly no doubt about the direction it had taken by the time it reached the tiny stage of the Royal Court. His provocative and challenging production, in line with the radical spirit of much of his work at the Court, focused squarely on the political elements of the play, highlighting the disintegration of the state as a result of Lear's behaviour.

The final act provided images of the kind of torment and strife then taking place in the civil war in Bosnia. To the sound of artillery fire, groups of fleeing refugees were shown seeking shelter from the battle in the middle of a shattered, barbed-wire city. Pursued by soldiers with automatic weapons, clutching a ghetto-blaster or a bicycle, their mattresses and other possessions stuffed into supermarket trolleys, they scuttled across the stage, desperate to avoid the explosions that took out chunks of the set's brickwork. At the end of the play two grave-diggers shovelled up mounds of earth, in preparation for burying the corpses of Lear and Cordelia. 'You always want to have an image that resonates with the play and takes it into present consciousness,' Stafford-Clark says.

He initially talked to Alec Guinness about playing the part, but he declined. It subsequently seemed like a wise decision, since Bill Gaskill, who had once directed Guinness in *Macbeth*, told Stafford-Clark 'Alec can't shout' – which would seem to be a minimum requirement for anyone playing Lear. Eventually he offered the role to Tom Wilkinson, whom he had previously directed in *Tom and Viv*. 'You needed a heavyweight actor, and I thought Tom had the right kind of gravity and purpose. I knew of course that at forty-four he was far too young for the part, but I felt that he had the range, and also the necessary energy, which is important. But rather than try to play him as seventy, he hit the mid-fifties.'

Wilkinson too was worried about his relative youth, but was also concerned with one of the central problems with Lear. 'I used to think the play was imponderable, because I thought you couldn't be moved by a character for whom you had nothing but contempt,' he said. 'But my job is to find his point of view.' Once he began exploring the character in rehearsal he felt more comfortable with the play, even to the extent of down-playing its difficulties.

> You just have to shake off the sense of fear. Some actors go, 'Oh the Everest', but it's not that bad. It's probably a bit tiring, but in terms of the problems to solve it's not that difficult. The text is so dynamic that once you've stepped on board, it's going to take you where it needs to go. It's incredibly forceful and if you act what's written, you don't have to add anything.

Stafford-Clark gave the beginning of the play an Edwardian setting. Inspired by the title character in Powell and Pressburger's film *The Life and Death of Colonel Blimp*, and the image of first world war generals such as Sir John French, he and Wilkinson created a ruddy-faced Edwardian squire, a Lear dressed in a riding coat, breeches and boots, with beetling eyebrows, a walrus moustache and a monocle. The court was a militaristic and predominantly male, public-school one, with more than a whiff of a gentleman's club: at the beginning of the play Kent and Gloucester take a pee in the gents' toilets while discussing the fun the latter had at Edmund's conception.

During rehearsals Wilkinson acknowledged the radical nature of the production: 'We're taking the play apart, spreading it over the carpet, washing it out with petrol, and putting it all back together again.' Unlike some other actors, he was opposed to the idea of the love test being just a game on Lear's part. 'That idea doesn't work; this is no game for him. Audacity, directness and courage are what have kept him in power, not deviousness or *realpolitik*.' A father of young children himself, he expressed anxiety about how he might conjure up Lear's state of mind when he carries in the dead Cordelia. 'There are areas you have to be very careful about. I don't want to do it, but maybe for just one rehearsal I have to see Cordelia as my little girl, and find out whether that can be useful.'

In preparing his production Stafford-Clark took advice from several people. They included Jonathan Miller, who had already directed the play four times, and the actor Norman Rodway, who had played both Gloucester and Edmund twice. For the question of Lear's sanity or otherwise he consulted his father David Stafford-Clark, an eminent psychiatrist and author of the best-selling *Psychiatry Today*. 'My father was very helpful. We talked about cognitive decline of one kind or another, what state Lear was in, and the nature of his arbitrary decisions. We discussed the element of eccentricity. How much is it eccentricity, how much is it cognitive decline or senile dementia, and how much is it madness?'

One of the more original features of his production was Andy Serkis' startling Fool. Played as a camp drag queen, a ukulele-playing jester in a shimmering satin frock and sheer black stockings with a bouffant hairdo, his voice switched from a feminine falsetto to ordinary cockney whenever he was moved by Lear's situation. He kissed Kent on the mouth, and indulged in mocking games with Lear, bending him over, pretending to spank him with a whip, and bugger him to the cheers of the knights. 'Andy was a very inventive actor,' Stafford-Clark recalls. 'I gave him the idea that the Fool was Lear's acceptable child, and he took it a little further.' Goneril's anger was seen to be more than justified by this and other incidents taking place in this atmosphere of an officers' mess. These included Lear goosing a serving-maid while she was setting the dinner table, and his delight when Oswald was kicked in the groin and his mouth stuffed with butter by two of the rioting knights.

Controversially, the Fool did not simply fade out of the action after his final line 'And I'll go to bed at noon'. Instead he reappeared in Act 5, wandering around Dover, uttering lines either not his own or moved from earlier in the play. He sprayed a graffiti on the back wall that read 'What a piece of ...', leaving it open as to whether the quotation should end 'work is a man' or 'rubbish'. For this subversive act he was hanged by the soldiers, his corpse dangling in a noose on the back wall, giving an extra resonance to Lear's 'And my poor Fool is hanged'. Stafford-Clark, who remarked at the time that he 'would have asked Shakespeare for a few rewrites if he were around today', describes this decision about the Fool's fate as 'a little bit of re-editing'. He considered cutting some of Lear's lines from the Dover cliff scene, but decided against doing so. In fact he cut little: 'I probably should have cut more of Poor Tom's lines, as it's hard to make any sense of them.'

Like other directors he found the storm on the heath problematic. 'It's an incredibly difficult scene, and I don't think I got it right. I had people up in what is now the extension of the dress circle in the Royal Court, spraying water down on to the stage. The actors certainly did get wet, but I dealt with it rather unimaginatively.' He was, however, pleased with the blinding of Gloucester, a notably ghastly staging during which one of his eyes, consisting of a piece of chewed Turkish Delight, was flung against the back wall, and sometimes stuck there. 'A woman fainted one night, which was very satisfactory,' he remembers.

In general the critics welcomed his production. Michael Coveney described it as 'invigorating, challenging; each scene is surely staged, and richly considered', while Charles Spencer thought it 'blessed with a clarity and emotional intensity that reach to the heart of Shakespeare's greatest play'. But Paul Taylor was not happy with the Bosnia references, feeling that 'these tremors of contemporaneity are sounded at the expense of the Edwardian context, and aren't easy to defend against cynics who will say they represent radical chic rather than a radical new look at the play's political horrors'. Peter Holland likewise felt that such images were 'intrusions into the production's play-world, over-emphatic additions to make a point more superficially than the resonances created elsewhere'.

Wilkinson's performance attracted mixed notices. Some critics felt he missed both the grandeur and the pathos of the part, and were unmoved by the end; Michael Billington decided he was 'good at the bullying, patriarchal coarseness, but fails to give us Lear's mental turbulence'. But for Spencer, 'His superb performance in the title role digs deep into the dark core of the drama. He's a great bear of a man, and his awesome rages are both terrifying and strangely moving ... His fear of madness is presented with heartbreaking simplicity.' Taylor was more limited in his praise: 'Tom Wilkinson was never going to convince you he was an infirm octogenarian. Some of the extremities of the role are, consequently, beyond his reach. Within a slightly constricted range, though, he is very impressive, especially in the hushed fervour with which he gives voice to a late-flowering recognition of social injustice.'

Stafford-Clark too admired Wilkinson's playing, though with one qualification. 'He made a good fist of it, and he was very clear. But because I set the play in Edwardian times I think the element of kingliness and the divine right of kings idea was missing; we rather shuffled that one off. Within those limitations, however, I think he was absolutely terrific.'

In 2006 Stafford-Clark had a stroke and was in hospital for six months. The experience, he says, would certainly have a bearing on any future production of *King Lear* he might undertake. Referring to a number of weird decisions he made during that difficult time, he observed: 'It reinforced my view that Lear had been in some form of cognitive decline. So if I were doing the play now I would take more specific decisions about his medical history.'

# Oliver Cotton
## *Jack Shepherd*

*In 1996 Oliver Cotton played King Lear in the Southwark Playhouse in London, in a production directed by the actor and playwright Jack Shepherd.*

For the first three quarters of the play we held the audience absolutely. We lost it at the very end, when it became extremely fragmented. We were struggling to show the catastrophe, the breakdown in society. In a small theatre you can only hint at that.

Jack Shepherd talks honestly about the limitations of staging *King Lear* in a venue such as the Southwark Playhouse. The tiny London theatre has a very restricted acting space, with just one tiny dressing-room for the twelve actors. So he inevitably concentrated on the domestic scenes and the dysfunctional relationships within the Lear and Gloucester families.

For most of the play you have a domestic tragedy, which breaks out of the palace where Lear lives and goes into the wilds. But then the scale of it suddenly shifts in the last quarter. If you look very carefully at the text it seems gratuitous after the intensity of the first two and a half hours. From Gloucester's jump off the cliff onwards it goes haywire. The playwright in me thinks that Shakespeare is suddenly having to force it into the formula of the time, in order to satisfy whoever was going to put the play on; to make it a revenge tragedy, to fit the bill at the time, he has to have the fight between the two brothers. And then it develops into a play about revolution and anarchy, which is not very easy to show in a small theatre. You can't show that Panavision version; all you can show well is the intense psychology.

The confined space and minimal budget had other consequences. The actors worked on a bare stage, with just tables and chairs as props. The costumes were modern, as no period ones could be afforded; nor did the budget allow for any extras, so Lear's knights were heard but not seen. The lighting was bright throughout, with no special effects. There was no wind machine for the storm scene, nor any recorded music or sound effects, but simply flashing light and noise made by the actors with bits and pieces of stage machinery. 'The Fool was hanging on to Lear's coat-tails,' Shepherd recalls, 'and we were imagining this maelstrom of weather around them. It was actually very effective. I rather liked having to put the play on with what you've got, without recourse to electronic backup.'

As with his other Shakespeare productions – which included *Macbeth* and *The Two Gentlemen of Verona* – he was keen to look at the text without preconceptions. 'I wanted to see the play for what it is, and not pay any attention to the world that's grown up around it, to avoid the clichés which are like barnacles stuck on the keel of a ship.' He set up a series of workshops with the actors to examine the play in detail.

> We went through it scene by scene, improvising around what the scene is suggesting, to try to find a way in. Sometimes with a piece that's written four hundred years ago there isn't a way in to what's happening; it seems remote, the language seems remote. It's a matter of finding the way in, so the audience can understand the social resonance of what's happening, and not feel alien to it.

He used improvisation to explore subjects like old age, homelessness, and the parent–child relationships.

> We looked intensively at the psychological nature of each family, what had happened to the mother, what had happened to the children who had grown up without a mother's influence. An improvisation might take place in a high-rise flat with a middle-class family, using the idea that the father is going to get Alzheimer's and become utterly dependent on other people, and seeing how people react to it.

He did similar work during rehearsals for the actual production, as Rebecca Lenkiewicz, playing various small parts, recalls. 'We explored psychosis and old age and mental breakdown with Jack. It was incredibly intense. We would improvise every scene at length before we tried to tackle the language in any way. Jack stressed that there was no need to speak in an improvisation, we could simply watch or just "be". It was so freeing.'

Like other actors, Oliver Cotton found Lear's opening scene difficult. 'The entire play depends on what happens there, and I've very rarely seen it work. There's so much information and emotion, and too much surprise to understand what is happening if you are seeing the play for the first time. If that first scene didn't work I found the rest of the play tough.' Aged fifty-two, he decided to play Lear considerably older. 'It's no use saying Lear is making it up when he says he is four score and upward. He's eighty years old, and you have to believe him. I didn't use any special make-up, it was more of a behavioural change. I decided he had a circulatory problem, and a slight Parkinson's shake.' He saw him as a man unable to be in touch with his own feelings. 'There's something very strange about his horror of sexuality. The madder he gets the more the imagery is sexual. He's obviously got very real passions underneath, which have been suppressed.'

He found acting in a tiny space a mixed blessing. 'It was not an easy one to play in: if you took one step to the right you'd covered a mile. So everything depended on the language.' Yet for some scenes he felt the limitation was beneficial. 'I suggested that in the scene in Goneril's house where Lear demands supper, the meal should be brought in. So the Fool and I sat on chairs, eating it like two old men, while the Fool scolded Lear about his foolish behaviour. It was a very domestic scene, which suddenly became very playable and immediate.' Jack Bywater, who played the Fool, was roughly the same age as Cotton, and played him as a seedy, has-been comedian. As Shepherd saw it: 'He had been a music-hall comedian that Lear had seen at some show and found hilarious, so he had him living in a bedroom at the top of the house.'

Actor and director were old friends from their drama-school days, and knew each other well. According to Shepherd, this meant they could talk freely to each other during rehearsals. There were a couple of disagreements, the most disappointing for Shepherd relating to the storm scene.

I knew that as a student Oliver was quite obsessed with Beckett and the despair of his characters. With *Lear*, I started thinking there's no point in having him standing in the middle of the stage in a howling storm shaking his fist at the sky in such a tiny theatre. So I said, 'Why don't you do it like a Beckett character, up a back street somewhere, like a tramp muttering a private monologue?' And it worked beautifully. But his heart wasn't in it, and with two days to go he said to me: 'The audience will be expecting me to emote at that point, and I can't let them down.' I was very reluctant to let go, but I had to in the end, because it would otherwise have badly affected his confidence. It was completely understandable, but it showed how powerful the pre-conception of Lear is: the actor feeling that if he denies them that moment, he's denied them part of the play.

Otherwise he was extremely impressed by Cotton's Lear. 'Oliver took the audience by the hand, and guided them through this harrowing experience. He was dynamic at the beginning, you saw the commander, before he disintegrated into insanity. I thought he was absolutely brilliant.' Cotton himself looks back at his performance with some satisfaction, but also a certain amount of frustration. 'Few actors get the part completely right. I got some of it right, but certainly not all of it. I don't think I ever quite got the mock trial right. I found Lear so interesting, but also very elusive. I'd like to have another crack at him in a bigger space.'

# Oliver Ford Davies
## *Jonathan Kent*

*In 2002 Oliver Ford Davies played King Lear in Jonathan Kent's production at the Almeida theatre's temporary London home, the converted King's Cross Bus Station.*

I don't believe Shakespeare altogether knew what he was doing when he wrote *King Lear*. Many great artists, particularly towards the end of their career, start experimenting and trying to get through to something, but they're not sure what it is. I think Shakespeare went on an experimental journey, and that's why we find the play so difficult to interpret.

Remembering the challenges he faced playing Lear, Oliver Ford Davies cites various reasons for this view. There is Lear's lack of soliloquies, reflecting his lack of self-knowledge. 'He has these occasional flashes – "I did her wrong" and "Fool let me not go mad" – and you think, "Go on, give him 15 lines on that subject, as you would for Macbeth." But no, that's all he can manage. I think it's incredibly brave of Shakespeare to do that, but it makes the part terribly hard to play.'
Then there is Lear's madness.

How closely did Shakespeare think about it? There must have been a lot of mad people in London at this time, he must have observed them in the streets and pubs, and been very aware of them. But did he quite think through what the nature of madness was? He's clearly recovering from it when he meets Cordelia again. But if this is a form of Alzheimer's, do you have that degree of recovery? I don't think so. It's a great puzzle.

He's puzzled too by Shakespeare's portrait of Cordelia. 'What is he doing with these Christian references? Is he trying to turn her into some form of Christ figure? "It is my father's business that I go about ...". And what did he think he was doing, killing her off? Was he in a dark place, down in some deep trough of nihilism?'
And then there's the last act, and his attempts to resolve the sub-plot.

Shakespeare sets himself extraordinary structural difficulties, which he can't really cope with. Gloucester and Goneril and Regan all die offstage, which is a terrible bit of plotting. Then it's as if he says, Oh God, we better have a duel to satisfy everybody. So he gives Edgar and Edmund these interminable speeches, which are usually heavily cut. It's all over the place. What is the play about? Is it about, 'As flies to wanton boys are we to the gods, they kill us for their sport'? Or is it that fate is just random, that it kills some people and not others? It's so difficult to interpret, which is what makes the play so difficult to direct, and Lear such a hard part to play.

A notably intelligent man, a former history academic and theatre critic, Ford Davies is well-known for his essential amiability, and for playing what he himself calls 'benign ditherers' and 'well-meaning failures'. He was therefore seen by many as a surprising choice to play Lear. But his director Jonathan Kent had no doubts about his suitability. 'He's a remarkable actor, and I have a huge admiration for him. He's not your conventional idea of a great leading actor, but he is one. He has an acute intelligence, emotional availability, a humanity which I thought was interesting, an intellectual disdain which he can call on easily, and a child-like quality which suits the second half of the play.'
An experienced Shakespearean director, with *Richard II, Coriolanus* and *Hamlet* among his previous productions, Kent sees *The Tempest* and *King Lear* as the most affecting of the plays.

In *Lear* there's a grandeur of expression of the human condition, the folly and the terror of being alive, that is unparalleled in any other of his works. It's the greatest expression of Shakespeare's genius. But it's like an out-of-control truck roaring down the M4, going speedily from 0 to 60mph, beginning straight away at crisis point. Lear's descent into madness and the beginning of his rage are very difficult to gradate effectively.

In rehearsal he tried to persuade Ford Davies to become more angry, and not stray into more congenial areas. 'There's a balance to be struck. Oliver was keen not to rant, but my worry was that he was becoming too rational and measured, especially in those obsessive scenes which aren't quite rational.' Ford Davies acknowledges the problem:

> Jonathan often wanted me to do more, to be more aggressive. I know he was trying to get a performance that nobody thought I had in me. I do have a tendency to be measured; I'm a very contained person: I find it enormously difficult in real life to get angry and lose my temper, whereas on stage I can let out emotions that have been buttoned down. So I was interested in going down the anger route, and Lear's anger is quite a release. The problem is, it's very difficult to find variety in anger, and also to *stay* angry.

Kent had no difficulty in deciding on the appropriate period for the production. 'I didn't see much virtue in setting it in Ancient Britain or in Elizabethan times. It seemed to me to have an immediacy that demanded a modern production.' So for the first scene the men were in suits, the women in sumptuous dresses, and Lear announced his retirement to a television camera, the moment being shown on screens placed around the auditorium.

Kent and his designer Paul Brown set the play in a low-ceilinged, oak-panelled room, a kind of baronial study complete with armchairs, a log fire, carpet, wall fittings and chandeliers, a mirror, desk and chair. As Lear's mind began to turn the set started to fragment in spectacular fashion: the desk became the hovel from which Poor Tom emerges, the walls collapsed as the storm began, and the rain bucketed down on Lear and his companions. 'It became a surreal world,' Kent says, 'a place where the normal is subverted by the ominous and the frightful, a contemporary world which suddenly loses its parameters, and spirals off. So Oliver had to deal with normal things that suddenly seemed threatening, such as the desk becoming a hovel with a voice underneath it, that of Poor Tom, and that it was raining in a study.'

Ford Davies had to express Lear's fury early on: when Goneril criticised his knights' loutish behaviour, he pulled a lamp violently from the wall and hurled it against the mirror. But he was not entirely happy with the notion of the collapsing set. 'From the outset I thought: "Oh I see, Lear's mind is splintering, crash, down comes another bit of the set. But this is doing the audiences' work for them." There was also a practical problem: in the technical rehearsal I had to work out exactly where to stand, because the various bits of the set had iron frames, and I had to make sure they didn't collapse on me.'

This image of the panelled room had been the first to come into Kent's mind. As the son of an architect, a brother of another one, and formerly a painter himself, his initial response to a play is to picture the world in which it might take place. 'I tend to spend a lot of time with my designer formulating my ideas, building a house for the play to live in,' he says. One impulse for directing *King Lear* was the plight of his grandmother, who suffered from Alzheimer's (as did Paul Brown's father) for the last eight years of her life. 'Those years were beset by terror and anger: it was terrible to see the disintegration of her personality. She just retreated into a shell, not speaking and just staring into space. But Lear in my production wasn't a precise medical portrait, nor should it have been.'

He and Ford Davies clearly worked amicably and creatively together in rehearsal. Ford Davies recalled:

> Jonathan is very strong on concept, design, pace, clarity, and the overall sweep of the story. He's also very good at thinking on his feet, and because he was once an actor he knows how to leave you quite a lot of room, but to give you a feeling of security that he knows where he's going, that he's got an idea that he wants to carry through – and he will. He's a very determined man, but always very clear.

The two of them sometimes differed over an interpretation or an action. One example involved the Fool's behaviour. Kent explained. 'Anthony O'Donnell didn't play him as a comic, he was just doing his job. He'd been doing it for a long time, so he had that carapace of slightly forced joviality. He had a great pink wig, which he would shove on his head to perform.' Ford Davies felt it was important that the audience feels the Fool loves Lear. 'But Anthony went very firmly down the sardonic route. I could see Jonathan thinking it was sentimental to think the Fool loves Lear, so we won't do that. He was very against sentiment.' He recalls another difference over Lear's entry with the dead Cordelia: 'Jonathan didn't want me to carry her on, he thought that was sentimental. It may well be, but it's fairly clearly there in the text. Instead he had this idea that I drag her on by one arm, like an old teddy bear. But you've got to be careful: there are some things that Shakespeare clearly intended.'

There was also disagreement about exploiting the comedy in the play. 'Jonathan allowed some of the comedy that's there, but he wasn't keen on it,' Ford Davies remembers. 'When Kent is in the stocks, there's a little bit of front-cloth comedy, which is almost like farce: "No. Yes. No I say. I say yea." And so on. I said to Jonathan, This is a strange little bit of comedy, but he absolutely wouldn't have it; he wouldn't let Paul Jesson and I play it as comedy.'

Kent had problems with some of the characters, notably Goneril and Regan.

> They are difficult ones to make work. It's like with Gertrude in *Hamlet*, it's as if there are a couple of their scenes missing. It's partly that their descent into evil happens so quickly. The danger is that it can make them seem to be just functions for the plot, rather than fully fledged characters. Both they and Edmund are not really allowed the journey

into themselves. Edmund is not quite explored; he explains himself but doesn't reveal himself, except as a kind of function for the story.

Looking back, Ford Davies reflects candidly on his performance.

> It's a very upsetting part, and extremely tiring to play. There were bits of it I just couldn't crack. Every Lear loves doing acts four and five, because they contain some of the greatest writing in world literature; they're easy because they're so wonderfully written. The difficulty is the first two acts. I never felt I got round the long scene before Lear goes out into the storm, and the 'O, reason not the need!' speech. Maybe I had exhausted my anger, but the argument is very difficult to follow. I also never came to terms with the set; I sometimes thought the thunder, lightning and rain belonged on a larger stage. I certainly had a feeling of failure, like most Lears do.

As so often with Lear, his performance attracted a range of critical reaction. Charles Spencer wrote: 'Ford Davies does full justice to Lear's spiteful rage and terrible fury in the first half of the play'; Kate Bassett thought he 'proved a Lear of startling authority and snarling ferocity'; while Benedict Nightingale thought 'he found the emotional truth, especially in the reconciliation scene, and at the end'. Others were less convinced. Rhoda Koenig thought he lacked variety: 'Lear arrogant, Lear affronted, Lear compassionate, Lear demented, all speak in the same curmudgeonly rant', while Susannah Clapp was one of several who thought his performance 'too fortissimo' and lacking in 'inwardness'. In general Kent's production won plaudits, for its invention, theatricality and intelligence. The coup de theatre of the collapsing set was widely admired. But there were some who felt Ford Davies had to battle too hard to compete with the aural and visual elements.

There were plans for the production to go on a world tour sponsored by the British Council, as well as the possibility of a transfer to the Old Vic, but both fell through because of the expense of transporting the set, as well as other problems. In retrospect Ford Davies saw this as a blessing. 'We did it at the Almeida seven times a week for twelve weeks. Quite soon after we finished my back gave out. It's as if the mind and body know, and they say, We'll hold out until the end of the run, and then we'll pay you out.'

# Derek Jacobi
## *Michael Grandage*

*In 2010 Derek Jacobi played King Lear in the Donmar theatre in London, directed by the theatre's artistic director Michael Grandage. The production made an eight-week tour of the UK before moving to America, where it played for six weeks at the Brooklyn Academy of Music in New York.*

> I knew we had in Derek an actor who would properly excavate the first third of the play in a way that would bring new insight into Lear's rage. Too frequently I have seen angry old men who are basically just shouting – at their daughters, at their servants, at their lieutenants.

Michael Grandage started to talk with Derek Jacobi about *King Lear* more than a decade before their Donmar production, after having directed him as Prospero in *The Tempest*. Their discussions over the years convinced him Jacobi would bring the kind of skills to the part that would match his own vision of the tragedy.

> Derek is famous for being able to make beautiful detailed choices on single lines in Shakespeare, sometimes even on single words. As a great interpreter of Shakespeare he has that ability to illuminate a line in a different way, which can make you feel you are hearing it for the first time. I thought he would bring great wisdom to a man losing his faculties. Like all great actors, as a human being he has a lot of anger in him, and he uses his art quite often to vent that anger. So he's suited to parts where you want a detailed examination of rage, rather than just bombast. I wanted to use his natural ability to express ferocious, forensic, powerful rage. But another of his strengths is his ability to form a bond with the audience, and with Lear it's important that they warm to this tyrant as he loses his power and prowess.

An acclaimed Hamlet – he played the part four times – and a hugely experienced Shakespearean actor – he has appeared in thirty of the plays – Jacobi had refused earlier opportunities to play Lear. 'I never felt old enough,' he explains. 'I'd seen various Lears, including Wolfit's, Holm's and McKellen's, and never felt I would be able to give off the age. Also I always came across younger than I actually was, which was a bit of a burden. I'd always wanted to have a go at Lear, but I wanted to be in the right frame of mind.' It helped that Lear's description of his age as 'Fourscore and upward' was cut at the Donmar.

Grandage was more interested in exploring the domestic than the political or social line, an approach that fitted the limited space of the Donmar. It was to be emotions, not politics, chamber music rather than a symphony. He set it in an abstract, pagan world, reflected in the simple dark costumes, and in Christopher Oram's stark, understated design, comprising white, daubed wooden boards enclosing the whole acting area, with scarcely a prop or piece of furniture in sight. 'Everything was concentrated on the people,' Jacobi says approvingly, 'what they were saying and doing, thinking and feeling.'

During the first week of rehearsal the company read each scene. Grandage then asked them to translate it line by line into modern English, 'to check that we all knew what we were talking about'. Jacobi was prepared for this exercise, and had gone through his part in the same way, writing down the meaning in his own words. He had also learnt it, and had been thinking about the play for some time, in particular what to do about the opening scene.

Grandage, who had previously directed him in *Don Carlos* and *Twelfth Night*, observed: 'There's a part of Derek that would just like to get on and do the work on his own. I think he sometimes sees directors as obstacles to be dealt with on a journey towards performance, but he also acknowledges he needs them.' But Jacobi recalls those five weeks of rehearsal as being very positive.

> Michael and I trusted each other, we were thinking along the same lines. As a director he is a benign dictator. He knows what he wants, he has a very strong idea of how the production is going to look and sound, and you fit in with that. He won't let you deviate too much from his vision, but up to a point he's perfectly willing to compromise. It's all very meticulous and thought out, but within that framework he's willing to accept what you're offering him if he thinks it's better than what he thought of. He's a good collaborator: he gave me my head, and we didn't disagree over anything much.

They came up with a striking idea for the storm scene. Grandage recalls its origin:

> It was a pragmatic decision. That anger, rage and power evident in the first part of the play was so great that I knew Derek couldn't sustain it vocally on the heath. So we decided he should whisper the storm, as if it was coming from inside his head, and was more a vocalisation of his thought than a man railing against the elements.

Jacobi fully supported this plan: 'It became what Lear was saying to himself, it was taken absolutely internally. Normally the storm scene becomes a contest between the sound design and the actor's vocal limits. This time the audience heard every one of those fabulous words.'

There was, Grandage remembers, considerable discussion of the characters' back stories.

> I always say to actors that it can never harm them, and sometimes it can help. It very rarely interferes with a performance. If you don't like it you can get rid of it. We wanted to investigate what had happened between daughters and fathers, between sons and fathers. Derek was quite obsessed about Mrs Lear, and working out whether Cordelia was the result of another relationship after his wife had given birth to his oldest two daughters.

Grandage was clear how they should tackle Goneril and Regan, played by Gina McKee and Justine Mitchell.

> We didn't want to make them super-bitches, who were just angry, nasty, vengeful and ambitious. Why couldn't they be daughters who were caring up to a certain point? That's much more interesting. They marry husbands who expect certain things, because their wives are daughters of the king. Out of that mix come conflicting emotions and confusions, leading to irritation with their father, which then leads to something else. An audience recognises this, not seeing these children as nasty pieces of work, but being like other families where they have taken on other things, and in doing so distanced themselves from the parent whom they love, with both sides suffering complex emotions as a result. We wanted everybody who had been a father, a mother, a daughter, a son, to in some way recognise the situation, and so see a way into the play.

Jacobi had no difficulty, as some Lears have, with his relationship with the Fool, played by Ron Cook.

> There's a traditional distrust between the actors playing Lear and the Fool, as there is with those playing Othello and Iago. It can be a trial of upstaging, but with Ron, who is a great comedian, there was none of that: we just clicked. We had confidence and trust in each other, we liked each other, and we decided to use that. I think Lear loves the Fool, so it became a lovely warm relationship. For me it was a marriage made in heaven, and those scenes almost played themselves.

Grandage was keen not to make Cordelia the sweet, passive character she can sometimes be:

> 'You have to put into the first half what you know she shows as a character in the second half, when she heads an army. Usually people who end up in that position are strategic, insightful, take power on their shoulders, and all that comes with it. So she's not a victim, she's not passive or innocent, she's just somebody who stands for right and justice in what she believes in. She's clear-sighted, and can only speak her mind, which of course is one of her negative traits, given the terrible place it gets her into at the beginning of the play.

Jacobi talks about the way to deal with obscurities in the text.

> However much you love Shakespeare, however well you know it, there are always archaic words that need to be made sense. So the way you say them is important. The audience may not hear or understand the precise

words, but they can tell by your body language or tone of voice, by your gesture or facial expression, what you are meaning, thinking and feeling. As long as it comes out as spoken thought rather than a revered text, they will get it. The Shakespearean rhythms, the end-stopped line, have never meant much to me. I prefer my own rhythms.

The role was especially demanding physically and vocally, since he was doing eight performances a week; between Thursday and Saturday he had to play Lear five times in forty-eight hours. As a result he lost his voice, once in London, once on tour in Llandudno, where three performances had to be cancelled.

I didn't do anything extra to keep fit: just playing Lear eight times a week did that. I've always been blessed with a healthy body, and a lot of energy. I didn't worry about my age; I was old enough. The anger was wearing, utterly exhausting. But you've got to get there, in order for the end of the play to work. I'm naturally very placid, very non-confrontational; I rarely show or feel anger, but it's there, and I think Michael successfully tapped into it.

Both director and actor found differences in the audience response when they took the production to New York. For Grandage the single biggest difference was the additional laughter. 'The Americans found more comedy in the play. We in Britain are a nation of tragedy, we're brought up on it over 450 years, and we have great respect for it. The Americans are a younger country without that tradition, so they just see it as it is. They found amusement and fun at all sorts of key moments.'

The critics in the UK were full of praise for this latest Lear. 'Derek Jacobi made the familiar lines new and shook the heart,' wrote the critic of *The Times*. Michael Billington saw

a tremendous Lear, to be ranked with those of Paul Scofield and John Wood ... What is truly astonishing is the way he combines Lear's spiritual trajectory from blind arrogance to impotent wisdom with a sense of the character's tumultuous contradictions. He is quite superb in the central mad scenes, taking us inside Lear's tortured mind without diminishing the king's residual moments of cruelty.

Charles Spencer concluded: 'Michael Grandage's production proves outstanding, the finest and most searching *Lear* I have ever seen, and in this small space it often achieves a shattering power. Almost every performance seems fresh-minted and psychologically persuasive.' But Michael Coveney had some doubts: 'There's something guarded and "worked out" about Jacobi's Lear, but it is most beautifully spoken and detailed.'

Recently Grandage asked Jacobi: 'Has Lear left your body?' Jacobi took this to mean whether he would play the part again. 'There are scenes I would like to re-visit, especially the Dover cliff scene. But the answer is I truly don't know.'

# Jonathan Pryce
## *Michael Attenborough*

*In 2012 Michael Attenborough directed Jonathan Pryce in a production of* King Lear *at the Almeida theatre in London, where he was the artistic director.*

Jonathan Pryce had been considering playing Lear for a while. But it was only when some critics likened his playing of Davies in Pinter's *The Caretaker* to a kind of lower-class King Lear that he decided the moment had come.

'Lear is a fabulous role, encompassing everything from tragedy to comedy,' he said. It's a view shared by Michael Attenborough who, in casting Pryce as Lear, was confident he had an actor who could handle both elements in the play.

> Jonathan is a very witty, funny man in life, and a ruthlessly realistic and earthy actor. He never sings the text, which a lot of people still do. Whatever he does on stage, he manages to play the comic and the ludicrous alongside the tragic and the moving. That's so central to Shakespeare. Comedy is always half an inch away, and will come peeping through, even in *King Lear*.

He and Pryce, who had played Edgar forty years earlier at the Liverpool Everyman, discussed certain aspects of the play before rehearsals began, particularly the way to stage the storm, and the casting of the Fool and Cordelia, key figures in relation to Lear.

> With Cordelia, we both wanted someone not in the usual mould of a rather simpering and nice character. I felt the daughter whom he loved most would be one capable of standing up to him. So in the first scene she becomes very fiery, she gives as good as she gets, and becomes very angry with him. For the Fool, I wanted him and Lear to be very old mates, someone who knew Lear and his history inside out, a plain-talking, blunt, earthy, all-seeing, jaded, not very young character, very close to Lear and very fond of him.

They discussed the back story at some length.

The crudest element of Shakespeare's writing is his means of exposition, which usually gets lumped into the first scene. He's got such a lot he wants to say, he doesn't show you very much of the pre-tragic life, of what Lear's court is like on a normal day. You have to decide that amongst yourselves. I had some preconceptions myself, but I was really interested to hear the actors' views.

Discussions focused on possible reasons for the absent mother. Phoebe Fox, playing Cordelia, recalled:

I put forward the idea that possibly she died while giving birth to me, which explains why I am the favourite; or that I have some sort of striking resemblance to the mother. I wondered if all three of us in some ways have been brought up as boys. We're quite strong and hot-headed and a lot of our attributes are quite male, which makes sense for girls who have been brought up without a mother.

Zoe Waites, who played Goneril, expanded on the idea:

What Goneril and Regan do can be perceived as so barbaric and savage and extreme that it's very easy to write them off as an evil duo. But Lear puts them in an impossibly damaging and difficult situation. It's a case of you reap what you sow. The outcome of his parenting is that when we get power, we want to take it away from him. Perhaps had he loved us a little bit more we wouldn't have chosen to do so.

As rehearsals progressed Attenborough found one particular theme coming in to focus:

I began to feel that Shakespeare was absolutely riveted by the idea of gender. It's a play dominated by power-oriented masculinity, and I became increasingly fascinated by a political and social world where femininity, gentleness, softness were simply not part of the landscape. There's no Queen Lear or Duchess of Gloucester. Of the three women, two of them virtually turn themselves into men in order to compete in the political struggle. And the one ruthlessly consistent woman is banished for telling the truth.

This world, he suggests, is reflected in Lear's attempts in the early scenes not to show emotion.

He talks about tears being women's weapons, and the need to resist them. He refers to emotions needing to be pushed down, to *Hysterico passio*, which is a female condition. So in a way the play is about Lear coming to terms with his emotional range. It's interesting that it's when he's finally stripped of all that power that he begins to discover his gentler, feminine side.

To reinforce his thinking about gender, Attenborough turned the servant, who after the blinding offers to fetch some whites of eggs to apply to Gloucester's bleeding face, from a man into a woman. She then stayed with Gloucester until they reached Dover, when he dismissed her, and Edgar as Poor Tom took over caring for Gloucester. 'She offers gentleness and support, and remains a benevolent character who looks after Lear when he is mad. I just wanted to be very specific about the things that men and women did in the play.'

Unlike many actors, Pryce preferred not to learn his lines in advance: 'Jonathan will think about a scene, and he'll have views on it,' Attenborough explains,

> but broadly speaking it goes into his system in rehearsal; he virtually learns it as he is working on it. So he held on to the script for quite a while. He doesn't reveal a lot early on, he's just exploring it. He would come to some of it quite late, but I had faith in him, so I didn't want to push him any faster.

Pryce liked to introduce new ideas unexpectedly in rehearsal. 'He's a great improviser,' Attenborough says. 'I never asked him whether the things he did were planned or not, but if they were he didn't tell me about it.' At one point he wanted to introduce the idea of a slightly abusive aspect to Lear's relationship with his two eldest daughters. During rehearsals Pryce suddenly came up with a way to convey this, as he explained:

> I went to kiss Goneril, and it lasted a bit too long. Then I kissed Regan, and it lasted even longer. We took it from there. We didn't go into the story saying, 'How are we going to make Lear appear a bad father?' But it began to make sense. Ultimately it was less about abuse than about the power parents can have over their children.

In deciding on the crucial question of the period setting, Attenborough ruled out a modern-dress production.

> I don't think it's a play that resonates in modern dress. I've seen that done, and I think it looks ridiculous. You've either got to go contemporary in Shakespeare's time, or go way back. It's a pagan, pre-Christian play: we never hear about God, we just hear about the gods. So I decided to go quite far back in time. But I didn't want it to be slavishly of a particular period.

Designer Tom Scutt shared this viewpoint: '*King Lear* doesn't like being designed,' he argued. 'If you try to pin it down or set it too tightly in time and place, it kicks like a mule. Any rigid period ultimately feels reductive.'

So the costumes he designed were a mixture of ancient and modern, with a stress on the ancient, using earthy natural fabrics such as felts, wools and canvas in grey, oatmeal and black.

Similar thinking went into Scutt's design of the set, which had the appearance of a medieval castle, but had electric lights flown in to be used in the storm. 'There was an element of the castle about it,' Attenborough says, 'but what we were really going for was a prison exercise yard. In the scene changes there were doors constantly slamming shut, and grills coming across. It was a brutal environment, and you didn't know whether it was a prison or a castle.' In the second half some of the bricks in the walls were removed, and pieces of greenery appeared, to suggest the outdoors. Attenborough had wanted the set to crumble, but the budget didn't allow it. 'As a result I don't think we captured the disintegration of the play.'

With the storm, he and Scutt had to make a decision about using water.

I believe that when you are doing Shakespeare, the less literal you are, the better, the more the audience's imagination is engaged, the better. Tom and I decided, for pragmatic as well as theatrical reasons, that we didn't want water. It carries all kinds of problems: you've got to produce it and get rid of it, and the stage has got people running around on it, which could be lethal. So we put water on the actors rather than on the stage: when they entered they were already wet.

Because the production was in the 325-seat Almeida, he concentrated on the family rather than the cosmic aspects of the play.

I wanted it more contained and more intimate. I'm becoming more and more interested in doing Shakespeare in small spaces. The difficulty with the main house in Stratford was that you played the scenery, and it ended up being shouted, bombastic and rhetorical. The richness and the three-dimensional quality of Shakespeare's writing is better in an intimate environment, where the detail really can come out. But an intimate space doesn't mean that people can do mumbling naturalism.

Pryce's relaxed, instinctive approach to playing Lear was revealed during a question and answer session after one performance. Attenborough recalled the occasion:

Someone asked him how he prepared each night for a part as titanic as King Lear. Jonathan said: 'You can ask any member of the company: I don't. I sit in my dressing-room, I put on my costume, get myself ready with the door open, usually with some fairly loud rock music on. I walk round the dressing-rooms, I say hello to everybody, and as I'm walking up on stage I say to myself, 'I am the king of England and I'm about to divide my kingdom in three,' and then I let the play happen to me.

Attenborough observes:

> Of course he wasn't improvising every night: he had it in his back pocket how he would react to the play happening to him, but he didn't try to pre-empt it, pre-judge it or prepare for it. You never got the feeling that he was walking on stage with five acts of tragedy ahead of him. It's very easy, even unconsciously, to let that enter your psyche.

The critics generally admired Pryce's Lear. The *Evening Standard* observed: 'He brings an impressive mix of tenderness, quivering insecurity and raw passion to his interpretation of one of Shakespeare's most exacting roles', while the *Daily Mail* critic wrote: 'I place this Lear higher than Ian McKellen's celebrated rendition.' Charles Spencer decided: 'When Lear's wits begin to turn, Pryce suddenly becomes both thrilling and deeply moving. As he rages in the storm, he brilliantly captures both the torment and the sudden glimmers of truth and humanity that Lear discovers in his insanity.' Michael Billington noted his comic skills: 'It is striking how, even in madness, Pryce's Lear remains sharp, quick and observant: the confrontation with the blinded Gloucester on Dover heath, which actors often milk for pathos, here has a wild comedy as Pryce cries, "Ha, Goneril with a white beard."'

Attenborough remembered an important element in the actor's performance: 'It grew amazingly through the ten previews, but also during the run. It wasn't about putting in new things, but increasing the richness of the detail and improving the flow.' Pryce himself recalled the physical challenge. 'Tradition dictates that you should play Lear while you're young enough to lift Cordelia up and carry her. I was 65, and I put my back out doing it. I was having a lot of trouble with my knees, too. But at least when you're a king there's always someone there to help you up.'

Attenborough's production was admired for its clarity and thoughtfulness. 'His staging has a beautiful, deceptive simplicity', noted the *Independent on Sunday*; the *Time Out* critic described it as 'pacey, vital and beautifully spoken'; the *Evening Standard* thought it 'lucid, well-spoken and confidently paced'. Attenborough points out: 'People often say about my Shakespeare productions that they're incredibly clear. It sounds like a backhanded compliment, but for me it's the highest accolade. Despite all the preconceptions and mythology, Shakespeare is incredibly accessible. The language, if the actors inhabit it properly, is very clear. He's not an obscure writer.'

Looking back three years later while rehearsing Shylock at the Globe, Pryce explained why he found Lear the easier part. 'When I played Lear I felt I knew him, knew the man, understood that descent into madness. Lear gets a chance to express himself. With Shylock you just don't: so much of him is in shadow.'

# 16

# Transatlantic Sessions

### Peter Ustinov
### *Robin Phillips*

*In 1979 Peter Ustinov took on King Lear at the Avon Theatre in Stratford, Ontario in Canada. The director was Robin Phillips, who since 1975 had been artistic director of the Stratford Shakespeare Festival. The production was revived at the same theatre the following year.*

On the first day of rehearsal Robin Phillips asked the assembled company to name themselves and say what they thought the play was about. When it was Peter Ustinov's turn, he said: 'My name is ...' (forgetful pause) 'and the play is about senility.' The director was the last to speak: 'My name is Robin Phillips, and I don't know what the play is about.'

Their responses say much about the two men and their approach to *King Lear*. Ustinov, then fifty-eight, was himself a director, a novelist and successful playwright, and an international star in films. He was also a man of great wit and mirth, a fiendishly funny mimic in several languages who once stated that he was 'irrevocably betrothed to laughter, the sound of which has always seemed to me the most civilised music in the universe'. It was an element that was to loom large throughout the six weeks of *Lear* rehearsals.

This was the first time in thirty years that Ustinov had acted in another author's play. He had long wanted to play Lear, but never any other Shakespearean role; he had declined Peter Hall's invitation to play Falstaff. He saw Stratford as 'the ideal climate for the enjoyment of physical and mental hard work. It had for me all the advantages of drama school, luxury of time and the possibilities of profound research.' It appears that he insisted on the play being staged in the Avon theatre seating 1,100, rather than the main Festival theatre, which had 2,300 seats. On his suitability for the role, he explained: 'I've got three daughters, which is a more thorough rehearsal for the part than anything Stanislavsky ever suggested.'

He had read how other actors had interpreted Lear, and had consulted several scholarly works. But his initial respect for the 'footnotes of distinguished professors' didn't last long into rehearsals.

> After two weeks you begin to doubt one or two of them, and then the doubt becomes fairly general. When you're actually playing the part, you feel you're rowing out to sea alone in a boat with Shakespeare, and the professors are like bungalows on the seashore; they are getting lost in the mist, and eventually they disappear altogether. Suddenly you realize that they unravel as much as they can without actually having played the parts, and that when you play them, something quite different becomes clear, because you're forced into contact with people that have to understand them, and not just in an intellectual way.

Meanwhile Phillips, while envisaging a 'voyage of discovery' for himself and the actors rather than an imposed directorial concept, had as usual already made extensive preparations. He explained his initial ideas to the company, talked about the play's structure, and revealed his decision to set it in 1850s England during the Crimean War period. He passed round source material to evoke the world he wanted to create, including Thomas Hardy's *Tess of the D'Urbevilles* and *The Mayor of Casterbridge*, which he considered prime sources; savage cartoons drawn during the Crimean War, featuring beggars and cripples; paintings of women by Ingres; and early photographs from the period.

Ustinov's initial reference to Lear's senility was not just a joke: it was a concept he went on to develop as he charted the king's state of mind. Later he outlined his idea:

> Through a series of absolutely ghastly events, including the heath scene in which he's suddenly, really, practically a naked man, he comes face to face with reality. Gradually, under that kind of pressure, his sanity returns, and he understands suddenly, with terrible and painful clairvoyance, all the horrible things that have happened to him. Then, when he is re-joined to civilization as a prisoner, he is absolutely sane. But for a man of that age, it's less trouble to pretend you're mad, because you don't have to use energy in trying to decide on things. Inside he's clear as a bell when he dies; that's the real tragedy.

Fortunately he and Phillips were in full agreement about such ideas. The director had now been in charge at Stratford for four years. A former actor who had recently run the Greenwich Theatre in London, he had set out on his arrival to revitalise the Canadian theatre, 'to make people sit up and notice, to startle them into realising that Stratford was more than this slightly old-fashioned jiggery-pokery, with velvet costumes spinning around'. Greeted initially with hostility from those who disliked the idea that after Michael Langham had run the festival for over a decade until 1967, another British director should be in charge, he overcame it with a series of productions, including several Shakespeare plays, that were marked by realism, attention to a wide range of classical texts, and a spare and muted design.

Described as inspirational, he was admired by many of the actors in the company. William Hutt, the previous Lear at Stratford, suggested he 'gave the Stratford Festival a soul', and that 'he seemed to know what actors wanted to do before they did it'. He talked a great deal, sometimes for five minutes at a stretch, 'but if you listen you will pick up something invaluable for you'. Martha Henry, who was later to take over as Goneril, recalled:

> Robin is a very complex man, and a complicated director, but without a doubt the most thrilling and brilliant one I've worked with. His rehearsals were terrifying, exciting, funny, devastating, humiliating, shocking, all by the force of his personality. Other directors seem to be slightly pale in comparison. I think that's because Robin is such an extraordinary teacher. It doesn't matter what age or experience you are at, he uses the rehearsal period to teach you about acting in a way that I've never known another director to do.

Ustinov described him as 'a director of genius'. One of his directorial techniques was to make the cast play games. Ustinov found these interesting, but later he was critical: 'You felt you were becoming part of a sect. Robin, instead of being another free spirit just particularly gifted at his job, which was the way he held our attention at the beginning, became a kind of guru, asking to be followed in all sorts of decisions that were not necessarily ours.'

Phillips' attention to detail was considerable, his focus on the text meticulous. In rehearsal he had the *Oxford English Dictionary* to hand, to check the meanings of words. His essential aim at all times was clarity. He once said: 'I direct plays for a fourteen-year-old who's never been to the theatre before, and I want them to understand it.' He made it clear that he favoured 'restrained acting'; better too little than too much. 'Don't be too emotional,' he told the actors. 'Emotions are fine, but when I get too much of them I don't get the text.'

In rehearsal he made use of improvisation. For example, when directing Lear's sixteen hearty and boisterous knights, he had them create a series of tableaux, in which they attended a horse-race, saw a goal scored in an ice-hockey game, took part in a cocktail party, and witnessed a bomb explosion in New York harbour. He built up their individual activities and movements, which, he suggested, 'is simply much richer than when you're merely thinking as a group'.

He was relentlessly interventionist, forever jumping on and off the stage to show the actors what to do. Sometimes he would walk them through their entrances, or ad-lib the thoughts of their characters while acting them. He played a drum during the bridges between scenes, and to help with the rhythm of the verse. Initially he provided the sounds of the storm with his own voice; later he mounted a stepladder with a watering-can, and poured 'rain' over Ustinov and William Hutt, who was playing the Fool as roughly the same age as Lear.

Ustinov was a predictably jovial presence in rehearsal, smoking a cigar most days, frequently cracking jokes, or mischievously ad-libbing *sotto voce* under the dialogue with Poor Tom. Often he did this to cover a continuing difficulty with remembering his lines. Sometimes if he missed one or more he would invent his own blank verse. Rather than take a prompt he preferred to paraphrase the lines – a habit which would still be in evidence on the first night. Later he recalled: 'One night I thought of a word that was tremendously good, better than the original, and it was very hard not to put it in instead.'

The set for the opening scene was an austere panelled room full of Victorian furniture, with comfortable upholstery, *chaises longues*, deep-padded chairs, and a desk, lamps and tables. The room was enclosed by three walls. For external scenes the middle wall was flown up out of sight, to expose a small amount of sky; otherwise the set remained unchanged throughout. The effect for most of the scenes was one of a cage, reflecting the starchiness of Victorian society – a feature reinforced by Phillips' insistence that the men should wear corsets. Their costumes were of a military nature, uniforms decked out with epaulettes and brass buttons, supposedly real ones from the Crimean War.

The production was domestic, not epic, the king a father rather than a Blakean archetype. The effects for the storm were simple, the focus being on the characters and their relations with each other rather than a man battling with the cosmos. Ustinov rejected the idea of Lear as 'a windswept old man of granite, outshouting the hurricane, outbelching the storm, outspitting the rain'. Instead he highlighted the king's senility which, he pointed out, is 'an inconsistent state' with 'moments of lucidity, moments of control, among the catnaps and the rages'. Lear was a man 'who has to live with the decisions he made during lapses of concentration, and is usually too stubborn by nature and by accident of birth to reverse these decisions'.

Not surprisingly given his roguish personality, Ustinov was able to provoke laughter with certain lines. Afterwards he denied he was 'playing for laughs', which he said would be stupid. 'What is possible, and even necessary, is to play it truthfully, according to Shakespeare's clues and the quirks of old men. If the public laughs, so much the better; if it fails on a given night, it is no great loss.' He added: 'Laughter humanises tragedy, making it poignant. A tragedy which only impresses, but does not move, is as outdated as a pterodactyl. Lear is a contemporary play if ever there was one.'

The critic of the *New York Post* described him as 'emotionally engaging, intellectually persuasive, and providing an unanswerable answer to the conundrum of Lear'. He also thought him 'one of the funniest Lears I have ever seen' who 'consistently provides a tragic edge of unlocated loss to his clowning'. Other critics evidently wanted a more traditional king: 'An honest Lear, but I fear too light, too naturalistic, not nearly massive, resonant or archetypal enough,' wrote the critic of the *Detroit News*. There were mixed views about the wisdom of the nineteenth-century setting, which was said either to make the play 'less universal', or to 'sharpen the visual focus for modern audiences'.

The production ran for only nineteen performances. Ustinov described it as 'one of the great experiences of my life', and agreed to play the role again at Stratford the following year. The production was subsequently due to be seen in London and be televised, but for a complicated set of reasons neither plan came to fruition.

# Christopher Plummer
## *Jonathan Miller*

*In 2002 Jonathan Miller directed his third stage production of* King Lear, *this time in North America, with the Canadian actor Christopher Plummer playing the king. The production opened in 2002 at the Stratford Festival Theatre in Canada, and moved two years later to the Vivian Beaumont Theatre in New York's Lincoln Centre.*

> Jonathan was going to direct *Volpone*, but he said he had decided to forget it: he had grown to hate it, it was so over-written. In the same breath he said we should do *King Lear* before I became too old for the part. He said it was one of the funniest plays ever written.

This last comment was enough to convince Christopher Plummer, an experienced Shakespearean actor who had already played Hamlet, Henry V, Richard III, Iago and Macbeth, that at the age of seventy-five he should tackle the most demanding part in the canon. '*King Lear* is certainly a very funny play, with very funny lines in it, and full of unbelievably black humour,' he says. 'And when we staged it I found the laughs we got relieved the pressure.' So the comedy in the tragedy became a strong element in Miller's production, mounted as the centrepiece of the fiftieth season at Stratford, with a cast consisting of the home company and American actors.

As in his earlier productions, Miller asserted that Christianity was essential to the play, 'although it's only there by allusion, not by explicit mention. The whole idea of gaining through loss is a specifically Christian notion – that it's only by enduring the hideous ordeal of loss that any of these people gain.'

He set the play in the seventeenth century, on an unadorned stage, with just a few stools and a table. The costumes, with large lace collars for everyone and elaborate hairstyles for the women, suggested the civil war period. By now he had changed his initial approach to rehearsals: 'I used to give long talks about my ideas on the text, but as I have got older and, I hope, wiser I have become less and less discursive. Creatively things might feel hesitant and blurred to me, but I don't want to foreclose the possibility of unforeseen elements emerging during the course of rehearsals.'

As before, he concentrated primarily on Lear's encroaching senility. As Plummer puts it:

> Jonathan being a doctor was enormously helpful, because he charted my performance medically. He was less interested in the staging than in matters of the heart and mind. So with his agreement I played Lear as deranged from the start: he couldn't remember Burgundy's name in his first line, and had to be prompted. For the reconciliation scene he insisted that Lear had had a stroke, so I slightly slurred my speech.

Plummer also approved of Miller's notion of Lear's relationship with the clown. 'Usually the Fool is capering around in an embarrassing way. Jonathan's idea was that Lear had seen him perform as a clown, recruited him, and he'd become his friend, the only one who could call him Lear. He was the same age as Lear, which made it doubly touching.' He insisted that Lear is not the most difficult part in Shakespeare.

> Richard III is much more difficult, and really exhausting – you have speech after speech and then you have to have a fight at the end. The first half of *King Lear* has a wonderful arc, but from then on Shakespeare suddenly gives up on Lear and deals with the Gloucester story, so that when he returns after forty minutes the audience can barely remember who he is.

The production moved at a brisk pace, with scenes spliced into one another to keep the narrative moving. Miller was felt to have lifted the standard of acting and directing at Stratford. The critic Christopher Hoile noted: 'The whole company seems to shine like new, almost everyone eschewing old habits and speaking the text with such understanding that line after line glossed over in previous productions makes sense.' Hoile wrote of the comic ingredients:

> Plummer has decided to make Lear's madness comic rather than pitiable or frightening. And Miller, too, emphasizes the comedy in the play, though in a highly controlled fashion. His strategy in playing so many of the lines for full-out humour is meant to coddle us along, until we wake up to the horror or distress of those who have been amusing us.

The influential *New York Times* critic Ben Brantley wrote approvingly:

> The overall clarity of the production – in diction, exposition, and dramatic logic – is remarkable. Its greatest pleasure comes from Mr Plummer's taking you step by step through Lear's enormous changes in temperament and insight, and justifying every turn on both an intellectual and gut level. I have never seen an audience so saturated in tears at the end of *King Lear* as this one was.

But not everyone was convinced of the picture of madness. While commending Plummer's stage presence, the clarity of his verse-speaking, and the range of his expression, Hoile felt that in the Dover scene with Gloucester he came over as 'merely crochety and eccentric'.

When the production moved to New York, the company encountered technical problems, as Plummer recalls: 'We had the same set as at Stratford, but the acoustics were appalling. We had to bring our own sound equipment, and have microphones placed discreetly all around the set.' He also remembered a problem with a member of the audience. 'One night I came in with the dead Cordelia, howling my heart out. A woman in the fourth row got up, and said very audibly: "All right, that's it, let's go." It seems she'd had enough of corpses.'

Plummer based his style of howling on the barbaric version used in Grigori Kozintsev's Russian film version of the play. He also came up with a novel way of bringing on the dead Cordelia. 'Neither of the actresses in Stratford or New York was light enough. It would have killed me to have had to carry them in. So I dragged them on in a sheet. Jonathan said it was fine, as long as we avoided making it look like I was bringing in the laundry.'

Many critics commended Miller's 'unfettered' and 'no-frills' production. There was praise for his minimalist treatment of the storm, which relied simply on a small amount of stage fog and some strobe flashes. Gary Smith praised 'the Spartan way it avoids excess … Miller's direction, clean and neat, focuses squarely on the text, making no attempt at imprinting debasing theatrical clutter.' Michael Feingold agreed, noting that 'the play is played for itself, not for Miller's or anyone else's crackbrained notion of it. You can actually see *King Lear*: not a concept, not an update, not a renovation, not a deconstruction, just a very great play.' Brantley again praised Plummer's 'lacerating, double-edged' portrayal of 'a man of prodigious will and fading powers', calling it the performance of a lifetime.

John Simon in *New York Theatre* took a different view:

> The king starts out as a blustering despot, which Plummer plays superbly. But then Lear must become a baffled, humbled man, a ranting malcontent, a madman humanized by suffering, a broken wreck, and, finally, a doomed, heartbreaking hero. None of this is the dashingly handsome, jauntily witty, musical-voiced, charmingly matinee-idolish

Plummer's meat. His Lear, instead of gaining in stature, decreases in it; if he grows in humanity, it is a rote, actorish humanity, not a transfigured, radiant warmth.

Other critics felt Miller had reduced the impact of the play by scaling it down, and demeaned Lear by reducing his nobility. Plummer defends his director's approach: 'Lear is not a noble man at all, he's an absolute bastard, and really a peasant king. I don't know how this idea of his nobility and majesty ever happened.' The production's value, he argues, lay in its simplicity: 'No gimmicks, just total starkness, the absence of music which was absolutely right, just the sound of the wind and the dogs barking, nothing to lean against or hide behind. That's the way you should tackle these great plays.'

He acknowledged the benefit he gained from the experience or working with Miller.

It takes many, many years before you can stand absolutely still on a stage, to say something so simply that you don't have to work at it or imbue it with emotion, because it doesn't need that emotion, it's given it to you the way it's written. I think I did achieve that in *King Lear*, but I give Jonathan most of the credit for that. His genius was to make the play as clear as the clearest diamond.

*Both actor and director were nominated for Tony awards, Plummer for Best Actor, Miller for Best Revival. Miller also directed a version with students and staff at the City Lit in London in 2002, and a rehearsed reading in 2013 at the Old Vic and the St James', with Joss Ackland playing Lear. His fourth full stage production, for the Northern Broadsides company, opened in 2015 in Halifax, with Barrie Rutter playing Lear; the production then toured the UK.*

# Frank Langella
## *Angus Jackson*

*Angus Jackson's 2013 production of* King Lear *at Chichester's Minerva theatre starred the American actor Frank Langella. The following year it moved to the Brooklyn Academy of Music in New York.*

One of the first things I brought to the role of King Lear is a fear of death, which I never had before. At 76 if you don't start to think about it, you're nuts.

Feted for his recent powerful portrait of the disgraced America president in *Frost/Nixon*, Frank Langella found playing Lear on both sides of the

Atlantic an even mightier challenge, and not just because of the role's vocal and physical demands. 'I have had to bare my soul in this part more than any other role I've ever played,' he said. 'When I was doing Nixon I felt I had to go there, but Lear – because of what his journey is – requires total soul-baring. Albert Camus once said that it takes the man in the audience a lifetime to emotionally travel the distance the man playing Lear travels in two hours, and that's true.'

He admitted that in his sixties he turned down the part more than once without actually reading the play:

> I just believed all the clichés about Lear being a self-indulgent, whining bore. But when I read it a couple of years ago I realised it's a play about a man finding his mind, not losing it. I'm at the age now to completely understand his plight, and to empathise with it. Before, I wasn't old enough to really understand what crawling towards death meant. Now Lear has taken me by the hand and said: 'It's time for you to drop the things you think you need.' There isn't anything else when you get older but the fundamental things.

The play's director, Angus Jackson, recalls their initial discussions about playing Lear.

> We talked about ageing: Frank said he didn't want to leave it too late, that you've got to have enough power in your belly and in your mind. He talked about mortality, and his own children, and his experience of life – he's a very forthcoming man, and also very sharp. He was very interested in Lear starting with everything and ending up with nothing.

They talked too about the different interpretations of other actors and directors, comparing notes after watching DVDs of earlier productions.

> You get an awful lot out of doing that, but ultimately you have to come back to the text. There's so much there that you don't worry about what somebody has done before. Our notion was that you can't tell the audience at the start that Lear is on a downward spiral. Frank is phenomenally powerful, both in mind and body, and a man of immense emotional depth. Our decision was to play him at the top of his game at the start, not to play him mad, because we wanted the journey to be the fall of a powerful man. I don't think that's a given; I've seen Lears walk out very fragile and old.

Tall and imposing on stage, with a strong, gravelly voice, Langella's previous Shakespearean roles included Prospero, Oberon and Iago. His strong personality was apparent during rehearsals, as Jackson recalls:

Frank is a very accomplished actor and easy to direct. We had certain lynchpins in our discussions, we shared the same big ideas. He's got a hell of a voice and presence, and a powerful intellect. He certainly dominated rehearsals, but I imagine Lears often do that. It was interesting to watch the women in particular fight for their territory. It was all absolutely courteous, but you could feel the dynamics playing out in their negotiations. Harry Melling as the Fool had to use all his abilities to do to Frank what the Fool does to Lear. Frank would say, 'In this scene I think I should have the Fool next to me,' and Harry would reply: 'No, I think I should hide behind a chair.' And then there would be a rather creative negotiation.

Melling was aged just twenty-four, so there was a fifty-year age-gap between the Fool and Lear. 'He became this son that Lear never had,' Jackson explains.

He had this notion that he had grown up with Lear as a child, so he had a real impish, childish quality to him. He was essentially a young urchin, with something of the wisdom of the child who says wise things almost accidentally, because they've got no filter. Harry played it with an awful lot of guile, which is exactly what Fools do.

Consciously influenced by Peter Brook's filmed version, and directing his first Shakespeare play, Jackson decided to stage an 'elemental' rather than a modern production. 'I wanted to do it with stone and wood and water and fire, a broad swords and boots production rather than suits and mobile phones.' The result in the small, intimate Minerva was an austere, stark set, with minimal scenery, and unfussy costumes reflecting a period setting of around 1600. The raked thrust stage made of brick, wood and stone had at the back a plain set of vertical wooden beams, to represent the castle walls and a forest. The floor of the stage echoed the outline of a map, and was later stripped away, foreshadowing the destruction of the kingdom.

In staging the storm Jackson decided to use water. He had the floorboards ripped up, and used a stone floor underneath which had the ability to drain rapidly, and had water-heads installed in the roof. 'Frank was against the idea at first, but then he saw the duplicate costume arriving. There was a curtain of rain, so he and Kent and the Fool were truly soaked.' There was no question of a totally naked Lear. 'Frank just had a loin cloth, and that was naked enough. You can see as he strips himself down that he is physically old. It was very effective to see him exposed in that way after having been so kingly. It's the poetic image that is interesting, the mortality and the vulnerability; you don't want to be thinking about the actor.'

Jackson spells out his approach to the key matter of Lear's madness.

What are often called the mad scenes Frank and I called the sane scenes. We wanted to keep away from any notion of mental degeneration, and focus much more on how a human being can handle being faced with reality as he finds out more and more about the world he lives in. We ended up with Frank playing these moments with absolute clarity and truth, rather than any 'crazy old man' acting. We hung on to Gloucester's 'reason in madness'.

Langella admitted he approached the part with trepidation, wondering if at his age he could learn it, and whether he had enough stamina to play it sometimes twice a day. 'I didn't think I was capable of it. The first two weeks I nearly killed myself trying to learn the part. It was unbearable. I came to rehearsals fully memorised because I was terrified.' The same feeling was to occur before he went on stage on performance days. 'At the beginning I don't want to do it. Around four in the afternoon I go into a very low place of energy. I just think I'm never going to do it. Then adrenalin and determination and ego kick in, and out I go.'

There's a deliberately instinctive aspect to his playing, which means his performance can vary from night to night. 'I believe what you owe an audience more than anything else is immediacy,' he suggested,

> the sense that 'I'm walking out for you this minute, and this moment is a revelation to me'. Every night within a certain framework – the framework of integrity – you must forget what you did the night before and create it anew. So you take a speech which you have done for forty performances at the top of your lungs, and you suddenly take it quietly.

He pointed out the difference between his approach and that of British actors. 'They have a tendency to value consistency over creativity: you get it, you nail it, you repeat it. I'd rather hang myself.'

Jackson appreciated this creativity that Langella brought to his performance: 'He enjoys doing that, it's part of his fundamental gift. But it wasn't that he would suddenly do something different for the hell of it; he lived it every time.' Melling, in his first Shakespearean role, found this unpredictability stimulating. During the run he said: 'Frank is a fantastic force and leads by example. I have no idea what he's going to do next. That changes you and makes you better, because the play is always evolving. The Fool and Lear are sort of yin and yang, and if he does something one way, that allows me to do it another.'

The critics found much to admire in Jackson's production, praising it for its swift, uncomplicated lucidity and its insights. 'After a glut of concept-driven productions, it makes a refreshing antidote,' Michael Billington stated. 'It is staged with great clarity as a timeless moral fable.' The response to Langella's Lear was more diverse: while the weight of his performance was commended – his terrifying rage, his thunderous power in the storm – more than one critic complained it was too high-voltage, with a tendency to deliver too many lines *fortissimo*. Charles Spencer felt his performance lacked vulnerability, arguing that 'he never quite captures the character's terrible fear of madness, those sudden, piercing moments when he seems to anticipate the horrors to come'. Yet several critics saw a Lear constantly craving for love, and were moved by Langella's final scenes

When the production moved to the Brooklyn Academy of Music in New York, the play and its star were warmly received, with standing ovations nightly. Jackson remembers the audience response:

> Being in a British company doing Shakespeare in America, you get plenty of praise for that. Frank is loved by American audiences: they were more ready to laugh, because they had a relationship with him, they could appreciate an actor who was part of their firmament giving a big, title-character performance. We tried to prevent them giving him entrance rounds, using various techniques to ride over the top of them. But he did get them once or twice.

Marilyn Stasio, the critic of *Variety*, noted: 'Super-clean staging and tight ensemble work provide strong support for Langella, who turns in a thoughtful, moving, and well-rounded performance that is only the teensiest bit hammy.' In his *New York Times* review Ben Brantley wrote: 'Mr Langella retains a mighty strength to command. The great revelations come from watching him translate the reflexes of tyranny into different keys. Other recent interpretations have suggested that Lear is already afflicted by senility when the play begins. With Mr Langella, the problem appears to be less physiological, or even psychological, than societal. This Lear isn't suffering so much from old age *per se*, as from having lived all those years without once being contradicted.' He concluded. 'For me, the evolution the king undergoes here is more intellectual than emotional. While I was often intrigued and stimulated by Mr Langella's Lear, I was only occasionally moved.'

Langella himself felt dissatisfied, confessing during the New York run: 'I don't think I have conquered Lear. It's one of the greatest parts ever written, and the most impossible. What I'm in need of is peeling this onion to a deeper, more profound place, a place to which I have not yet been able to go.'

# Michael Pennington
## *Arin Arbus*

*In 2014 Michael Pennington played King Lear in New York, at the Theatre for a New Audience in Brooklyn. The production, with an otherwise all-American cast, was directed by Arin Arbus.*

A greatly experienced Shakespearean actor, an acclaimed Hamlet of his day, Michael Pennington muses on the changing times.

There used to be what was called the Shakespearean career, where you progressed from Romeo to Hamlet to Macbeth to Iago and ultimately to Lear. But nowadays you don't have the same control over the theatre world as Gielgud's generation had. There isn't much logic, it's pretty much a bazaar. It so much depends on being asked by a director you feel sure of, who feels the same about you.

In fact he and the American director Arin Arbus had not seen each other's work until she saw him playing in New York with Natasha Parry in *Love is My Sin*, a two-hander consisting of a selection of Shakespeare's sonnets, assembled and directed by Peter Brook. 'I was immediately knocked out by Michael's sensitivity with Shakespeare's language,' she remembers. 'It was clear that he was able to create complex and vivid relationships onstage.'

They met after the opening night and talked about *King Lear*. At the age of seventy Pennington felt ready for the challenge. 'You've got to be convincingly enough that age, but you also have to have the energy and the memory for the part.' Arbus, however, had serious doubts about the project. 'The thought of directing it terrified me,' she admits.

It felt foolish and arrogant to tackle what is arguably one of the greatest and most difficult plays ever written. In it Shakespeare challenges the very foundations of western civilization, pointing out the absurdity of privilege, entitlement, social and economic hierarchies, and man's assertion of his power over nature. Many smart people told me one has to be in Lear's phase of life to really understand the play. I was 31 at the time.

A meeting with Peter Brook in Paris persuaded her to think differently. 'He asked about my instincts about the play, and spoke of his own. He very lightly dismissed my anxieties; his warmth was encouraging. He suggested as a first step that I explore the play in a workshop. I ended up doing several.' She held one with graduate acting students at New York University, another with prisoners in a medium-security facility in upstate New York. Finally she and Pennington got together with a group of actors for a week-long workshop in New York. 'It was a covert way of finding out whether we would be good collaborators,' he recalls. 'We trusted each other on a hunch, and also surprised each other: there was more and more about each other's work and approach that meshed. It was most invigorating.'

Once committed to a production at the newly built Theatre for a New Audience, they had a rare opportunity of rehearsing on the stage. 'We read each scene, and then read it again moving about freely,' Pennington remembers.

We'd improvise the movements on the big open stage, until half way through rehearsals it was clear it needed organising. So it got staged relatively late in the process. As a director Arin gave me terrific freedom. I think she felt I was a dog who could be allowed out on a loose leash, just to see how my instincts played with the part.

Arbus found him to be an excellent company leader. 'Michael was incredibly open and generous. He was the dream collaborator: hard-working, curious, unsentimental. He was interested in what everyone in the room had to say. And yet he also had instincts which were unwavering. He was immediately able to portray a powerful man losing his grip on power, on his mind, and on his sense of self.'

Like most Lears, Pennington found the opening scenes the most demanding.

Within minutes you find yourself shouting your head off. Those first two scenes are inevitably taxing both physically and technically. I used to come off after the first one saying to myself, 'Quieten down! Why are you yelling again? There must be another way of doing this. It's technically boring.' Then you have to do the same thing with Goneril. From then on it's like riding a horse that keeps bucking, and you try to control it. But after a while the horse settles down, and by the time of the storm the horse and you are one. The second half, if you're any good as an actor, you ought to be able to do in your sleep. You have just four scenes, two of them very short. They're a beautiful piece of writing, and just heaven to play. You can't fail.

In exploring Lear's character and actions, he examined the key question of the king's madness.

The first thing he says after 'My wits begin to turn' is directed to the Fool: 'How art thou my boy?' It's the first time he's shown the slightest interest in anybody else. It's a most wonderful moment of humanity, the first of those sorts of passages in the play. So he associates going mad with being nice to other people. And like many of Shakespeare's madmen, he actually goes sane rather than mad. Being curious about the world is to him being part of the vocabulary of losing his wits.

What is obvious is that he learns something as a result of his experiences. But because it's Shakespeare it doesn't happen sequentially, it's not one thing after another. He is blind and then he suddenly sees. And even after he's supposedly clear-witted he's mad as well. And when he's mad he makes superb common sense. For instance, there's a kind of logic to the scene on Dover cliff. He's supposed to be free associating, but at that piercing moment when he says 'I know thee well enough, thy name is Gloucester', he suddenly makes complete sense. It's as if he has completely recovered. Shakespeare didn't know much about neuro-science, but he obviously had a hunch about what happens to the mind, and it's very close to what doctors reckon happens now.

In rehearsal he developed his ideas about Lear's motives for giving up power.

> My reading was that his decision to split the kingdom is not a bad idea. He clearly feels less confident than he did. He's aged a little, he thinks perhaps it's time to retire, and a triumvirate in the country is probably better than two children fighting against each other. His huge mistake is wanting to find out how much his daughters love him, because he wants to be loved. I don't think anybody knew he was going to do that. And I think it's more interesting if you play it that he only decides to do it that moment, so that it's happening in front of the audience.

Arbus believed that Shakespeare saw a young boy as the Fool, so she cast nineteen-year-old Jake Horowitz in the part.

> There is little information in the text about the Fool's history, where he came from, how long he's been with Lear. But one senses that he knows and loves Lear deeply, that like Kent he lives for Lear. I imagined he was orphaned and living on the streets, using his wits to survive, and Lear happened upon him and employed him. So he became a surrogate father to the Fool, and the Fool a surrogate son to Lear. It becomes terribly painful and frightening for him to watch Lear fall apart, and in despair he abandons Lear. There is no place left for him in the world, and he knows it. So as the sounds of war are heard in the distance, he commits suicide.

Pennington was happy with the notion of a boy Fool. 'He was a little bit like a Dickensian street waif with a cap, he was scarred and had a limp. So the relationship with Lear became a mutually protective one. His effrontery at criticising his master was more acute because he was so much younger.'

The two of them agreed the play should be set in no particular period. 'I wanted the production to feel like our world,' Arbus explained,

> as I think these characters exist now. But finding the right balance between ancient and contemporary is incredibly tough, though I think we accomplished it. The designer created a rusted steel floor and a large rusted steel back wall, so that it was at once modern and ancient, brutal, militaristic, simple and epic. We used a table in one scene, a chair in a few others, a crate in the barn scene, some dead animal props in the hunting scene, and that was about all.

For the storm her aim was to make it both external and internal, literal and metaphorical, to reflect the tempest in Lear's mind. She experimented with a rain machine, but eventually used language, sound and lights to create the storm, as well as live musicians onstage playing abstract sound music. This suited Pennington well:

> I'm not very keen on the idea of whispering the speech and not actually having a storm. Shakespeare intended there to be one, but it has to be controlled. Otherwise the actor just yells his head off and can't be heard. So we made a score of the storm, which meant that I always knew when the sounds were going to happen, and that was extremely helpful. Rain is difficult to control, and creates too much interest of the wrong kind in the audience, so we simulated it with lights.

The new 265-seat theatre proved an ideal setting, since it had a large and deep stage area where the more epic scenes could be enacted, and a thrust forestage where the more intimate moments could take place. Arbus points out the benefits: 'We staged the blinding of Gloucester as far downstage as possible; the front row was less than two feet away, and the violence was horrendous and unavoidable. And when Lear was grieving over Cordelia's body, Michael could whisper into her ear and the audience could understand his every word.' This possibility of intimate contact with the audience was useful for Pennington, since it enabled him to compensate for Lear's lack of a soliloquy. 'The fact that he has none tends to make him a little cut off from the audience. Here you could make certain lines into a kind of soliloquy, and let the audience in more. It was miraculous to be able to tackle Lear on an intimate scale, and still have the opportunity to play the storm and the bigger scenes upstage.'

The critics praised both his performance and the production. 'The gifted Shakespearean Michael Pennington plays the role with valiant sensitivity and insight,' wrote Alexis Soloski of the *Village Voice*, while Joe Dziemianowicz of the *New York Daily News* picked out the actor's 'uncanny depth of connection with his fellow actors in quieter scenes, which feel more intriguing and honest than ever.' In the *Broad Street Review* Carol Rocamora observed: 'Performed on a bare stage in the theatre's sleek black box, director Arin Arbus has delivered a stately, toned-down production that allows the beauty of Pennington's honest performance to shine. I've seen a dozen Lears over the years, but none match the clarity, simplicity, and humanity of Pennington's.'

Ben Brantley of the *New York Times* welcomed the way

> the production gives the impression of talking to, rather than yelling at, its audience. Ms Arbus is here to remind us just how much *Lear* is a story not only of dynasty but also of families, with all their mixed-up rivalries and affections. Starting with Michael Pennington's delicate portrait of a

paterfamilias who has never taken the time to know his daughters but now expects the world of them, this *Lear* is less electrifying epic tragedy than absorbing domestic drama.

Arbus herself was unstinting in her praise of Pennington's Lear.

Michael was brilliant and heartbreaking in performance. It was thrilling to see him embody Lear's continual evolution, the dismantling of the king and the emergence of an incredibly vulnerable, broken and wise man. I don't know how he did it playing seven times a week, but through the course of each performance he seemed to age thirty years. He was terrifying at the beginning: invulnerable, wild and capricious, a loose cannon, ever on the verge of violence, and yet still remarkably human. There was also a dark and fantastic sense of humour in his performance.

Pennington was delighted with their collaboration.

I think we brought the best out of each other. I certainly don't expect to do anything better, and I'm immensely proud of the work. I would like to think I got all eleven scenes right at some point, but not always on the same night. But your performance is always in a state of flux, and each thing has to be invented every night. It's like serving at tennis: some of the balls are aces, and some go into the net.

# 17

# At the National

## Anthony Hopkins
### *David Hare*

*In 1986 David Hare directed Anthony Hopkins as Lear in the Olivier at the National Theatre.*

During rehearsals Anthony Hopkins, then forty-eight, spoke feelingly about the challenge of playing this supremely difficult part.

> It would be slightly abnormal not to have any anxiety about playing Lear. *King Lear* is a great piece of writing by a great genius, but I think once you look at it as an Everest, you can never begin to climb it. There's a great danger of looking on it with awe. It is a challenge, but if I saw it as too monumental, I'd never do it. I prefer to just get up there and get on with it. I have contempt for fear in myself; it embarrasses me. But being human I am occasionally prone to it.

In his battle against this fear, he made sure he came to the first rehearsal word-perfect. 'I hate walking around with the book in my hand,' he explained. 'My approach is very crude: I belt the lines out in rehearsal with tremendous energy. I just smash through to block out the fear that I'll make an idiot of myself. I go over the top, and then gradually relax into it.'
Nevertheless the fear sometimes got to him:

> Sometimes I wake at four in the morning with everything racing in my mind. So I get up and come here to the stage or the rehearsal room, and just pound through my lines in a very aggressive way. I get all the consonants working. I just shout my voice into shape. I go over and over the lines, disciplining the tongue and the brain and the lips to get everything coordinated so that I don't have to think about it anymore. It's an unorthodox way of working, but it helps me.

This was David Hare's first Shakespeare production. Looking back, he reflects on Hopkins' acting skills: 'What Tony's got is the ability to take certain characteristics which lie at the heart of whoever he's playing, to take these hints in the text and exaggerate them, and by exaggerating them to play both the inner and the outer man. He always finds some external expression of the inner man.'

Like Hopkins, he found rehearsals demanding. 'I discovered how different it is to have an idea of a play, and to face the reality of realising the idea,' he admits.

> I thought if you had an idea of what you wanted to do you were half way there, whereas you are only a thirtieth of the way there. The most daunting thing with *Lear* is that there is no other play with eleven epic, major, complex scenes. As director I felt that no sooner was the beachhead captured than it was lost again. You would think, 'I've nailed that passage, I've finally got that scene the way I want it.' But when you went back to it, it had mysteriously gone. You feel you are pushing, pushing, pushing interpretation, but you're not holding it, you're not gripping. I found it hard to keep myself fine-tuned to that level of intensity. There are no 'unimportant' scenes, so there is no relaxation. It was more exhausting than anything else I've done.

This was not his first attempt to stage the play. Earlier in the 1980s he had wanted to do a small-scale production at Riverside Studios in London, 'a kind of Pocket Lear', with Bill Patterson as Lear and a cast of under-35s. That scheme didn't work out, so with the agreement of Peter Hall, then running the National, he had the chance to stage a full-scale production in the Olivier. He set the play in an unspecified period, with the costumes by Christine Stromberg a mixture of ancient and modern, including balaclavas and stark military outfits. 'I wanted to strip it back to a European sensibility, and make it look as much like a European production as possible. By European I mean working primarily through light and space and texture, in a very limited colour palette.' Pressed by some academics to use the Folio text, he eventually decided on a hybrid version. 'If something didn't work I just cut it. I cut all that boring stuff, such as the offstage reporting. It seemed drowned with words, so I cut whole swathes, to make the tragedy seem to come faster.'

It had been Peter Brook's Stratford production, which he saw while at school, which had made him want to work in the theatre. 'I have a very clear memory of it, the tangible excitement in both the production and the performances. The way it was spoken and staged with what appeared to be realism just wasn't how one assumed Shakespeare to be.' But when he came to direct the play himself he had no time for Brook's linking of the play to Beckett and the absurdist theatre, describing as 'nonsense' Jan Kott's theories, 'the idea that Shakespeare was some sort of unknowing fore-runner of Beckett, when the poetry of one is bleak and pared down, and the other is lush'.

He did, however, agree with Brook that the first half of the play was about indoors, and the second half about outdoors. 'But you have to have some intimation of the outdoors in the first half, and the outdoors has to have some memory of the indoors. Connecting the two is tricky.' He was also keen to follow Brook's view of Goneril.

> I buy into his argument that Goneril is reasonable, and believes herself to be reasonable. You can make that case for her but not for Regan, who is simply irredeemable. So the deep psychological damage still hurts between Lear and Goneril: whatever that relationship is, to be shouted at by her father hurts her profoundly, whereas Regan has gone over and become a stone, and is incapable of being reached. So Goneril has more to lose by the events of the play. It's a more rewarding part, because you can show that your father's behaviour both distresses and shocks you, and makes you behave the way you do, whereas Regan is a truly bad person, and there is no other way of playing it.

He felt strongly that the play was not about old age, or a medical treatise on Alzheimer's. 'I wanted to get rid of this feeling that it's about senility. I don't see it that way at all. Although he loses his wits, he remains a powerful figure, not a pathetic one.' He was also concerned with the problem of imposing light and shade on the production.

> Of all Shakespeare's plays, *King Lear* is the one that can most easily become monotonous. My note to Tony, which we were never able to achieve, was that Lear has eleven scenes, and they're like a series of one-act plays, each one with a different tone. I asked him to find as many different colours and variations as possible, so that it doesn't become one monotonous stream of suffering.

Hopkins sought advice from two other actors who had played the part, Michael Gambon and Clive Swift. During rehearsal he spelt out his take on Lear:

> I see him as a hard, virile, stubborn old bugger, a man with an iron will, unable to let go. His relationship to Cordelia is a relationship with an ideal woman. She's the mother who he wants to nurse him. I find there is something touching about his relationship with her. She sets him on the spiritual path and lets him discover himself, walking towards absolution and self-discovery. I'm sure he thinks she's not going to marry, so he's just going to stay with mother. What she says rips him in half – not because he's senile or old, but because he's too young in heart.

Hopkins drew inspiration from his Welsh family background. 'My grandfather was that kind of man, a real tyrant.' He spoke of Lear's 'volcanic rage, bound into some form of subterranean nature, so colossal that it cracks him wide open; I have that rage in myself.' His difficulty was to express the range and depth of feeling Lear needed to show. 'You've really got to put yourself out on a limb and whip yourself to pieces.' In trying to achieve this he recalled the death of his father five years previously. 'I don't like showing emotion or grief. When he died I was very stalwart. But on stage I feel like him as he looked in his last days. I remember how deeply disturbed and emotional he was, how frightened. It comes powerfully into my mind.' But as the previews approached his anxiety continued: 'It was a bit nerve-wracking. I started speaking too fast, not observing the verse, and for a while my voice cracked. It was deeply disappointing.'

He was probably not helped by a letter he received about playing the part from Olivier, who wrote enigmatically: 'It can be quite undifficult if you make it easier for yourself.' There was a further factor in his struggle. In his previous role at the National he had achieved a huge success playing Lambert Le Roux, the monstrous South African newspaper tycoon, in Hare and Howard Brenton's play *Pravda*. During the previews traces of that performance were still evident in his Lear, prompting an anxious Peter Hall to write to Hare:

> It is a clear, classical, savage interpretation, beautifully staged, with a very strong cast. But it doesn't have a Lear at its centre yet ... There is a slight tendency for everyone to shout. One needs full voices fully extended, but not strangled. They almost seem to catch it from Tony – Kent, Edmund and Edgar ... It is extremely uncomfortable to listen to a great actor mangling his voice for two hours and playing everything staccato. Tony under pressure seems to have no sense of 'line'. And one longs to hear the natural music of his voice. The danger is that he will be accused of playing King Lear in his *Pravda* style, as a series of barking one-liners. We have to get him out of that. You can't get inside an actor unless you can relax with his vocal ease and presence – particularly when he has long rhetorical speeches. So the sympathy just wasn't there until the third act. You know all this, but I can't stress how important it is. I think the success or failure of the whole venture depends on it.

Hare was very conscious of the problem, recalling:

> Tony was so deep in Lambert Le Roux he didn't know how to pull himself out of it. He knew immediately how to play that part, but he didn't have that security with Lear. He's like Olivier, a physical actor who likes the voice. If he knows the clothes, the voice and the wig on that first day of rehearsal, you will then go on a thrilling journey with him, going

deeper and deeper. But if he hasn't got those things, he can't go on that journey. He wanders round the stage like a wounded animal, looking for the part and not finding it.

During the previews he could see Hopkins was frightened of giving Lear the full emotion. 'The audience watched a performance that was technically adroit, but they were not moved or involved. He needed to draw on his personal pool of grief.' On the first night he reminded Hopkins of this, telling him: 'The personal pain you take on to the stage will be what distinguishes the performance, not any rehearsal process we've been through.'

Many of the critics were impressed. Irving Wardle thought his Lear 'stupendous'; John Peter thought him 'more of a primitive chieftain than a king', but praised his 'magnificent, harrowing animal performance'. Michael Billington wrote: 'Hopkins combines the strength and rage of a bull with an extraordinary capacity for pathos. He is a genuine heavyweight endowed with emotional finesse ... He conveys both Lear's brutishness and his emotional vulnerability.' Milton Shulman admired his 'virile pugnancy'.

Others were less convinced: while admiring Hopkins' power and vigour they criticised what they saw as his limited range and vocal limitations. Eric Shorter felt that 'his gravel voice mars the poetry'; Andrew Rissick that 'he had the diaphragm, but not the heart'. Anna Massey, playing Goneril, concurred: 'He was a bullish Lear, and revelled in the physicality of the old man, but sometimes he missed out on his spiritual side.' Alarmingly, Lambert Le Roux, complete with South African accent, still found a way into some early performances; Robert Cushman spotted the traces in 'the bullet-head jutting forward in quest or challenge, the thunderously elongated syllables ("O, reason not the need-ah!")'.

Some reviewers thought it the best production since Peter Brook's, while Jim Hiley thought it 'oozes belief in the play and its modernity' and praised the director's 'uncompromisingly spare but incisive' staging. Others felt the actors were too isolated on the vast Olivier stage, making it difficult for them to establish anything more than a fleeting sense of their relationships. The criticism was particularly made in relation to the Fool: Rosan Seth made his pronouncements in a detached and hectoring manner, and rarely came close to Lear.

Hare explained his thinking about the Fool:

I don't find him funny; I've never seen one that makes me laugh. He doesn't have the lines to be funny with, so what's he supposed to do, roll over and make them funny? I think it's more interesting to play him as a *savant*, as someone who has knocked around a lot, and is essentially a wise person. I wanted him to be an alien, not a member of the court, somebody from outside rather than inside. I chose to make him grave, to reflect the spiritual experiment that Lear embarks on. But I don't think it worked.

He says the Dover cliff scene between Lear and Gloucester was the best he had seen. 'That's where the heart of the play lies, with its extraordinary poetry, sweetness, and its statement of a spare Christian ethic, that of the Sermon on the Mount. Contrary to expectations, Tony was intensely moving in that scene. His way of showing insanity came out in feathery gentleness, which I don't think anyone had seen in him before.'

Hopkins later admitted he 'couldn't touch the part'. He was unhappy throughout the season, during which he played both Lear and Antony a hundred times each. His state of mind was reflected in the waywardness of some of his later performances. Anna Massey recalled his lack of discipline: 'When David was not there during the run, he altered his performance, and some nights ran amok.' Dominic Dromgoole remembers his indiscipline: 'He had that wonderful casualness of giving up on a scene if it wasn't going well. If he wasn't happy he just mumbled fast, and then walked off smirking.'

Although Peter Hall initially had doubts about allowing Hare to choose *King Lear* for his Shakespearean directing debut, he told him afterwards that it was the best-spoken Shakespeare production he had heard at the National.

# Brian Cox
## *Deborah Warner*

*In 1990 Brian Cox took on the role of King Lear in a production in the Lyttelton at the National Theatre, directed by Deborah Warner. The play subsequently went on a world tour, including visits to Europe, Japan, Egypt and Ireland, as well as a UK tour.*

It's a monstrously difficult part. Lear is quite brutal about himself, he's relentlessly self-castigating; he just doesn't let up. That's what makes it so hard to play, and so exhausting.

Looking back a quarter of a century from his year inhabiting Lear, Brian Cox compares the role to that of Titus Andronicus, which he had played three years earlier for the RSC.

There were nights when *Lear* was great and it went well, but at other times its depressing nature really got me down. *Titus Andronicus* is a younger man's play, written with a kind of freefall. Lear is not like that: he's falling, but he keeps hitting things on his way down, he keeps bouncing off things, which makes it really painful. It's a great deal more difficult mentally and spiritually than Titus.

Though only forty-four at the time, there were occasions when his immersion in Lear overwhelmed him.

I was going through a crisis in my own life, which became exacerbated in the play, which is so much to do with Lear's rejection. That rejection, his solitude and death at the end, and the realisation that his life has been a mistake, were very difficult to bear. The strain was destroying me, and I wondered how I was going to shake it off. During one matinee I had just done the 'O, reason not the need!' speech. When I came off I said to David Bradley, my understudy: 'You do it. Go on, you do it.' It actually got so bad that he did play for me in Nottingham, because I had a sort of mini-breakdown, and my voice went, just through the stress of it all.

At other times he broke down in tears, both onstage and off, notably when playing the last two scenes with Cordelia.

*King Lear* was being rehearsed and played by a company working in repertoire with Richard Eyre's production of *Richard III*, with Ian McKellen taking on Richard and Kent, while Cox doubled his Lear with the Duke of Buckingham. This second role added to the pressure on him, and during the tour he seriously considered withdrawing from it. The set-up meant an extensive, thirteen-week rehearsal period in tandem for the two plays, during which the actors were exposed to two very different styles of production. While Eyre preferred to do a significant amount of preparation beforehand, mapping out the ideas he wanted to follow through, the images he wanted to use, Deborah Warner adopted a more free-flowing, spontaneous style that had been a feature of her work since her pioneering Kick Theatre days.

'I begin from an actor's idea rather than my own,' she explains. 'I urge actors to try anything, to use and explore everything. I keep quite quiet. If the actors are not allowed the chance to find their own way, or are asked to repeat, demonstrate or copy something, the performance will be dead.' But she also points out: 'Having a vision of the way ahead is fundamental, although this mustn't be confused with having a concept; it's something rather like a well-trained hunting dog having a sense of direction, a sense of smell. Once a director and a group of actors are on this path following their instincts, the real rehearsal process starts to happen.'

As was her practice, she began work on *Lear* by having a read-though of the play, in which everyone read someone else's part, the aim being to reduce the pressure on the actors to give a performance at this early stage. There followed three days of games designed to break down the company's

inhibitions and encourage them to bond together. They then worked on
the text, with Warner encouraging them to paraphrase their speeches to
demonstrate their understanding of them. She then had the forty-five-strong
company sitting on one side of a huge circle, with the other side acting as
a playing area: each actor joined it as it became their turn to read, and a
performance began to take shape.

Warner had directed Cox in *Titus Andronicus*, and he speaks admiringly
of her way of working. 'She always gives you the freedom to explore, to
take risks and go as far as you can with your own abilities. She has a sense
of humour and a sense of the ridiculous. She doesn't impose anything on
us. Everyone used to tell me to hold myself back, to restrain myself. But
she always asked me to let myself go.' But during the *Lear* rehearsals, as
he wrote in the diary he kept of the production, he sometimes found her
method problematic.

'The actors do all the work, and in a sense she selects and edits, but she
waits for us to offer it up – most exhausting.' On the other hand, 'Once
we get the ideas she's very good at saying, "I don't want this, I do want
that," but it can be frustrating if you're asking for impetus and you don't
get it.' Later in rehearsal he observed that because she relied on the actors'
ideas until quite late in the day, 'you have to take the play by the scruff of
the neck and do something with it' and that 'sometimes you require the
director to have done a little more homework on the inter-relationships of
the characters'.

Warner suggests a reason for Cox's occasional irritation.

I don't think Brian would have baulked at anything in rehearsal if he
hadn't had to rehearse two productions at the same time. The actors
were running from one rehearsal room to another, and working in two
very different ways. If you're playing a part like Lear, maybe it would be
better if you didn't take on another role at the same time. You have to
risk exhaustion to play it well. I think the original concept was that Ian
would play Richard III and then play the second spear-carrier on the left
in *King Lear*, and the same arrangement would apply to Brian. But of
course once you've got those wonderful heavyweights in the company,
you don't want to do that.

Before the opening Eyre watched a run-through of *King Lear* in the
rehearsal room, and wrote in his diary:

The play is overpowering, huge and inchoate. Brian is very affecting;
he just goes for it with unqualified gusto. A charging bull, with
occasional shocking moments of extreme gentleness. The production
is shapeless, and large areas of it are entirely generalised. Somehow
Deborah's ethos seems to preclude intervention: all is intended to grow

like mushrooms in the dark, but the actors need help and the play needs shaping.

In outlining her directorial approach, Warner later told Eyre: 'I want the audience's expectations to be turned on their head the moment they walk through the door.' She certainly achieved that aim with *King Lear*. On his first entrance a geriatric Cox careered onto the stage in a wheelchair propelled by a nurse, a rug over his knees, ready for a jolly family party, wearing a paper crown and a red nose, and bringing party hats, whistles and paper trumpets for his daughters. He made the test of their love for him a jokey parlour game, played out in his living room. His Lear was a vain, spoilt, self-indulgent man, already old, and living through a kind of second childhood.

Warner suggests this surprise opening was the real strength of her production.

> We were very committed to the idea of it being a party game that's gone wrong, set up by a man of great vanity and sense of self-worth who is then humiliated. He couldn't really be serious: it was an absolutely insane plan, and completely unnecessary. You can't imagine for one moment that anyone in their right mind would ask his daughters which of them loves him most.

The wheelchair idea came to Cox before rehearsals began, after he played Burgundy to Olivier's Lear in the Granada Television version. During rehearsals he noted: 'The big discovery of the afternoon was the tremendous advantages of the wheelchair. Unlike a throne fixed in the centre of the stage, it is a shifting focal point which allows interesting stage variations.'

Reflecting on his Lear, Cox recalls: 'I played him as having a form of dementia and loss, especially in the scene with Gloucester. But I didn't go down the naked Lear route; I thought that would be a distraction.' In his diary he stated that he wanted to give Lear

> a sense of faded grandeur, combined with the idea of an old man who spends a lot of time loping around the corridors of the palace in dressing-gown and slippers ... I wanted to heighten the humour and the fantastical. Much of the mechanics of *Lear* is in the humour, and we need to exploit it to the full, and keep up a buoyancy – a reflection of the madness – and suddenly switch and make people cry at the same time.

Warner greatly admired his eventual performance:

> It was not the easiest time in Brian's personal life, but I think his trouble and pain helped him to produce a very good performance. He's a great and very instinctive actor, and he had a real understanding of Lear; he

found a superb humanity in his every vein. And I don't know if I could have had a more perfect Kent to play alongside him than Ian McKellen. The dynamic between them was fantastic.

The Fool was played by David Bradley as a bitter, laconic northern comedian, to whom Lear was tied like a child to his toy, caressing and hitting him almost simultaneously. Cox remembers: 'We were contemporaries, two old men who had grown up together. I had seen that idea work brilliantly with Michael Hordern and Frank Middlemass in Jonathan Miller's production.' Warner, in her Kick Theatre production, had doubled the parts of the Fool and Cordelia, as she felt Shakespeare intended. At one point she wanted Fiona Shaw, with whom she frequently collaborated, to play the Fool, but Cox resisted the idea. 'I thought the part was particularly male, and the relationship between Lear and the Fool one of male intimacy, which is very different from intimacy with a female.'

Warner decided to have the Fool suffer a quiet death rather than simply vanish: exhausted by the storm, shivering uncontrollably, left behind unnoticed by Lear, he fell asleep in a wheelbarrow in the darkness of the hovel, and never woke again; at the interval that followed he remained visible on stage, lifeless. As with her Kick Theatre production, the storm scene was understated, though not to such an extent as before: thunder-sheets were used, and torch beams were flashed across the black stage to the accompaniment of drumming. Cox ended up with a cymbal on a stick as an umbrella, which he had been using in rehearsal, and a bullwhip with which he created the storm. 'It was a great image of the show,' Warner remembers.

When he first saw the set designed by Hildegarde Bechtler, Cox described it as 'a large empty white space on a slight rake, fractured by a series of cloths lowered to change locale and climate – a leaden sky, the white cliffs of Dover – and a white floor cloth which can be torn up at the beginning of the storm, leaving a vast muddy underlay.' This pared-down design reflected Warner's radical approach to the question of setting and period, her belief that the setting of a production is not the way to unlock the play.

> How do you costume *King Lear*, how do you place it? Those matters aren't important. It needs no costume, no placing: those elements get in the way, and you do your head in thinking them through. Stonehenge? Seventeenth century? Neither of those are a good idea. But if you think this way, you have to choose very carefully where you stage it.

Not surprisingly given this view, she found the Lyttelton stage problematic.

> It was a very difficult space to go into with a bare setting and what I wanted to be an actor-led *Lear*, a *Lear* which would be all about the psychology. The stage is quite pushed back, and you really need to

throw it forward. It was tough for the actors. I think the canvas we were showing it on was too big.

Many of the critics agreed with her. About Cox's Lear they were divided. Michael Billington wrote that 'he has a battered shaggy authority and the gift of pathos', while Paul Taylor felt that 'Lear's tragedy is all the more piercing because Cox so magnificently conveys, before madness, his perplexed comic humanity'. But Benedict Nightingale posed the question: 'How are we to believe in the spiritual and moral regeneration of someone who seems not just immature, but suffering from near-psychotic infantilism?' And Michael Coveney observed: 'Cox is both wonderful and curiously dull. It is something to do with a lack of spiritual and intellectual energy at the core of this production.'

On one occasion while playing at the National the company took the play to Broadmoor Psychiatric Hospital in Berkshire. Here they performed *Lear* to an audience of ninety patients, many of them murderers, who were at the beginning of the parole process. The visit was designed to help them with their rehabilitation; such visits were felt by the staff to be purging and healing.

Cox found the experience exhilarating, and was fascinated by the audience's response.

> They had such intelligence and understanding, particularly of the humour, and the relationship between Lear and the Fool. All these situations were familiar to them. I'll never forget this young woman in the front row, who we learned afterwards had slashed and disfigured her sister. She was aphasic, so she didn't speak very much. I got to the line 'Is there any cause in nature for these hard hearts?' And this woman shook her head and said: 'No, no cause, no cause.' It was very eerie, and it stopped the play in its tracks. Afterwards I was introduced to two relatively young patients, who were saying how much the reconciliation between Lear and Cordelia had affected them. One of them said: 'I wish I could have had that moment of reconciliation before I murdered my parents.'

Warner remembers the performance as one of the best the company gave.

> It was an incredibly rewarding day, and unquestionably revitalised the company. We had to leave all the props in one room, and all the knives with two guards at the door. We dropped costume and set: it was like being back again in the rehearsal room, but fully rehearsed. It was a tiny room, the actors weren't having to project, so it was probably more intimate than the Kick *Lear*. The patients were very attentive to the fierce performance going on right in front of them. Afterwards we were told that they included a woman who had killed her father, and somebody who had put another person's eyes out.

# Ian Holm
## *Richard Eyre*

*In 1997 Richard Eyre directed* King Lear *in the Cottesloe at the National Theatre, with Ian Holm in the title-role. The production subsequently toured to Istanbul and Salonika.*

When a director or actor approaches a new play, they are free from the weight of critical opinion, and come with no baggage. With Shakespeare, as Richard Eyre observed, it's quite the opposite.

'You arrive with pantechnicons; you cross continents of critical prose. When I thought about *King Lear* I felt as if I was balancing the summit of an inverted mountain on my skull.' But as his confidence grew, he found the critical prose becoming less of a burden. 'I became aware of the comparative rarity of commentators – all convinced of the greatness of the play on the page – to concede, or perhaps even to understand, the singularity of Shakespeare's genius.' His plays, he argued, were written for performance, not for 'publication or reflective analysis'.

Peter Brook also helped lighten his load. Brook's iconoclastic production with Scofield had been the first *King Lear* he had seen, and he had been 'knocked sideways by its savagery, its bleakness, and its prescience'. Now, as he and Brook discussed the play while walking in Paris, Brook told him that it seemed unapproachable until you started to think of it as a play about a family. This became the focus of Eyre's production, which he decided to treat as a domestic rather than an epic drama, a central theme being the young supplanting the old. Before rehearsals began he reflected: 'More and more I think of it as a play about a father being locked out of his house by his children.'

This decision was one reason why he insisted, against considerable opposition, that the play be staged in the intimate and flexible Cottesloe theatre rather than in the much larger Lyttelton or Olivier. Another was his desire to retain the great intensity of the play. He was also affected by his recent experience of directing *Hamlet*, when he felt that, after a very good rehearsal period, the vastness of the Olivier stage had drained the production of substance.

In choosing Ian Holm to play Lear he was taking a risk. After several seasons at Stratford, during which he had played both Richard II and Henry V (as well as the Fool to Laughton's Lear), Holm had not appeared in a Shakespeare play for thirty-three years. Perhaps more crucially, he had barely been on stage for twenty years: during the final preview of *The Iceman Cometh* he suffered a terrifying breakdown, and walked off the stage in the middle of a monologue. But Eyre had 'boundless admiration and great affection' for him, and felt instinctively that at sixty-five he was ready to take on the part.

'How do you play an eighty-year-old man with manic energy?' Holm asked when he and Eyre first met to discuss the play. They agreed early on that, for a man on the edge, Lear's outbursts should be taken at full throttle. 'The arias can't be ducked,' Eyre said. He decided that Lear's madness was not senile dementia. 'His madness is an overload of remorse and pain and anger. It's a purging.' Holm assured him that, having grown up next to a Gothic asylum run by his father, the notion of madness held few terrors for him. 'I did not feel a need to "play" madness, perceiving it as extreme but not necessarily unnatural behaviour,' he explained. He also insisted that Lear should end up naked in the storm, an idea with which Eyre agreed, believing: 'Anything less than "unaccommodated man" would be dishonest.'

In their early discussions they talked about families, about parents and children. 'Our parents cast long shadows over our lives,' Eyre admitted to Holm, echoing the opening of his autobiography *Utopia and Other Places*, in which he wrote of his difficult relationship with his autocratic father. He realised he had previously shied away from directing *King Lear* because he didn't know enough about its subject-matter: with the death of his parents, and with the experience of being a parent himself, he felt ready to understand it. He also told Holm that as he grew older he found his sympathies moving away from Lear, enabling him to understand better his wronged daughters. For his part Holm stated that although he had three daughters, there would be 'no cross-referencing between life and art'.

On the first day of rehearsal Eyre offered the actors some advice. In essence he said:

- Trust your own knowledge of the world. This is a play about two fathers, one with three daughters, the other with two sons. Everyone is an expert on the subject of families.

- Shakespeare was a playwright, an actor, and a theatre manager. It doesn't help to treat him as a sort of holy fool or a messianic seer. He was utterly pragmatic.

- Treat the verse as an ally, not an enemy.

- Don't make judgements on the characters. Let us, and the audience, discover what the moral scheme of the play is.

- Rely on the evidence of the text, not speculation or psychological theory, or spurious historical research.

- Try to be simple. Trust that Shakespeare is trying to do the same, however profound, eloquent and complex his intention is. Be specific.

Eyre admired the 'extraordinary daring and ferocity' that Holm displayed throughout the six weeks of rehearsals. The actor claimed to find Lear quite a straightforward role, difficult physically, but mentally not so difficult as, for instance, Antony in *Antony and Cleopatra*. 'The teasing of family, the loss of position, the madness, and the production's internal momentum, appeared to me entirely logical and sensible. All I had to do was learn the lines, allow the rhythm of the words to push me forward, and be "me", sort of gremlin-like.'

Eyre and his designer Bob Crowley opted for a traverse stage with entrances at both ends, and the audience on three sides. For the first scene they had a simple, bare set with red walls, and a long conference table, with Lear at its head, providing what Eyre hoped was 'an image of order, of hierarchy, of family, one that would resonate with everyone in the audience'. As the action moved from the warm interior of the early scenes to those outside, they came up with the idea of having a collapsing wall at each end. 'We wanted the audience to feel a visceral fear when the walls fell and the thunder cracked.' His aim was 'to use scenery not to decorate and be literal, but to be expressive and poetic'.

He decided that part of the play's meaning 'lay in the sense of the young needing to be liberated from the oppression of the old – the universal feeling of the child towards the parent'. He wanted there to be four old men in the play: Lear, Gloucester, Kent and the Fool. So as Gloucester he cast Timothy West, as Kent David Burke, while the Fool, whom he saw as Lear's alter ego, was given to Michael Bryant, who was slightly older than Holm.

During rehearsals Eyre resisted Holm's suggestion that Lear might have Parkinson's disease, arguing that to give him any form of illness would weaken the power of the play. 'The story is about a father, a man, who is selfish, self-absorbed, impatient, irascible, a domestic autocrat.' This was precisely how Holm played him in the opening scene: barking orders and impatiently drumming his fingers on the table, waspishly treating the test of his daughters' love as a game, then unleashing his rasping fury when Cordelia refused to play, and standing imperiously on the table as he banished Kent.

His performance was convincing at every stage, providing beautiful transitions between the different emotional moments, from his initial fury to his rare glimpses of self-knowledge. He began the reconciliation scene in an agonised state, 'bound upon a wheel of fire', then conveyed with great subtlety his gradual realisation of Cordelia's presence. His howls while carrying in Cordelia were delivered with a great snarl of horror.

He later claimed to have had no qualms about appearing naked. 'It was something you got used to. Once you did it in rehearsal, that was it. You went on and it just became part of the action.' It felt, he said, entirely impersonal. 'I didn't feel I was revealing anything of myself. Ian Holm had long ceased to exist by the time I appeared.' He did, however, feel awkward during the interval, when he stood naked as himself, while a couple of stage hands smeared his body with mud. 'Nobody likes to have his balls smeared with sludge by a complete stranger in more or less full view of twenty other complete strangers.' His nakedness excited a good deal of comment from the critics as well as members of the audience, who saw it as a distraction from the drama. Michael Blakemore observed: 'The person who should be naked, if anybody, is Edgar. Nakedness is very dangerous on stage because of our curiosity about other people's genitals. Something that is happening both in front of you and in your head, it suddenly makes it a spectacle. You're no longer contributing something in your head, you're just looking.' Julian Glover recalled: 'One ghastly critic said how small his appendage was. So he pinned the review to the notice-board backstage, and wrote beside it "Every inch a king."'

Although some critics had reservations about the wisdom of staging the play in the Cottesloe, arguing that the Olivier was its natural home, the production was widely acclaimed, as was Holm's Lear. Benedict Nightingale thought it 'may be the best Lear I have seen', explaining: 'Holm never slackens in his determination to show us a man whose make-up consists both of seismic anger and of surpassing love.' Jasper Rees called it 'an immensely subtle performance', while Michael Billington noted: 'This is Lear seen, unsentimentally, as a capricious tyrant.' John Peter judged Holm to have entered a special hall of greatness. 'It is reserved for actors who have conquered this physically and spiritually exhausting role, and left on it their personal imprint.'

Michael Pennington noted: 'Ian always had that bunched energy, and a way with the language that you just don't see these days.' Afterwards Holm stated: 'I try to be emotional and big, and at the same very true to the verse.' He described his performance modestly as 'unfussy'; while Eyre thought it one of 'sustained brilliance', suggesting people would marvel at 'his speaking and thinking at the speed of light'. In the years that followed he and Eyre occasionally talked of reviving the production. Eventually Holm concluded: 'I think we're both glad nothing has happened. The prospect of achieving perfection is tempting, but of course unrealistic and unattainable.'

*Ian Holm gained both the Olivier and Evening Standard awards for Best Actor.*

# Simon Russell Beale
## *Sam Mendes*

*In 2014 Simon Russell Beale appeared as King Lear in the Olivier at the National Theatre, in a production directed by Sam Mendes.*

It's a very violent and dark play, and I was determined to have a Lear who had power and authority, who could cause fear in those around him.

In casting Simon Russell Beale as the king, Sam Mendes was drawing on their shared professional history, a theatrical association over twenty-five years that had previously involved them working together on six Shakespeare plays, in which Russell Beale had played Thersites, Richard III, Ariel, Iago, Malvolio and Leontes. 'What I knew from Simon in similar roles – I'm thinking of Richard III, and in particular Iago – was that there is a darkness in him, and I felt we could tap into that. That's an aspect that isn't often called upon, because as a person he is a very benign, gentle and sweet-natured presence. But he can be very scary.'

That fear-inducing quality was certainly in evidence in his opening scene in the Olivier, which was staged as a very public state occasion. Playing Lear as a shaven-headed, thuggish, Stalinesque dictator, flanked in the opening scene by rows of soldiers, Russell Beale addressed his daughters sternly through a microphone, then reacted with unremitting rage at Cordelia's refusal to speak, turning over tables and manhandling her in his elemental fury.

Reflecting on this interpretation midway through the run, Russell Beale admits:

> Sam was more enthusiastic for me to play him as a dictator than I was. I understood why he wanted to do that: one of the puzzles of the play is that we only ever see Lear being cruel. But we've got to believe that Kent, who is a good man, has some reason to love him, as does Cordelia. Of course he has killed people or ordered their death, and torture was probably used as a weapon in his state. So he's not a nice man.

There was another reason why he was less keen to portray a despotic Lear. 'I don't naturally play high status very easily. That sounds as if I am a very modest man, which is not necessarily true. But I think that first section is hard: those blind outbursts of self-indulgent rage are difficult to manage. I have had to look very hard to find that rage and power in myself.'

Now fifty-four, a hugely experienced Shakespearean actor, who played Edgar to Robert Stephens' Lear, he believes *King Lear* is the greatest of the plays.

> It has a technical bravura in telling two very big stories side by side; I don't think he ever does it with such a broad canvas, except perhaps in *Henry IV*. But more importantly, it digs deeper into the nature of human existence than any of the other plays. *Troilus and Cressida* is just cynical, *The Winter's Tale* is redemptive, but *Lear* is somewhere in the muddled middle of the way we see our lives.

Mendes first planted the idea in his mind of playing Lear when he was forty-five, but he felt then he was too young. In their discussions in the intervening years, Mendes expressed his intention of highlighting the political as well as the family aspects of the play.

It's about the gradual stripping away of power and home and family, and the gradual isolation of a leader. It's an enormous play, the movement of nations, the movement of people, the breakdown of an entire nation because of a single human act between a father and a child. Our decision to mount it on the large Olivier stage informed every decision that followed: the scale of the production, the way it moved, the use of 30-plus supernumaries.

Anthony Ward's design reflected the atmosphere of a non-specific postwar dictatorship, with harsh tectonic screens dropped on to the large Olivier stage to create smaller acting spaces. In rehearsal there were discussions about the behaviour of dictators such as Gaddafi, Mubarak, Ceausescu, Tito, Lenin and Stalin, and the similarities with the autocratic way Lear exercised power. To emphasise the dictatorship idea, Lear's soldiers became a private army of Mussolini-style blackshirts, while Kent was put into the stocks beneath a huge, heroic Soviet-style statue of Lear.

Mendes took an unsentimental view of Lear's situation. 'I have always felt that when he says he is a man more sinned against than sinning, he's talking bullshit. He's a self-pitying man who is not misunderstood, a bad man who has done terrible things.' Russell Beale agrees: 'That statement is a complete delusion. At that stage nothing can be regarded as good behaviour on his part. For example, his treatment of Goneril is horrible: I hadn't realised before how much venom he shows her.'

In developing his Lear he made other discoveries:

The major one was that the end was not at all redemptive for him. I always thought that in the last beat of the play it was, but the playing with the audience's sympathy was much more complicated than I thought it was going to be. I became fascinated by the thought, What happens if a dictator loses his daughter and you're supposed to feel sympathy for him? I found that a very interesting question. And are we allowed to feel sorry for Lear? How to make him sympathetic is tricky.

Working on the awakening scene with Cordelia also proved revelatory: 'I thought it was some kind of marvellous reconciliation, but it's not that. He's bound upon a wheel of fire: he's uncomfortable and ashamed, and so he's angry; he knows he's done something terrible, and his guilt means he doesn't want to see her. It's a very difficult scene.'

The scene he found the hardest to settle on was the brief one with Cordelia before they are taken away to prison, which includes the 'birds i' the cage' speech.

They never get the chance to forgive each other. Their damaged and fractured relationship needs time to heal, and they don't get any. That's what's so devastating. In rehearsal we tried hundreds of ways of doing it, because I didn't know why he was allowed to speak at all at that moment. One idea was to do it like those scenes you see in second-world-war pictures, of Jewish people queueing up to be registered by an enemy officer. I had the idea that it should be whispered in the night through a prison cell. But the ideas became immensely complicated. I think there are moments in Shakespeare when a character should just be allowed to speak.

In preparing for the role, he opted to learn the part before starting rehearsals.

That was partly because my memory is marginally slower than it was. But I'm always pretty quick off the book, because I hate getting up on to the floor while I'm holding it. With Hamlet I never stood up with a book in my hand; knowing the lines already just releases me. The danger is of course that you learn it wrong. I now learn a part before rehearsals in as neutral a way as possible. It helps with the sense if I've understood it before I start, so that even if I haven't made those decisions about profounder matters, I know what the text means.

Having played Lear at school at seventeen, he was surprised to find how many of the lines he had retained in the back of his mind. 'I remembered Lear's lines more clearly than anything else I've done.' Adrian Scarborough, who was playing the Fool, remembered the first time the actors were on their feet: 'Simon just went for it. I've been in first previews that were no better than that.'

The first two weeks of rehearsal were spent poring over the text, talking about the verse and the metre, looking at sub-text, making cuts, and re-ordering scenes. In the third week Mendes introduced his method of exploring the play, which involved placing the actors in a large circle on chairs, rugs and cushions:

It actually emerged when I was directing *Othello* at the National. I keep the whole company together, and we experiment with scenes. Sometimes we play games, or do simple things like having people swap roles. I had the full company of twenty-one act as Lear's knights for six weeks of rehearsals, until the supernumaries arrived. By the time they did so we had experimented with many different ways of using them. A lot of this way of rehearsing is about losing self-consciousness. People are willing to try things and be free with things because they know there is no right or wrong.

He and the actors looked at various options for the short opening scene with Gloucester and Kent, setting it among other locations in a urinal and an airport waiting-room. For Lear's first scene they considered staging it in the form of a cocktail party, a birthday party, as a men-only meeting, with the daughters placed right at the back in the dark, or not having Goneril and Regan there until they are called in. Various exercises were also used: for the scene where Goneril and Regan insist Lear's knights should be dismissed, Goneril and Regan (Kate Fleetwood and Anna Maxwell Martin) gradually removed Russell Beale's possessions, starting with a duvet and ending with a bean bag ('What need one?'). Mendes was keen for anyone to contribute ideas: 'You have twenty other imaginations in the room, and you'd be an idiot not to use them. There are some incredibly intelligent people there, who see it with every bit as much insight as you do. So my job is largely an editorial one.'

In one session they considered how to deal with the disappearance of the Fool. 'Sam hates loose ends,' Scarborough explained. 'He felt there had to be a purpose in his leaving.' Russell Beale recalls: 'My original thought was that he might hang himself. Then Sam said, What if Lear kills him, as a sign that his mind has almost gone?' The idea proved controversial, prompting the criticism that this was not what Shakespeare wrote. Mendes defended his decision: 'When Lear goes mad his only means of communication is violence. He uses the language of violence throughout the play, and the currency of the society he governs is violence. So for him in his madness to turn round in the mock-trial scene and club the Fool to death with an iron bar is because his means of communication is non-verbal.'

In trying to identify the nature of that madness, Russell Beale took the unusual step for him of consulting outside experts, in this case about dementia.

I sensed that Shakespeare must have known someone with dementia, or watched people who had that sort of breakdown. He's such an acute observer of humanity. My nephew who was training at St Bartholomew's Hospital told me that there were three types of dementia, and the one that caused shaking hands and hallucinations was Lewy Body dementia. I also consulted a geriatrician, who told me the symptoms were shame, wandering, and anger. It seemed to fit with what Shakespeare was writing about. The psychotherapist Mike Brearley disagreed with me about using the idea, saying you can't recover from dementia. But of course I wasn't using it as an exact blueprint, just a useful guide.

He has remained open to new ideas during the run, some of which have happened instinctively, such as during the Dover cliff scene with Gloucester, played by Stephen Boxer: 'In that marvellous moment when he recognises Gloucester, I now hug him. That just happened one night, because Stephen looked so upset. I had resisted doing that before because I thought it might be too sentimental, but I think that was probably wrong.' He's also varied the way he plays the 'O, reason not the need!' speech: 'It changes in terms of the amount of grovelling I do, and how Goneril and Regan are behaving.

Sometimes it's an aggressive fury, sometimes I'm begging on my knees, sometimes I'm affectionate to them; I even hug Goneril. It's a moveable feast.'

He found a similar changeability in his Fool: 'Adrian does something different every night, every single performance, and sometimes it's substantially different. I've had genuine joy watching him and being on stage with him. I genuinely am laughing at him. Last time on his entrance he pretended to be a super-model, and he's done air guitar and much more. His capacity for invention is extraordinary.'

Like every actor in the part, he's found it a formidable challenge, both physically and in other respects. 'It's certainly challenging vocally, but less so than *Timon of Athens*, because Lear has a little bit of a rest for forty minutes in the middle. Timon really whacked me, it just battered me. Lear is tiring, but the second half is not a vocal challenge, it's an emotional one. Those last four scenes are about absolute despair.'

His performance was generally welcomed by the critics. Charles Spencer wrote: 'Russell Beale movingly captures Lear's terrified intimations of madness. His insanity is often harrowing to watch, and his final scenes are beautifully achieved.' Henry Hitchings felt that 'his performance becomes fascinating in his aching soulfulness. There is perhaps no actor better at conveying the shapes and sounds of grief.' Maxie Szalwinska decided that 'he draws out Lear's dottiness and dementia beautifully, and brings a disarming trailing pathos to his final moments'. But Dominic Maxwell demurred, stating: 'Russell Beale cannot keep irony and intimacy out of his performance, and the king's rage feels like mere indignance.' Michael Billington thought the production exceptional. 'It combines a cosmic scale with an intimate sense of detail and is neither imprisoned by an intellectual concept nor by an actor's temperament ... Russell Beale is a magnetic and unorthodox Lear.'

Among actors, John Shrapnel observed: 'Simon achieved a wonderful balance of huge lethal dominance and areas of horror and madness. I will remember especially the big brooding darkness and obsession.' Reflecting on his experience of working on the play, Mendes stated: 'Although it's a really nihilistic, bleak play, there was something purifying about doing it, something exhilarating about going to that extreme, and pushing it as far as we could.' For Russell Beale too it's been a rewarding experience: 'I'm proud of our work, I think we've done the best we could. I hope it will be remembered as a good production.'

# SOURCES

These are the main sources for the productions described. Full details of the publications referred to can be found in the Further Reading section. All interviews are by the author unless otherwise stated.

## 1 A Stage History

Several publications, and introductions to editions of the play; Michael Bogdanov, *The Director's Cut*.

## 2 The First of the Moderns

*John Gielgud*   Croall biography; Gielgud autobiography.
*Randle Ayrton*   Beauman, *The RSC*.
*Donald Wolfit*   Harwood biography; Wolfit autobiography.
*Laurence Olivier*   Various biographies; Olivier autobiographies.

## 3 At the Old Vic

*William Devlin*   *Old Vic and Sadler's Wells Magazine*, April/May 1936.
*John Gielgud*   Interview with Alan MacNaughtan; Croall biography; Gielgud autobiography; Stephen Haggard memoir and letter to his father.

## 4 A Stratford Decade

*John Gielgud*   Interviews with David Conville, Jocelyn Herbert; Croall biography; Gielgud autobiography.
*Michael Redgrave*   Findlater biography; Strachan biography.
*Charles Laughton*   Interviews with Michael Blakemore, Zoe Caldwell, Julian Glover; Callow biography; Lanchester autobiography; Hall autobiography; Byam Shaw notes.

*Paul Scofield*   Interview with Clive Swift; O'Connor biography; Brook memoir; Williams, *Theatrical Casebook*; Marowitz, 'Lear Log'.


# 5 For the Royal Shakespeare Company

*Eric Porter*   Interviews with Diane Fletcher, Tim Pigott-Smith, John Shrapnel.
*Donald Sinden*   Interviews with Donald Sinden, Barry Kyle, Michael Pennington, Paul Shelley; 'Conversation with John Barton' in Ford Davies memoir; Brochure for the Renaissance Theatre Company's radio production of *King Lear*.
*Michael Gambon*   Interview with Adrian Noble; Gussow biography; *Players of Shakespeare*, vol. 2.


# 6 Around the Regions

*Michael Hordern*   Interview with Jonathan Miller; Hordern autobiography; Miller *Subsequent Performances*; Miller/Bassett biography; Miller/Romain biography.
*Kathryn Hunter*   Interviews with Kathryn Hunter, Helena Kaut-Howson, Marcello Magni.
*Warren Mitchell*   Interview with Jude Kelly.
*Pete Postlethwaite*   Interviews with Rupert Goold, John Shrapnel; Postlethwaite autobiography.
*Tim Pigott-Smith*   Interview with Tim Pigott-Smith; press interview with Ian Brown.


# 7 At the Old Vic 2

*Anthony Quayle*   Interview with Isla Blair.
*Eric Porter*   Interview with Jonathan Miller; Miller *Subsequent Performances*; Miller/Bassett biography; Miller/Romain biography.


# 8 In the Round

*Paul Shelley*   Interviews with Paul Shelley, Sam Walters.
*Clive Swift*   Interview with Clive Swift.
*John Shrapnel*   Interviews with John Shrapnel, Andrew Hilton; 'Edgar I nothing am', a talk by Andrew Hilton given at the Bridge Foundation for Psychotherapy and the Arts conference, 2012.

# 9 For the Royal Shakespeare Company 2

*John Wood*   Interview with Nicholas Hytner; Interview by Michael Owen, *Evening Standard*.
*Robert Stephens*   Interviews with Adrian Noble, David Calder, Simon Russell Beale.
*Nigel Hawthorne*   Interview with Adrian Noble; Hawthorne autobiography.

# 10 At the Globe

*Julian Glover*   Interviews with Julian Glover, Barry Kyle.
*David Calder*   Interviews with David Calder, Dominic Dromgoole.
*Joseph Marcell*   Interviews with Joseph Marcell, Bill Buckhurst, Dominic Dromgoole.

# 11 On the Road

*Timothy West*   Interviews with Timothy West, Stephen Unwin, John Shrapnel; West autobiography and letters.
*Anthony Quayle*   Weston *Covering Shakespeare*.
*Richard Briers*   Interview with Kenneth Branagh.

# 12 In Wales and Scotland

*Nicol Williamson*   Correspondence with Terry Hands.
*David Hayman*   Interviews with David Hayman, Dominic Hill.

# 13 Young Audiences, Young Players

*Tony Church*   Church autobiography.
*Richard Haddon Haines*   Interview with Cicely Berry; Carson *Shakespeare and Me*.
*Timothy West*   Interviews with Timothy West, Alan Stanford; West autobiographies.
*Nonso Anozie*   Interview with Declan Donellan.
*Paul Copley*   Interviews with Paul Copley, Tim Crouch.

## 14 For the Royal Shakespeare Company 3

*Corin Redgrave*   Interview with Bill Alexander; Letters to Annie Castledine.
*Ian McKellen*   Ian McKellen interview on DVD film of 2007 production.
*Greg Hicks*   Interviews with Greg Hicks, David Farr, Kathryn Hunter.

## 15 In Smaller Spaces

*Robert Demeger*   Interview with Deborah Warner; Russell Brown *Routledge Companion*; Giannachi and Luckhurst *On Directing*.
*Tom Wilkinson*   Interview with Max Stafford-Clark.
*Oliver Cotton*   Interviews with Oliver Cotton, Jack Shepherd.
*Oliver Ford Davies*   Interviews with Oliver Ford Davies, Jonathan Kent; Ford Davies *Playing Lear*.
*Derek Jacobi*   Interviews with Derek Jacobi, Michael Grandage; Jacobi autobiography; Grandage memoir.
*Jonathan Pryce*   Interview with Michael Attenborough.

## 16 Transatlantic Sessions

*Peter Ustinov*   Miller biography; Good memoir.
*Christopher Plummer*   Interviews with Christopher Plummer, Jonathan Miller.
*Frank Langella*   Interview with Angus Jackson; Langella YouTube interview with Charlie Rose.
*Michael Pennington*   Interview with Michael Pennington; Correspondence with Arin Arbus.

## 17 At the National

*Anthony Hopkins*   Interview with David Hare.
*Brian Cox*   Interviews with Brian Cox, Deborah Warner; Cox *Lear Diaries*.
*Ian Holm*   Holm autobiography; Eyre Lecture to Royal Society of Literature, 1998; Eyre *National Service*.
*Simon Russell Beale*   Interview with Simon Russell Beale; Sam Mendes NT Platform.

# FURTHER READING

## Editions of King Lear

These all have introductions covering stage performances.
Elspeth Bain, Jonathan Morris, Rob Smith, Cambridge School Shakespeare, Cambridge University Press, 1996.
Jonathan Bate and Eric Rasmussen (eds.), RSC/Macmillan, 2009.
R.A. Foakes (ed.), Arden Shakespeare, Bloomsbury, 1997.
Jay L. Halio (ed.), New Cambridge Shakespeare, Cambridge University Press, 2005.
George Hunter (ed.), Penguin Shakespeare, Penguin Books, 1972.
Stephen Unwin (ed.), English Touring Theatre, Oberon Books, 2002.
Cedric Watts (ed.), Wordsworth Classics, 2004.
Stanley Wells (ed.), Oxford World's Classics, 2001.

## Autobiography/Memoir

Michael Blakemore, *Arguments with England: A Memoir*, Faber & Faber, 2004.
Peter Brook, *The Shifting Point: Forty Years of Theatrical Exploration 1946–1987*, Methuen, 1988.
Zoe Caldwell, *I Will Be Cleopatra: An Actress's Journey*, Norton, 2001.
Tony Church, *A Stage for a Kingdom*, Oneiro Press, 2013.
Brian Cox, *The Lear Diaries: The Story of the Royal National Theatre's Productions of* Richard III *and* King Lear, Methuen, 1992.
Dominic Dromgoole, *Will and Me: How Shakespeare Took Over My Life*, Penguin Books, 2007.
Richard Eyre, *National Service: Diary of a Decade at the National Theatre*, Bloomsbury, 2003.
Richard Eyre, 'King Lear', in *What Do I Know? People, Politics and the Arts*, Nick Hern Books, 2014.
Oliver Ford Davies, *Playing Lear: An Insider's Guide to Text and Performance*, Nick Hern Books, 2003.
John Gielgud, *An Actor and His Time*, Sidgwick & Jackson, 1979.
Maurice Good, *Every Inch a Lear: A Rehearsal Journal*, Sono Nis Press, 1982.
Michael Grandage, *A Decade at the Donmar 2002–2012*, Constable, 2012.
Stephen Haggard, *I'll Go to Bed at Noon*, Faber & Faber, 1944.
Peter Hall, *Making an Exhibition of Myself: The Autobiography*, Sinclair-Stevenson, 1993.
Nigel Hawthorne, *Straight Face: The Autobiography*, Hodder & Stoughton, 2002.

Ian Holm, *Acting My Life: The Autobiography*, Bantam Press, 2004.

Michael Hordern, *A World Elsewhere: An Autobiography*, Michael O'Mara Books, 1993.

Derek Jacobi, *As Luck Would Have It: My Seven Ages*, HarperCollins, 2013.

Else Lanchester, *Elsa Lanchester, Herself*, Michael Joseph, 1983.

Kika Markham, *Our Time of Day: My Life with Corin Redgrave*, Oberon Books, 2014.

Jonathan Miller, *Subsequent Performances*, Faber & Faber, 1986.

Laurence Olivier, *Confessions of an Actor*, Weidenfeld & Nicolson, 1982.

Laurence Olivier, *On Acting*, Weidenfeld & Nicolson, 1986.

Edward Petherbridge, *Slim Chances: NT Fifty Years: Personal, Partial, Unofficial*, Indepenpress, 2013.

Pete Postlethwaite, *A Spectacle of Dust: The Autobiography*, Orion Books, 2012.

Robert Stephens, *Knight Errant: Memoirs of a Vagabond Actor*, Hodder & Stoughton, 1996.

Irving Wardle, *The Theatres of George Devine*, Jonathan Cape, 1978.

Timothy West, *I'm Here I Think, Where Are You? Letters from a Touring Actor*, Nick Hern Books, 1994.

Timothy West, *A Moment towards the End of the Play: An Autobiography*, Nick Hern Books, 2002.

David Weston, *Covering McKellen: An Understudy's Tale*, Rickshaw, 2011.

David Weston, *Covering Shakespeare*, Oberon Books, 2014.

Donald Wolfit, *First Interval: The Autobiography*, Odhams Press, 1954.

# Biography

Kate Bassett, *In Two Minds: A Biography of Jonathan Miller*, Oberon Books, 2012.

Bill Bryson, *Shakespeare*, HarperCollins, 2007.

Simon Callow, *Charles Laughton: A Difficult Actor*, Methuen, 1987.

Jonathan Croall, *John Gielgud: Matinee Idol to Movie Star*, Methuen Drama, 2013.

Richard Findlater, *Michael Redgrave, Actor*, Heinemann, 1956.

Mel Gussow, *Gambon: A Life in Acting*, Nick Hern Books, 2004.

Ronald Harwood, *Sir Donald Wolfit: The Life and Work in the Unfashionable Theatre*, Secker & Warburg, 1971.

John Miller, *Peter Ustinov: The Gift of Laughter*, Weidenfeld & Nicolson, 2002.

Garry O'Connor, *Paul Scofield: The Biography*, Sidgwick & Jackson, 2002.

Piers Paul Read, *Alec Guinness: The Authorised Biography*, Simon & Schuster, 2003.

Michael Romain, *A Profile of Jonathan Miller*, Cambridge University Press, 1992.

Alan Strachan, *Secret Dreams: A Biography of Michael Redgrave*, Orion Books, 2005.

# General

John Barton, *Playing Shakespeare*, Methuen, 1984.

Sally Beauman, *The Royal Shakespeare Company: A History of Ten Decades*, Oxford University Press, 1982.

Michael Bogdanov, The *Director's Cut: Essays on Shakespeare's Plays*, vol. 1, Capercaillie Books, 2003.

John Russell Brown (ed.), *The Routledge Companion to Directors' Shakespeare*, Routledge, 2008.

Susannah Carson (ed.), *Shakespeare and Me*, Oneworld, 2014.

Gabriella Giannachi and Mary Luckhurst (eds.), *On Directing: Interviews with Directors*, Faber & Faber, 1999.

Harley Granville Barker, *Preface to King Lear*, Batsford, 1930; Nick Hern Books/National Theatre, 1993.

Andrew Hiscock and Lisa Hopkins, *King Lear: A Critical Guide*, Continuum, 2011.

Peter Holland, *English Shakespeares: Shakespeare on the English Stage in the 1990s*, Cambridge University Press, 1997.

Jonathan Holmes, *Merely Players: Actors' Accounts of Performing Shakespeare*, Routledge, 2004.

Russell Jackson and Robert Smallwood (eds.), *Players of Shakespeare*, vol. 2, Cambridge University Press, 1998.

Alexander Leggatt, *King Lear: Shakespeare in Performance*, Manchester University Press, 2004.

Charles Marowitz, 'Lear Log', in *Drama Review*, vol. 8, no. 2, Winter 1963.

Michael Pennington, *Sweet William: A User's Guide to Shakespeare*, Nick Hern Books, 2012.

Elizabeth Shafer, *Ms – Directing Shakespeare: Women Direct Shakespeare*, Women's Press, 1998.

Robert Speaight, *Shakespeare on the Stage: An Illustrated History of Shakespearean Performance*, Collins, 1973.

Kenneth Tynan, *Curtains*, Longmans, Green, 1961.

Stanley Wells, *Great Shakespeare Actors: Burbage to Branagh*, Oxford University Press, 2015.

Stanley Wells and Sarah Stanton (eds.), *The Cambridge Guide to Shakespeare on Stage*, Cambridge University Press, 2002.

David Williams (ed.), *Peter Brook: A Theatrical Casebook*, Methuen, 1988.

# INDEX

*Numbers in bold indicate sections dealing in detail with a specific production, reflecting the ideas and memories of the actor or director in question.*